# Humble Pie

# Humble Pie

St. Benedict's Ladder of Humility

## CAROL BONOMO

MOREHOUSE PUBLISHING
*A Continuum imprint*
HARRISBURG • LONDON • NEW YORK

Morehouse Publishing
P.O. Box 1321
Harrisburg, PA 17105

*Morehouse Publishing is a Continuum imprint.*

Design by Corey Kent

Library of Congress Cataloging-in-Publication Data

Bonomo, Carol, 1952–
    Humble pie : St. Benedict's ladder of humility / by Carol Bonomo.
       p. cm
Includes bibliographical references.
    ISBN 0-8192-1960-6
    1. Benedict, Saint, Abbot of Monte Cassino. De humilitate. 2. Humility—Christianity—History of doctrines. I. Title.
    BX3004.Z5B66 2004
    241'.4—dc21

                                                      2003012404

*Printed in the United States of America*

03  04  05  06  07  6  5  4  3  2  1

*For Felix*

who stopped to consider the lilies of the field
but decided he liked roses better.

The LORD is our savior;
     we shall sing to stringed instruments
In the house of the LORD
     all the days of our life.

*Isaiah 38:20*

# Contents

# Acknowledgments

The best thing about acknowledgments is that they force you to remember that you never accomplish anything meaningful alone. St. Benedict would approve of this insight and wonder what took me so long.

At Morehouse Publishing, Debra Farrington and later Nancy Fitzgerald provided enthusiasm, clarity, and insight to my initial flourishes on humility, as well as good humor to my morning e-mails.

My long-distance volunteer researchers were my mother, Barbara, in Rhode Island, and Blanche Monacco, my sister-in-law, in Arizona. Arlene Ruiz, my coworker and prayer partner, was a living biblical concordance—better, faster, and much nicer than any on-line Bible for finding specific references that I could only remember in generalities. My colleague and stringed instrument guru, Richard Riehl, was a thorough reader of the draft manuscript, as well as my backup music coach.

I am blessed with extraordinary teachers. The old abbot pulled me into Benedict's fold graciously but firmly. Auntie Margie of Kamuela, Hawaii, taught me more than she can possibly imagine.

Special acknowledgment to my best friend and life companion, my husband Felix. And I always need to acknowledge my patron, Blessed Joanna Mary, who must have been praying overtime on this one.

—Carol Joanna Mary Bonomo

# Prelude
## *The Preparation*

## Advent

I thought humility would be fun. Maybe it wouldn't be holding-my-sides-laughing *fun*, but fun, as in different and daring and darling to look at. It's not exactly like I'm an expert on humility—nor could I admit it if I were.

Humility is *that* kind of fun—the weird, backwards kind that had Alice in Wonderland questioning her luncheon mushroom.

With a subject like humility, you've got to start somewhere, and Advent is as good a starting place as any. Advent is the beginning of the Church's liturgical year, the time of preparation before Christmas takes over. I need a little time of preparation before jumping head-first into humility.

Humility is terribly important to understand if you're a Benedictine monk or even a lay Benedictine oblate. St. Benedict must have cared deeply about humility. It is by far the longest chapter in the little Rule he wrote, and he gives us twelve steps to achieving humility. If he cared, I care. If he thought humility was that important in the sixth century when he wrote his Rule, then maybe it's still important in this century as well.

Until I became a Benedictine oblate, the only steps I'd ever heard of came from all those Twelve-Step programs: Alcoholics Anonymous[1] and its dozens of anonymous spin-offs, from nicotine to overeaters to sex to shopping. I think that's where the idea of looking at Benedict's steps of humility as some sort of fun originated. I thought it must be an ancient self-help model—Humility Anonymous—where you got up and bragged about your humility until everybody yelled at you to sit down.

Well, it sounded fun at first. But there was trouble right off the bat. For one thing, the twelve steps bored me—been there, *done* that, in AA for four or five years until I ran away looking for something more fun and stumbled into the Catholic Church. For another, the self-help twelve steps and Benedict's twelve have nothing in common other than their twelveness. Who knew?

Some things take a while to figure out. Apparently, humility is one of those things, even though St. Benedict breaks it out into twelve steps. But I'm a slow learner. I was an oblate for a couple of years before I began to grasp the Benedictine charisma—its marketing brand, its distinction, what makes it Benedictine instead of, say, Franciscan. Abbot Antony, our oblate master at the monastery, told me early on, "Our life is the liturgy"—the Divine Office, or Liturgy of the Hours that the Church has prayed since the earliest times. That should have been a clue.

Reading the Rule should have been another clue about what makes Benedictines Benedictine. Humility is the longest chapter, but the biggest number of chapters in the Rule dictates the prayers of the liturgy. Humility may lie at the heart of a Benedictine life, but the liturgy of hours, weeks, and years wraps around that life like a well-worn habit.

Maybe it's less fun to structure a look at humility, but at least it's tidy, and I like tidy nearly as much as fun. This Advent I am preparing to look at the humble heart of Benedictine life and wrap it in the cloak of the memories and liturgical practices of my life in the world. I have a perfectly good reason for this plan: I know absolutely nothing about humility in any form or under any conditions. Jamie, my coworker at the university, is in the same boat. In college, she was theatre and I was opera, and our long-ago choices of college majors, overwritten many times, probably suit our dispositions as well. Old performers never die; they just keep reaching for that applause button like a rat in a cage pushing a lever for food pellets. These days I'm a lobbyist and Jamie's a fund-raiser, and we are both late bloomers enjoying the afternoon sun on our careers.

Jamie tells me, "So I looked around and said to myself, 'Should I walk into the room and take it over because it's fun and I can do it, or should I grow up and try to take myself seriously?'"

We look at each other, full of the thrill and power old perform-ers know of what it's *like* to walk into a room full of people more important and powerful than we'll ever be, and know that within minutes we'll be the only person there who matters. Who wants to grow up anyway?

"Nah," we both say. Showmanship over sincerity every time. *Anything* over humility *anytime*. Humility's steps are perfect for me: *haven't* been there, *haven't* done that.

And with that decision, I just need to find wallpaper, which is what I call the place where I study and the people in that place. I'm sure it's not respectful to think of a monastery or church or retreat house—and the good people who work there and make me feel wel-come there—as wallpaper, but that's what I do. I need a place of interactions for humility, and not just any old place.

I want to find once again the wallpaper I knew too late as a kid. Growing up Episcopalian in Rhode Island, I went to church camp one summer in Pascoag, a wooded retreat with cabins, crafts, daily chapel, and evening prayer, plus a lake for brisk daily swims.

The walk from cabin to lake took us into the woods and past the House of Silence, where we had to hold back our chatter and our gig-gles till we got past the no-talking zone and on to the final freedom of the lake.

The camp counselors told us we could visit the House of Silence during free periods, but they never told us why we might want to, and I didn't know any campers who did. Twice a day we walked to the lake, shushing when we got to the reduced-noise zone and sometimes even tippy-toeing through the silence area.

After ten days of camp, we were retrieved by our parents, who got the grand tour before we all headed back home. For the first time, I went off-road with them and into the House of Silence. There was a library with books for young people and desks to sit at and write, which filled me with desire, and a simple chapel with a few pews, a tiny altar, a plain wooden cross, and two lit candles. I had never seen a chapel before and never been in a church without stained-glass win-dows before. Here, you could see the trees outside. I was a small per-son with a limited imagination, living in a small state. Now I knew *why* I should have come here. Suddenly there was a place to pray that was my size. I heard what quiet sounded like for the first time. The tour moved on to show off the chilly lake, but as we left the House of Silence, my ten-year-old self was heartbroken: why didn't I come here when I had the chance?

At our monthly oblate meeting, I was sitting deep in my favorite chair, half-snoozing, half-listening to the old abbot, half-ruminating over places to study and wondering where all the good libraries have gone—and I snapped to attention. Abbot Antony was talking about libraries.

"I am so pleased to announce that you have outgrown the little oblate library. We have petitioned for, and received, a larger room," he was saying. "Brother Patrick, our carpenter, is building the bookshelves, and our librarian is arranging to have the books moved. We will even have a VCR and collection of tapes for when you are here, and I hope you will make good of it."

"When, Father Abbot?" asked Mary in the front row. "When will it be ready?"

"Well, I don't quite know," he answered. "I suppose in God's time."

Great. How am I supposed to put *that* into my Palm Pilot? But I'm hearing something hopeful, and in the meantime, I'll just hide out in the cafeteria, drinking coffee and pretending I'm in a Starbucks for Spiritual Endeavor. At least it's a beginning. Advent is about beginnings and preparations for the journey. I'm short on humility. I've still got a lot of preparation to do.

## The Ladder of Humility

St. Benedict believed in preparation, too, especially when it came to humility. You have to build a ladder of humility, he said, to take you to the heights of Christian service. *Now the ladder erected is our life on earth*, he explains, *and if we humble our hearts, the Lord will raise it to heaven.*[1] Calling the sides of the ladder "our body and soul," Benedict fits into this metaphor twelve steps of humility and discipline to help us ascend into perfect love.

It's an ambitious project, these steps of humility. In fact, even *ambitious* seems like the wrong word. I'm glad to be reminded of the homely necessity of a ladder to reach where I cannot on my own. When I left my parents' house to go off into the world, my mother presented me with a stepstool. "Keep it handy," she said. "You'll be surprised how often you'll use it."

She wasn't speaking metaphorically. This was Practical Life 101. My mother is barely over five feet tall; my father was only three inches taller than that. And they both *towered* over me, whose sole ambition in life as a teenager was to reach five feet in height, and who never even came close. My mother knew that in a world designed for average-sized people, I'd need a boost just to keep up.

Benedict knows the same thing. I will never reach the heights of humility without a ladder. It's an image Benedict takes straight out of the book of Genesis: "Then [Jacob] had a dream: a stairway rested on the ground, with its top reaching to the heavens; and God's messengers were going up and down on it."[2]

I can understand the lonely place where Jacob rested his head on a rock and dreamed his dream. He's cheated his own brother out of the rightful blessing of the eldest son. As his mother's favorite, he's done his dirty work with her help. Now he's got a brother planning to kill him, a mother who's afraid he'll marry the wrong kind of girl, and a father who sends him away for his wickedness.

I've been in situations like that, playing one person against another, causing trouble, as my mother would put it, aggravating and infuriating innocent and not-so-innocent people in my quest to get my own way. And I've been banished for it, too. I like to say I've been thrown out of more respectable, church-fearing institutions than most people have ever walked into. I don't know why I would brag about it. Besides the hurt I've inflicted, there's the banishment, which hurts me. Sometimes I know full well I'm causing trouble; sometimes I'm blissfully unaware. Either way, like Jacob, I'm out on the street with a rock for a pillow, trying to sleep and forget.

Esther de Waal, an Anglican writer on Benedictine ways, says the ladder is "an ancient classical symbol of unity and integration" and adds that "to work through Benedict's ladder is therefore going to be a journey into freedom."[3] I can accept the sturdy symbol, but I worry about a ladder whose sides are constructed of body and soul. I know how weak mine are, and how easily my ladder can collapse.

And besides, isn't it weird that a ladder to humility should go in the "up" direction? Some sort of worldly common sense tells me that humility takes a downward dive. But wait—I could be mixing up humility, a virtue to strive for, with humiliation, a punishment to be inflicted. Benedict understands the differences and lays out the direction pretty clearly: *We descend by exaltation and ascend by humility*,[4] he says, and cites the Gospel as his guide: *For everyone who exalts himself will be humbled, but the one who humbles himself will be exalted.*[5] So up is down, and down is up for Benedict.

I'm just glad to know there are messengers from God no matter what direction I'm moving on the ladder. Sometimes it seems like my ladder is one of those whirly exercise wheels that hamsters use, and I'm the fulcrum, turning between exaltation and humility fast and furious.

But for Benedict, the image is clear and straightforward: our ladder to humility begins on earth and reaches to heaven. In Genesis, the Lord God stands above the ladder and promises his forsaken Jacob land, descendants, and a beautiful comfort: "Know that I am with you; I will protect you wherever you go. . . ."[6] Even when we are exiled or abandoned, it is not God who exiles or abandons us.

Jacob wakes up from his dream and exclaims, "Truly, the LORD is in this spot, although I did not know it!"[7] The Lord has been a surprise resident in lots of places I would least expect: in hidden, hurtful silences, awaiting my fall, assisting my climb, in defeat far more than in victory when my crowing tends to crowd him out.

For Jacob, this place where the ladder touched the earth of his dream is now sacred. "How awesome is this shrine!"[8] he cries. In the morning, he takes the rock that served as his pillow, pours oil on it, and consecrates it, naming it Bethel, the house of God. My own ladder to humility connects me to God, too. Where my ladder touches down, just as it did for Jacob, is where I begin. God is in this spot as I start out, this Advent, preparing to examine the first steps of humility.

## Advent

It is the beginning of the year for Christians, minus the resolutions, the noisemakers, and the champagne.

The start of the liturgical new year is quiet: an older pregnant woman named Elizabeth meets up with a younger one, a cousin named Mary, and a few beautiful songs are sung: "My soul proclaims the greatness of the Lord," sings Mary, according to the Gospel of Luke. "My spirit rejoices in God my savior."[9] The *Magnificat*, Mary's song of praise and acceptance, is sung or spoken every day in the Evening Office of prayer, called Vespers.

Barely a few verses later in Luke, there is a second song burst, this time by Elizabeth's husband, muted by God for his disbelief in God's words. Silent for months, Zechariah is filled with the Spirit of God after the birth of the child of his old age. "Blessed be the Lord, the God of Israel," he sings, as we all do each day in the Morning Office of Lauds, "for he has visited and brought redemption to his people."[10] At the end of his song are some of the most beautiful and comforting words of God: "to shine on those who sit in darkness and death's shadow,/ to guide our feet into the path of peace."[11]

And so Advent begins, as every day begins, in darkness and the shadow of death, with the knowledge that God will guide our feet into the way of peace. I like that in a New Year celebration. It's a lot better than noisemakers and popped corks and bursts of loud "Happy New Year!" shrieked in rooms of strangers, as if we're hurling ourselves over another barrier to face the open pages of the year before us. Advent as beginning, as preparation, makes a lot more sense.

Sometimes I feel that the kingdom of God is not-sense—as topsy-turvy as Alice in Wonderland. Ladders go up where you'd think they go down; the season before Christmas is all about penance, not celebration; and if you're going to glory in anything, it will be your weakness instead of your strength. Hello?

It is not too early in this study to wave my hand from the back of the classroom and ask for the teacher's help. I don't get humility, I want to tell the teacher. For that matter, Advent's a bit of a mystery, too. What am I preparing for again?

My teacher of things Benedictine is old Abbot Antony. When I was young, there were Sunday school teachers and church ministers to teach me the way, but my primary teachers were my parents. Now, much older, I still have parish priests and weekly homilies, but as a Benedictine oblate, I also have an abbot, "a surrogate parent," as oblate Norvene West clarifies the relationship.[12] And the old abbot is not just surrogate for my earthly parents, but for my heavenly one as well. *This is advice from a father who loves you . . .*[13] as Benedict begins.

Abbot Antony retired as the abbot when he was eighty-five years old and took on the role of oblate master at the abbey. Instead of being the superior and spiritual CEO of several dozen monks—with the full weight of Benedict's Rule behind him—he serves as mother hen to several hundred chicks called oblates. We scatter in hundreds of directions and come in a full range of spiritual conditions. But once a month about half of us are rounded up by his letter of invitation to come home to the abbey to consider our calling to Christ, ponder our affirmation to follow Benedict's Rule, and nibble cookies and cakes and spoil our appetites for dinner.

"What are you working on?" the abbot asks as I sit in the retreat cafeteria, feeling uncomfortably exposed and unhappy, trying to study.

"Humility. And if you ask me if I'm an expert, I'm going to get mad!" It's starting to feel like a stupid topic to study, and there's no place to study and get away from the stupid jokes.

"Try the chapel," he suggests, as if he's reading my mind or my soul's discomfort. "Nobody *there* to interrupt humility except Christ, and He will be pleased with your company, I am sure."

I gather up my things and head for the Retreat Chapel, where I made my vows as a Benedictine oblate, the same chapel the monks used until they built their church. It will be quiet there, but not lonely. With the consecrated Host demurely covered with a gold shroud, there is a Presence here. There is a choir section of just fourteen stalls on either side of a plain, bare altar and behind it, two candles burn on either side of the consecrated Host. There are only four rows of pews, and when you look up or out, you see the movement of the trees outside. It is a chapel small enough even for me. It is my House of Silence, after all these years, a place I can appreciate, visit, and work. In a little while, in God's time, our own oblate library will be ready, like the other room of that long-ago House of Silence. But for now I'm happy to be here in God's presence.

It is quiet here, even by monastic standards, at three o'clock on a Friday afternoon in Advent. The weekday retreats and recollection groups have cleared out. The weekend ones have not yet arrived. The rooms are cleaned, the grass is cut. All is readiness and calm.

Into this quiet, Abbot Antony slips in by the side door. I don't know if he remembers that he suggested I use the chapel, but he doesn't see me anyway. His eyes are fixed on the Host. This becomes the sound of silence in my newfound House of Silence: the crispy rustle of winter breeze against palm fronds, twittering birds, an old man's soft murmuring against the click of rosary beads, the Presence of God in all of it, the preparation for the gift that is to come.

# −1−
# The Gift

## Christmas

Well, I just hate Christmas, and nearly always did, ever since the faith was broken. I hear how kids wise up to the Santa Claus routine but pretend otherwise because the goods seem connected to keeping their parents' fantasies flowing. I've seen the parents trying to pretend for the same reason—not because otherwise the gifts stop, but to maintain the innocence a little longer—even when both sides *know* the other side knows.

I didn't know. Maybe in the fourth grade somebody at school recess took a survey of who did and who didn't believe in Santa Claus. The idea of not believing had never occurred to me before that survey. "Of course there's a Santa Claus," I said in absolute disgust. The survey-taker yelled to her friends, "Okay, that's two for Santa!" and took off to find another kid to question. *What a dope*, I thought. Her disbelief would get *her* into trouble. And the incident completely left my mind.

Until my mother took me aside the following year and said, "Hey, listen. About Santa . . ."

I was horrified at the revelation. It made no sense to me. How could some obnoxious creep at recess have the inside goods, the real truth about something this big and my own *parents* were in on the scam?

It took me three days of chewing on this new world order before I came back and asked, "Then where do the presents come from?" The sharpest crayon in the box I have never been.

9

"From us," my mother said. "Don't tell your sister. She's too young to know."

My sister already knew. The wise kids at recess had filled everybody in, including the kids in kindergarten and first grade. It was a matter of who believed and who didn't. All Christmas Day that year, my mother or father would say, "And see what *else* Santa brought you!" I would look guilty and stammer, while my sister would mutter, "There isn't any Santa Claus, . . ." under her breath so they didn't hear.

The fraud was exposed, and it wasn't about Santa. It was about an entire culture coercing themselves into the experience of wide-eyed faith. After that, all bets were off. Why believe any of them?

And why buy into Christmas at all? For me, Christmas was a solo affair, as I rushed off alone to sing at the 10:00 A.M. service at St. Luke's Episcopal Church. My parents had already gone to the Christmas Eve service and slept late on Christmas Day, so the presents were barely opened when I set out on the half-mile walk to church, carrying my freshly starched robe to stiffen even further in the chill. With the junior choir, I would sing to a half-filled church devoid of anybody I knew, and then walk back home alone. By then it was already Christmas noon, and relatives were arriving, and the food smells were starting to win over the pine spray on the artificial tree. Without knowing it, I knew when I got back to the house that the Christmas moment had already come and gone—and once again had left me hanging.

So it was only fitting that in my college years as a music major I took the solo nature of Christmas and turned it into a profit-making gig. The organist at my church was ill one year so I played all the services and ran home for a turkey sandwich in between. Another year, when the senior choir director gave me the solo parts to sing, I pre-empted the elderly soprano who'd *always* done the solos and created hard feelings and a few resignations. The joke in college was that "old sopranos never die; they just sound that way." But poor Bella was a wounded soul cast away after years of faithful service for a younger, fancier, flash-in-the-pan. Our college joke did not allow her humanity.

By my junior year in college, I had moved my Christmas to other church gigs, ones that paid, leaving behind my parents' more parsimonious parish. Bella returned to her faithful role as soprano soloist at St. Luke's while I hop-skipped to all the paying jobs I could round up. One Christmas Eve, I sang soprano solos from the *Messiah* for a radio broadcast the Methodist Church recorded at 6:00 P.M. in down-town Providence, got picked up outside in the icy cold to haul butt to an Episcopal service at 8:00 P.M. in Fall River (more *Messiah*), and made it back to Providence in time for midnight Mass at the Catholic cathedral as a member of the Peloquin Chorale. My parents heard the radio broadcast of the *Messiah*, went to their own Christmas Eve service, and caught up with me on television for the midnight Mass. It was great fun, but it didn't have much to do with the simple Gospel story, with the enormity of Mary's perfect obedience and God's incredible gift.

My last year of college was also my last year of Christmas gigs. A music professor got me a lucrative job as a soloist in a Presbyterian Church near the college campus. It meant an hour's drive from home each way on roads that turned mean with frozen ruts, but the money was great. So was the novelty of solo work with orchestra.

It wasn't only the roads that turned mean and rutty either. My vocal chords did, too. What started as a bit of hoarseness and a slight cough turned into laryngitis by Christmas Eve day.

"You have to manage," said the music director when I called and croaked at him. "It's too late to get anybody else, and we've spent too much money on the orchestra to start cutting back the music."

So even though I could barely say *Presbyterian*, I bundled up, drove alone on Christmas Eve to sing in front of a church full of Presbyterians who didn't know me or have a clue how sick I felt. I learned that even with laryngitis you can push out a half-decent sound by the second or third beat. When I was done, I was finished. I couldn't even whisper. It took a January in bed to get over a case of pneumonia.

Christmas and its magical moment! I was pretty sure there was one such moment every Christmas when everything suddenly hushed and you stood on the sacred ground called Christmas. But it always escaped me, even in my blind faith that such a moment actually existed.

The church of my childhood did not accompany me into adult-hood. The faith of the child cracked and splintered under the weight of a searching, restless, half-mad adult. When I moved to San Diego, I lost even the external clues that led to Christmas as I had known it. ("So what do people do about Christmas dinner here? Really? Shrimp on the barbecue? How very interesting. . .") We had our house up for sale in Massachusetts, so Felix and I lived in a two-room cabana (a motel room with cooking space) in Pacific Beach that first year. The

Charlie Brown Christmas special came on even there, and when I heard there was "no room at the inn," for the first time I really got being unwanted in a strange place and went on a major crying jag. Felix decided we would drive to Tucson to visit his family. We spent Christmas Eve that first year in San Diego driving the great desert wasteland east of San Diego for 400 miles to Tucson, listening to a "Jews for Jesus" broadcast coming out of a Mexico radio station—the only station we could get in the wastelands. Having established a precedent, we were expected in Tucson every Christmas thereafter. It wasn't my Christmas moment, but who knew that it even existed after all these years of waiting?

Twice in fifteen years I returned to Rhode Island to spend Christmas with my parents. The first time, the temperature dropped below zero by the Christmas Eve service, and I threw style to the winds and burrowed in anybody's extra winter clothing to listen to endless songs, a spin by the bell choir, and a sermon that lasted more than half an hour. As we left the service, my father started to introduce me to the minister, who seemed to have other, worldlier concerns that Christmas Eve. "Say, Al, would you consider heading up the church capital campaign in January?"

I hadn't been inside a church for a while, but I realized that this wasn't the Christmas moment I was looking for either.

I came back to Rhode Island one more time for Christmas. By then I was a Roman Catholic and a regular church-goer, and Christmas is one of the holidays they say you *have* to do, so the church is always packed with strangers, not only to each other, but to the liturgy as well. By now, in the month since he'd gotten strangely, seriously sick, and still a few weeks from being diagnosed with cancer, it was clear that my father was dying. He was sixty-five years old, and the suddenness of it terrified him. Once in a while, his big blue eyes would fill with tears, and he'd make a horrible gasping sound like he couldn't breathe. But he *could* breathe. The sound was his sobbing.

In the middle of that horror, Christ was born and the angels sang alleluia at a Catholic Church near my parents' home. Christmas was still a lonely solo affair, but this time the priest sang the most radiant music I had ever heard, and everybody in the congregation was lifted up by his enormous, determined caring. It became Christmas then, because of his gift. There had never been anything under the tree I really wanted, from Santa, or my parents, or Felix. But this lovely,

THE GIFT • 13

lonely, singular priest in Pawtucket, Rhode Island, was singing like his heart would break for joy at Christmas.

My heart broke, too.

Old habits die hard, and hating Christmas has been one of my oldest habits. There was that one Christmas of terrible beauty with the lovely priestly voice singing, but the rest were the awful ones, the forgotten ones, the adulthood ones of standing outside smoking alone listening to people inside fight over which TV show to watch and thinking, "There's a real Christmas going on somewhere else. Not here, but somewhere it's a real Christmas." Not in the jingle-jangle lane of the mall, or in the lite-jazz radio version of "chestnuts roasting on an open fire." Not here. But somewhere.

While I was waiting for the real Christmas moment to find me, Felix suggested, "Maybe you'd like Christmas better if you had a Christmas tree and decorated the house. Maybe you'd like the season better if you participated in it."

I wanted to snarl out a few choice remarks: how all my years of marathon Christmas services hadn't done the trick, and how Christmas trees were pretty secular after all. Should I get a picture taken with Santa Claus at Nordstrom's while I'm at it?

But this amazing thing happened. What I heard him say inside his words, almost wistfully was, "*I* sure would like Christmas better if we had a tree. *I* sure would like a few decorations, a little participation, a little spirit of the season."

Poor Felix has traveled all these years of exile from anything resembling Christmas with me because of me. Never a tree, or a gracious word about spending the holidays with his family, or a twinkle of fa-la-la-la—just me, hoping that if we shut our eyes, maybe the whole thing would go away. Even Charlie Brown finds the answer every year as the multitude of the heavenly host sing, "Glory to God in the highest and on earth peace. . . ."[1] I could have sung those words every year, too, when I sang the Messiah. But that was the chorus section, and I only knew the solo parts.

Christmas—how could I not know this?—is not about me. It is a celebration of that breathless moment in time—for *all* time—when God entered into the story and became a character, not just the author. It is that moment I loved when I was on a ski lift in New England, when the world seemed to drop away behind me and a hush settled on my shoulders as light as snowflakes. It is the yes moment, the moment of total commitment between God and his people, when he becomes one of us to free us.

Isn't that the Christmas moment I've been waiting for all these years? Suddenly it was mine when I heard another voice and listened to another heart's need and figured out that Christmas is all about duets and quartets and even the occasional full-bodied chorus.

So I got a tree and put out a crèche. Felix put wreaths on the doors. As he strung the lights around the tree, he began taking a look at the ornaments.

"Where did this one come from?" he asked.

"The one that's a heart that says, 'Our First Year'? Open it; our pictures are in it. My mom made it and gave it to us the year we got married."

"Oh." He smiled at the young skinny kids pictured inside. "This one?"

"Cape Cod, the year Jennifer got married."

"Who stitched this one? You?"

"No. My mom, when we moved to Encinitas."

"Okay. What about the shiny ones?"

"My sister, my mother, and I used to make an ornament at Christmas. We bought kits with styrofoam balls, sequins, and pins, and stuck that styrofoam until we didn't have any fingerprints left. Mom divvied them up between the sisters a few years ago."

"This?"

"You made me buy it at St. Benedict's Church on the Big Island the last time we were there."

"I *made* you buy?"

"Made. You did, even though you said we'd never had a tree and probably never would. You wanted it anyway, just in case."

"Well, I did good," he said virtuously, spearing the stuffed dove of peace onto the top of the tree. "You have a nice memory for your tree now that you've got a tree." He stood back to survey the effect. "Actually, you've got a lot of memories on the tree." He began to sound a little indignant. "For somebody who's never wanted a Christmas tree and never decorated and never liked Christmas, you sure have a lot of special ornaments here. What were you saving them for?"

Oh, Christmas, I guess. A Christmas moment, maybe. I'd lugged them from Rhode Island to Boston to San Diego to Encinitas, and now to Lake San Marcos. They've been packed and waiting, as I've been packed and waiting for Christmas. And now, for whatever reason, and undoubtedly in God's own season, my time, too, is at hand . . .

*Step 1: Obedience to All God's Commandments*

I joined Felix for one of his many business trips to Korea and out of the overwhelming foreignness to my eyes, one detail consistently caught my attention: the buildings that weren't done yet, complete in nearly every detail, but missing one feature, most often the front stairs. The door, sitting three or four feet from the ground, would be unanchored by stairs.

Felix had noticed this phenomenon, too. He suspected cultural and financial operatives: the philosophy of work-in-progress versus a Western "done-and-get-on-to-the-next-thing" mentality, or the bad luck of actually completing something, or the desire to forestall taxes until the building was really finished.

I would look at those houses and office buildings, with a door sticking somewhere in the middle of nowhere and say, "but that first step is a killer."

So it is with Benedict's first step of humility. Later steps rate a sentence or two with little or no explanation, but Step 1, beginning with the command to *keep the fear of God always before his eyes*[2] is a doozy. It's a door three feet up, a killer first step that continues for twenty-one verses, dense in language (Benedict's) and scriptural references (God's).

Humility is off to a rough start. It's like the slogan that shows up sometimes on the marquis in front of the community church I drive by every week: "God didn't give us the ten suggestions."

Well, no, but there certainly are a *lot* of commands in the Bible, and the Church surely added a few that God missed. How am I supposed to even round them all *up*, let alone obey them, and fear God for good measure?

The fear part gets easier by the minute. If this is on the final exam, where was I on the day of the lecture? The step itself says very simply, *obey all God's commands* and *fear God*,[3] and adds the following, like bulleted items in a Power Point presentation:

+ keep your thoughts on God,
+ do not do your own will,
+ do not follow the desires of the body, and
+ be vigilant.[4]

Not that I'm counting, but that seems to add up to more than just one step.

Alcoholics Anonymous introduced me to steps and to humility. The twelve steps of AA not only keep you sober, but also transform you from a "dry drunk"—the same person you were drinking, only now not-drinking—to somebody entirely different, someone who has reached a state of serenity. That's why we loved the Serenity Prayer so much. Even the *word* had a soothing, edgeless quality that we edgy perfectionists found appealing—and impossible. For Benedict, though, the ultimate achievement is not serenity but humility. It's a state that conjures up images of downcast eyes and meekness, and it doesn't seem nearly as appealing as the floating, angelic sound of serenity.

One of the founders of AA, Bill W., doesn't mention humility until you get to his Step 7: Humbly ask Him to remove our shortcomings. Like Benedict's obedience to God's commands, Bill W. knows self-reliance isn't the answer no matter how our culture exalts it. "As long as we placed self-reliance first, a genuine reliance upon a Higher Power was out of the question," he writes. "That basic ingredient of all humility, a desire to seek and do God's will, was missing."[5]

Although my fling with AA only lasted four years, it turned out to be invaluable preparation for becoming a Benedictine oblate. The AA twelve steps introduced a dedicated, isolated loner like me to the idea of community, gave me a set of rules to follow and steps to take, and perhaps, most importantly, showed me that *humility* was not *humiliation* dressed for takeout. *Humiliation*, Bill W. suggested, comes to us unwanted. Humility, on the other hand, is something we should embrace. "It was only by repeated humiliations that we were forced to learn something about humility," he suggests. But from force to embrace, he becomes lyrical:

> We enjoy moments in which there is something like real peace of mind. . . . Where humility had formerly stood for a forced feeding on humble pie; it now begins to mean the nourishing ingredient which can give us serenity.[6]

*Humble pie* would take some force to get down anybody's throat. It doesn't really have anything to do with humility, although we've come to use it that way. Humble pie was originally a dish made from animal "numbles"—entrails or other internal organs. Passing from the old French to old English, it became *'umble* pie. The dialect of the old English dropped the initial "h," so *'umble pie* and *humble pie* shared the same meaning. It remained the dish that poor people ate. I could see—and certainly smell—the humble residue of that history when my grandmother would cook kidney pie for my grandfather.

That gorgeous, placid-surface value, *serenity*, now offers a way in. There's a door, and the door is humility, and like those not-quite-finished houses in Korea, I need steps to reach it. In a way, AA has been my introduction to Benedict's first step of humility.

This first step on the ladder of humility reminds me to remember God's presence in my life all the time: *Let him recall that he is always seen by God in heaven*, says Benedict, *that his actions everywhere are in God's sight and reported by angels at every hour.*[7]

That's a little too close to Santa Claus and his busy elves for my taste: "He knows when you've been sleeping, he knows when you're awake, he knows when you've been bad or good, so be good for goodness sake!" But perhaps Benedict is simply trying to remind us never to forget God. "We forget the presence of God and so act as if God were not present," writes Benedictine nun Joan Chittister on this step.[8] This is real; this makes sense to me, the way AA's Higher Power never did. In order not to leave anybody out or turn anybody off to a group that was founded out of fragments of a Christian revivalist movement, we found ourselves tripping over our Higher Power and our personalized, small-time definition of it. "I pray daily to my Higher Power, who I define as the bottle of booze," said Gail in a small step meeting in the tiny town I lived in. "It's the only thing I've met that was stronger than me."

The Benedictine approach is more solid. Chittister breaks it out wonderfully in her analysis of what this forgetting of God's presence gets us—not fewer presents under the tree, but less remembering of what lasts in this life, what matters. And because we're not remembering God's presence, we go looking for something to replace it with. "We make so many little things into little gods," she says.[9]

Oh dear. And I thought they were just charming obsessions. One of my favorite little gods has always been time itself, the fourth dimension, and my attempts to manage it with organizers. A quick skim through my diaries reveals the embarrassingly small nature of my little, quirky god:

*January 7, 1990.* Seven days into the decade and I have already changed organizers. This is typical behavior for me—I change organizers the way some people change underwear.

*March 3, 1990.* I bought myself another organizer, so I will be wildly re-copying information for the rest of the weekend. Third organizer of the year. They are marketed for the Control Freak Club, of which I am a charter member. I know I'm not a bad person, or even an inherently disorganized one, but I keep trying like hell to get control over something I don't understand and haven't named.

*April 30, 1996.* Found the perfect organizer at the Chamber of Commerce board meeting. I lusted after it all 90 minutes of the meeting and never heard a word until I could rush up to its owner and ask where it came from. She told me. I told myself I would skip the retreat at the Mission I was going to sign up for if only I could have an organizer that perfect. I told myself I would never ask for anything ever again if I could keep such an orderly, planned life as that organizer promised me.

It took forty-five minutes to drive to La Jolla, and a mere twenty minutes (but ah, such blissful minutes!) to spend more money on a time-management system than I had ever spent on such an item before. For $83 I got the basic insides, plus add-ins that I had to have (a zipper pocket, blank pads that fit the holes), and the absolutely unbasic "lady golfer edition." Each month has a two-page pictorial spread of a different golf course. Each day has a golf quote or tip. One of my six numbered databanks is labeled "Golf" (the number-one slot of course!). There is a little golf caddie book that fits in the front (although why I want to track my golf scores and keep them with me at all times is beyond me), and the place marker is the silhouette of a lady golfer.

I fell helplessly in love with it. Then I bought the purse/briefcase that all this wonderfulness can slip into for another $200. Then I bought the all-day time management seminar to learn how to properly use all this wonderfulness for another $185.

Felix says he knows how I am about organizers, but he still can't believe I would be willing to cancel God (my retreat) for a new Day Timer. Where are your priorities, woman?

In database #2 of my organizer, I tell him . . .

It was funny then, even to me. Now I'm using a Palm Pilot, a change in technology, not a change of heart. My priorities are still kind of askew. If I substituted "Christ" for "organizer" in a sentence, would I lust to find him, ask the way from those who already knew him, promise anything and everything if only I could have him in my life?

Hardly. I would consider myself a religious fanatic. So would my friends and neighbors. Organizers are harmless, but too much lusting after God can make you strange.

I knew I could find my thoughts on the little time-management god in my diary because it has been my lust and love for so long. But the intensity and frequency of my diary entries on the subject surprised me. The slavish care I devote even to writing details *about* the organizers surpassed anything I devoted to family and friends and bodily lusts—not that I don't have any. I'm just prudish about writing them down. But my organizer worship was totally without shame.

How can God even *fit* around the small gods we create, not to mention the theologically challenging issue of why he would want to? I am more willing to learn and follow Day Planner's decrees than God's commandments or Benedict's Rule. But the first step of humility doesn't say "obey time planner and schedule time for yourself." It doesn't tell us to follow the dictates of a Higher Power *we* may choose (or not) to call God—or the bottle. The first step of humility isn't about us at all. It's about God—obeying God, fearing God.

So where was I going to find *all* his commands to remember and obey? My god of time management at least came with an instruction manual. I was at least open to the *idea* of obedience to God—but alarmingly fuzzy on the details—when the oblate retreat came around. Abbot Antony arranged for several monks to give conferences to the thirty-five or so of us who showed up, and Father Martin was first on the docket.

"Let me give you a quick overview of what God expects from each of us," Father Martin began. "Please take one sheet and pass the rest behind you." Like little kids, we took and passed, and my eyes grew big when I saw the title of his handout: "Growth in Holiness." Father Martin's point was that love is supreme and charity feeds love, and charity is fed by the sacraments, prayer, self-denial, service, and the practice of all the virtues.

"How do I know what all the virtues are?" I asked, wondering if somebody else had lifted all the commands out of the Bible so I wouldn't have to go searching.

"Good. Turn the sheet over. On the other side where it says, 'A Traditional Catalog of Christian Living' are all the commands to follow: the commandments of God, the precepts of the church, the corporal works of mercy, and the spiritual works of mercy."

That's not funny, God, showing up at my oblate retreat with an instruction sheet just one page long!

All told, there are twenty-seven items in the catalogue, and none of them are particularly surprising (feed the hungry, comfort the sorrowful). If all I did was remember the ten commandments of God, and the Golden Rule of the Gospel ("You shall love the Lord, your God, with all your heart, with all your soul, and with all your mind . . ."[10]) that Jesus claimed as the all-embracing command, I'd have reached the first step of humility, and it would still be easier to remember than trying to live by St. Benedict's entire Rule.

But, as Jesus taught in parables, so I, too, find that a good story will remind me of what I need to remember in a way that a bullet-pointed list never does. If obedience to God is more than ourselves, our bodies, our self-made gods and interpretations of higher powers, what is it?

Felix gave me the story after one of his trips to China. Once upon a time, he said, there was a rich merchant with four wives. The fourth wife was the youngest, the most beautiful, and the most loved. The merchant showered her with delicacies and beautiful robes. He loved his third wife very much and always wanted to show her off to his friends because she was so accomplished, but he was afraid she might run off with one of them.

The merchant loved his second wife, too, Felix continued. She was patient and wise, and always helpful in difficult times. His first wife was deeply loyal and devoted, but the merchant did not love her, and scarcely paid attention to her, despite everything she had done for him over their long years together.

The merchant fell ill and realized he was near death. Not wanting to be alone, he summoned his fourth wife to his side. "I loved you the best and gave you the finest," he said. "Will you now follow me in death?"

"Absolutely not!" she answered in a tone that cut like a knife into the merchant's heart. She swept away without another word.

The merchant then summoned his third wife and said, "I've loved you a long time. Come with me in death."

The third wife laughed her tinkling, clever laugh and answered, "I'll belong to someone else as soon as you're gone." The merchant's heart sank and turned cold. His second wife was nearby, so he called her to his bedside. "You were the one I always turned to when I needed help and advice. I need your help again. When I die, will you follow me and be my companion in death?"

"I can't help you with that," his second wife said regretfully. "At the very most, I can only see you to the grave."

The merchant was devastated and deserted. Then a voice spoke out: "I'll go with you. I'll follow you wherever you go." It was the first wife, shriveled, starving, neglected, and unloved, who had spoken in the dark. Greatly grieved at the sight of her, the merchant cried out, "You, of all of them, I should have taken the best care of while I could!"

Felix's eyes got red around the edges as he explained the old Chinese story he found in an English-language bookstore in Hong Kong. We all have four wives, he said. The fourth wife is our body, and no matter how much money and care we lavish on it, it will be the first to leave us in death. The third wife is our possessions and wealth, and when we die, they will be quickly dispersed to others. The second wife is our family and friends. No matter how close they've been in life, they can't follow us past the grave.

But the first wife, neglected and unloved, she's our soul. She's the only one who can continue with us in our journey beyond life—if we take care of her while we can.

I think of that first wife and realize that she is the neglected, unnoticed part of me as well. If I ever get everything else nailed down right and organized, I'll have time for this God-stuff, I think.

But God, through Benedict's steps of humility, insists on being the first wife: *Obey my commands, never ignore them, fear me—obey me always.*

## Christmas

Here at the abbey, the Christmas season is in full bloom, but down in the valley, it's history. There, everybody knows that the Christmas season begins with the after-Thanksgiving sales and ends at three o'clock on December 25 when the holiday music stops, the gym reopens, and the post-Christmas sales start. Down there, everybody knows that Christmas is a time for giving, a time that brings out the best in us.

Here at the abbey, the monks don't know anything like they do down in the valley. Here it is, days past Christmas, and the place is still lousy with Christmas trees, red and gold tinsel, electric candles in the windows, and a half-life-size crèche in the narthex, with one of the shepherds sporting a cowboy hat. (This is the southwest, after all.) The monks are all walking around praying, working, presumably relaxing out of sight of the retreatants, and looking so pleased you'd hate to be the one to break the news to them: Christmas is over. Just listen to the radio.

*They* know it's just begun, and won't conclude until Epiphany. *They* know the shocking truth about what Christmas means, and how it isn't really about giving, but about *getting*. And, unlike most of us most of the time, *they* think that what they got for Christmas is absolutely perfect and all they could possibly want: a baby.

How can a bunch of celibate guys get this gift so well, compared to the rest of us, presumably normal, worldly types?

I've been thinking a lot about this kind of gift giving here at the monastery, it being the Christmas season and all. St. Paul, easily my favorite saint, with his tough love and good-hearted ways, talks about gifts a lot, especially in his first letter to the Corinthians—not the kind under the tree, but the kind that God gives, the kind of gift that makes the monks so nearly giddy these days. "There are different kinds of spiritual gifts," he writes, "but the same Spirit."[11]

I think about gifts because it's a lofty excuse to talk about all my good attributes. I think about my gifts and come up with health, a great husband, a good job, a nice house—all the things you think of around the Thanksgiving table while you're contemplating the turkey with half your mind and your blessings with the other half. And those are gifts—one-way, God-to-us. But gifts of the Spirit are the ones that need to make a return trip, from us and back to the world—otherwise how does the world see God among us?

I hatch another list, quick and dirty, of the variety of God's gifts that I also turn around as gifts to the world: prayer, patience (sometimes), cheerfulness, baby quilts. Those are the gifts I get that also keep on giving, that seem to come from an inexhaustible well—I'm surprised to see in the life of a childless, aging woman how many babies manage to make themselves known to me on a regular, quilt-making basis.

But these gifts I give because I have them to give. "You cannot give what you do not have," Abbot Antony has told me more than once. That usually comes when I'm deploring the uselessness of responding to the world's needs by prayer, patience, cheerfulness, and baby quilts. "I should be *doing* something," I will say, and then comes the gentle reminder that we can only give from what we have to give.

Here's my two cents' worth. We also give what we want others to receive—not necessarily what the recipient wants to get. Felix buys me a gorgeous, too expensive, and far too sophisticated suit for Christmas, when I was hoping for a blank book to write in, and maybe some colored pens. And Felix gasps at the state-of-the-art downhill skis when a bottle of wine and a good book would have made him perfectly happy. We can make cute lists of our Christmas gift desires and post them on the fridge, but in the end, we get what somebody else wants to give us. And then God gets in on the act, too. As William Williamson, an American preacher and pastor, writes:

> God wanted to do something for us so strange, so utterly beyond the bounds of human projection, that God had to resort to angels, pregnant virgins, and stars in the sky to get it done. All we could do, at Bethlehem, was receive it.[12]

Let's hear it for God. His chosen people, sorely oppressed, wanted a mighty king who could take over the Romans and win freedom for the Jews. Two thousand-plus years later, we want pretty much the same thing: to *know* that God is on our side against our enemies, and while we're at it, peace on earth and goodwill to men. And does God give us what we want, that Christmas, this Christmas, *any* Christmas? Noooooooooooo.

God gives us what God wants to give us.

A baby.

Felix and I were driving through the almost-town of Honomu, on the Big Island of Hawaii. Honomu survives because it's between Hilo and Akaka Falls, and there's not a whole lot of competition to being between the two. All the tourists have to go to Akaka Falls, basically because it's there on the map, and if you're driving counterclockwise around the Big Island, it's the last site to see for a while. Honomu sells high-end Hawaiian crafts and art as well as ice cream and pastries as you're coming back from the falls.

We got a pastry at Shimagura's General Store, and then Felix said, "Let's see what we can see next door." The Odaishan Temple was a Tibetan Buddhist temple, exotic to a kid from Pawtucket, Rhode Island, or even a woman from southern California. But on the islands, it's about as exotic as a small-town Protestant church—which it is, in its Buddhist way. Felix had just returned from a lengthy trip to his great love—China—and I think he was missing old Buddha.

When he pressed his nose against the glass door, it suddenly opened. "Please come in." We certainly couldn't say "no, thanks" at that moment, so we removed our shoes and entered. The young man who brought us in introduced us to an even younger wife with a large baby on her lap and to a parishioner sitting with them.

Felix walked to the elaborate altar area, with its bags of rice offerings in front, its gold hangings, incense pots, candles, and large gold Buddha. "May I show you around?" the young man asked.

I waited behind. "Are you tourists?" the parishioner asked politely. "We don't usually see many tourists here." She was being kind for not adding, "—especially white people from the mainland." The young man and his family were from Japan via Honolulu, and the parishioner was originally from Japan, too, "but very long ago," she said.

"My husband has a Buddhist soul," I said, not even knowing if Buddhists believe in souls, but also not knowing how to explain his deep reverence and awe of things Buddhist.

"That's very good, then," she answered approvingly. "He will explain," she added, pointing to the young man, who was, it turned out, the minister for the Odaihan Temple.

"How do you do the incense?" Felix asked him.

"We light three sticks of incense: one for Buddha, one for our ancestors, one for ourselves—for health, a safe trip home." The minister showed Felix the palms-pressed bow. "The right body is Buddha, the left body is self. We press our palms together and join Buddha to ourselves," he says. He showed Felix the photos on the wall of his honorable ancestor ministers of the Temple, all venerable with age and wisdom.

"I am too young to be among them," the young minister said. "I am just twenty-eight. I have so much to learn." He learned English two years ago in Honolulu, and did not feel ready to lead this remote temple after just two years as an assistant minister. "But the bishop said yes to here or back to Japan. So I try yes."

It reminded me of St. Benedict's Rule, where Benedict says that if you're given an impossible task, you must, *in complete gentleness and obedience*, accept it.[13] This young man is doing that, with great gentleness and obedience. "But I have been studying since I was ten years old," he added, as much to shore up himself as to reassure those who depend on him.

Felix wrote a little prayer that the young man would successfully lead his congregation and see his picture on the wall someday along the other ministers. He dropped it in the offering box with some money. We all bowed the bow of joining the god to us, and our hosts wished us well on our journey.

It took us a few minutes to gather up our shoes and hit the road again. But we were quiet for a long time in the car, gathering up our thoughts.

"What are you thinking?" Felix finally asked.

"Well, what just happened there? Was that a gift or an answer to something you were seeking?"

"Oh, definitely a gift," he said promptly. "Who would know to look for that experience? I thought maybe I'd get a photo opportunity. That's all I was looking for."

A book I was reading at the time—about Buddhists reflecting on the Rule of St. Benedict—confirmed Felix's instinct: "Buddhist and Christian monasticism are compelling case studies of the idea that real community is a gift, not something you fabricate."[14] That's what our half-hour at the Odaishan Temple was—a gift of community, kindness, hospitality, teaching. It was a gift that pulled Felix inside from where he stood outside, nose pressed to the window.

It's Christmas, the season of giving, we think. I saw Felix receive something so wonderful just a few weeks ago, when we were on the islands. Maybe that helped soften me up for the silly happiness the monks at the abbey seem to be experiencing this week. Or maybe it's the present of the baby himself. We got a call in Kauai, telling us that Felix's first grandson had arrived, a month-early surprise.

"It's good, it's all good," the phone message kept saying. Arriving just a few weeks before Christmas, the baby made the pretty artwork of the Nativity more real to me. This new baby and Jesus share the same humanity, the same helplessness, the same hopes for the future and continuity from the past.

Babies and I have always inhabited different worlds, but this one became real and entered my self-enclosed world when his proud grandmother gave him context: "Wait until you see him; he's absolutely darling, just the most darling baby you will ever see; and the parents are so sweet, and their instincts are so good."

"And the word was made the flesh and it dwelt among us." All I seemed to need was a little human context to boost me into the divine. The beautiful, serene Madonna and Child of countless artists will never look so untouchable to me now that I've seen a digital photo of this baby all swaddled on the shoulder of a proud, fiercely protective mom (who is also a successful investment analyst, but in this photo is *all* mother, and you really wonder where the baby ends and mother begins). That's the kind of event—ordinary to everybody except the direct participants—that really changes you. Those are the best gifts.

As the preacher William Williamson continues, "This is often the way God loves us: with gifts we thought we didn't need, which transform us into people we don't necessarily want to be."[15]

We probably wanted any kind of God-gift than what we got: a baby. And if that wasn't shocking enough, Benedict's first step of humility talks about obedience to this Baby God, and this Baby God's commands.

As I walked into the abbey church last night for Vespers, I almost stumbled over Brother Maurius, kneeling in the alcove by the big nativity set. Brother Maurius, easily one of my favorite monks, once upon a time was a professional magician who still has a magical sense of humor. Brother Maurius can make all the salt and pepper shakers disappear in the retreat cafeteria by magic, and has a steady supply of really bad puns for every possible occasion. He's been a monk for a long time, but old showmen die hard, and watching him work the cafeteria will remind you of an old vaudeville comedian running through the same old material.

So it's a surprise to come upon him, because, unfair as it is, I take his light-heartedness and assume that's his only heartedness. And there he is with his beautiful features as immobile as the statuary around him, kneeling in the straw, lost in prayer before the manger.

There is a story told in the south of France of the four shepherds who visit the child. One brings eggs, one bread and cheese, one wine. The fourth, called *L'Enchanté*, brings nothing. The three with their gifts sit with Mary and Joseph, offering their congratulations, saying how well Mary looks, telling Joseph how cozy the cave is, and how nicely he's fixed it up, and weren't the stars beautiful tonight, and if ever they need anything else, well, just ask.

When it's time to go home, they all realize *L'Enchanté* is missing. They look inside and outside, and finally peek around the blanket Joseph hung to protect the crib from drafts. And there he is, the enchanted one, kneeling in adoration, as he had the entire visit, whispering, "Jesu, Jesu, Jesu."[16]

Obedience to God is a good thing. This gift of God, this crazy, insane idea he had of giving the world this baby we didn't ask for, didn't want, and don't know what to do with now that we've got him, is a good thing. It's good. It's all good.

# −2−
# The Star

## Epiphany

At the abbey, the monks offer a silent, stubborn gift: the holiday decorations are still up in mid-January. The manger scene, now moved inside the abbey church, is replete with the added statues of the three Wise Men who have finally breezed in to town. Down below, it's January, drab even in San Diego with post-holiday let-down, abandoned New Year's Resolutions, and credit card statements in fat envelopes full of regret for the excesses of holiday giving.

Christmas, the great feast of Christ's birth into human history, is blindsided by the holiday season wrapped around it. Down below we're recovering from Christmas with our January blahs. But up at the abbey, the monks are deep into Christmas II: Epiphany, when the three Wise Men—Caspar, Melchoir, and Balthazar—followed a star to Bethlehem to worship the newborn king and leave their gifts of gold, frankincense, and myrrh.

Growing up, I thought it was all one story, one gala event. Jesus is born in a manger and a star guides the eastern kings to the scene of his birth some time around midnight, December 24 at the Christmas Eve service, since that's when we sang "We Three Kings of Orient Are." Then it's Christmas Day—gifts, turkey, family visits. By three o'clock in the afternoon, the carols disappear from the radio station, the relatives pack up, the turkey remains get wrapped in aluminum foil and Tupperware. Santa heaves his last weary ho-ho and the feast is over.

But Christian writer and mystic Evelyn Underhill sorts it differently. "The Christmas mystery has two parts: the Nativity and the Epiphany," she writes. "A deep instinct made the Church separate these two feasts."[1] In Christmas, we celebrate God's entry into His creation. In Epiphany, we celebrate the *knowledge* of that event into the world.

It shouldn't be that hard for me to make the distinction. It reminds me of the dichotomy at the university where I work. The fundraisers scramble to secure gifts; the PR and legislative types like me proclaim those gifts and acknowledge what they mean to the rest of the world. We're the Magi.

Epiphany first looked interesting to me when I paid a shopping visit to Nogales, Mexico. On the main drag of Nogales right after Thanksgiving, the stores were full of cheap Nativity scenes and figures. Before that, I'd only seen the pretty, elaborate ones in churches and New England village squares. But these were different—so unprettified, so un-*white*. Jesus, Mary, and Joseph were clearly Spanish; cheaper versions had even darker, Indian features. It had never occurred to me until then that Jesus, the infant God, could enter history and look like us, when *us* meant non-white, non-European. It was a moment of illumination. "I want one," I said, always willing to purchase illumination wherever it might be sold.

"Next year," said Felix quickly, looking over at the rows of junk I was entranced by. "It would be hard to pack for the plane home. Maybe next year."

I went on to look at other things. I got the joke. Next year we'd be sitting around a fireplace in New England, celebrating Christmas (or not) as we always did, saying, "Remember that *awful* crèche we saw in Mexico last year?" Har, har, har—we'd dodged another bullet of tasteless impulse.

The joke was on them. The next year we were living in San Diego, a trolley ride from Tijuana. The day after our first Southwestern Thanksgiving, we went with friends by trolley to Avenida Revolution to see what Christmas shopping looked like in pesos. We returned lugging *two* garish sets of Nativity figures *and* wooden stables with straw glued in. I must have looked like the gringo from hell, but I didn't care. I had my Nativity scene—plus another as a gift for the poor souls back east who might not have visualized Mary and Joseph as brown Indian peasants with badly angled halos wired above their heads.

Italian writer Giovanni Papini, trying to impress the homely truth I felt for the first time in a seedy Mexican tourist trap, reminds us that Jesus was not born in a "holy stable made of plaster of Paris, with little candy-like statuettes . . . a neat, tidy manger, an ecstatic ass, a contrite ox, and angels fluttering their wreaths on the roof. . . ."[2] Gosh no—not *my* crèche, *my* Jesus. The cows in my crèche looked slap-happy because their red lips were painted askew, the beautiful black king had a white beauty mark on the side of his face, and Mary's halo was slipping down over one eye, giving her a rakish, French-beret effect. There was a painted bird on the thatched stable roof instead of a star because Felix negotiated it as an extra since I was buying two sets of figurines.

Although I never bothered with Christmas trees until this past year, I pretty faithfully put out the crèche each holiday season, and managed to keep it through four moves in eight years, including the year it stayed in a storage facility when we were between houses. It was so honest and humble; it had to mean something, although I wasn't quite sure what.

When I began attending Catholic churches and tried singing in the choir, I met Maria, another soprano. Maria loved Epiphany. I never heard of anybody who loved Epiphany before, or who even knew it was different than Christmas. But Maria's family was Mexican. "See, we put up the stable in Advent," she said. "But we leave Baby Jesus in the box until Christmas Day, because that's what we're doing in Advent—waiting for Jesus to come. So it's just Mary and Joseph and the animals and the angels. On Christmas, we put Baby Jesus in the manger and the shepherds outside to pray, but we put the Magi on the top of the stairs. Every day one of the kids moves the kings down one or two stairs, getting closer and closer to the manger while they followed the star. Finally, on January 6, the Magi arrive at the manger. We all give each other gifts to celebrate, and then everybody goes home the next week, after the Feast of the Baptism, and we put everything away until next year."

You can almost *hear*, and certainly feel, the approach of the kings that way. In the Divine Office, there's a similar drumbeat in the changing antiphons that open the day's prayer from the beginning of Advent until the end of Epiphany. The first half of Advent begins with, "Come, let us worship the Lord, the King who is to come." The second half of Advent opens with, "The Lord is close at hand; come let us worship him."

On December 24, the Office starts with, "Today you will know the Lord is coming, and in the morning, you will see his glory." From December 25 until Epiphany, the joyful news is proclaimed: "Christ is born for us; come let us adore him." And from Epiphany itself to its ending feast, the Baptism of the Lord, we say, "Christ has appeared to us; let us adore him."[3]

You can almost hear the slow, measured clop-clop of the camels moving closer with each antiphon's beat, zooming in on a baby's heartbeat that grows stronger and more real with each passing day. *Come, let us adore him!*

This is living theater, in living color. I wanted to celebrate that way, in liturgical time, the birth of Jesus and his manifestation to the world.

But there was a problem. If I was the last one to learn the truth about Santa Claus, I wasn't the last one on Epiphany. Early on in my Catholic journey, there was a book sale after Mass and I chose my first Catholic Bible because it was small, sturdy, hard-covered, and thumb indexed. The translation and commentary, prepared for the Christian Communities of the Philippines and the Third World, was an eye-opener, starting with Matthew's Gospel story of the Magi.[4] "In order to understand this chapter, we have to remember it belongs to a kind of literature in vogue among the Jews of that time," the commentators wrote. "History and fiction were intertwined so as to teach in a figurative way."[5]

"The Three Wise Men are fakes!" I howled to Felix when I read it. It was Santa Claus all over again and I felt betrayed.

"No, really?" Maybe Felix was the last one to know. He had to balance off the sense of loss at a beloved holiday story moving from history to myth against the vain hope that maybe those lopsided smiling cows and cross-eyed Marys might never again grace his home at Christmas.

The Wise Men represent not kings, but pagan seekers and seers, we're told, and the star tells us that God calls each of us according to our personality. The Philippine commentators continue, "So for the pagans who look at the stars, God calls by means of a star." The commentary closes with the provocative question: "But those who do not seek truth, justice, and forgiveness, how will they find Christ?"[6]

How indeed do you ever know what you've found unless you knew what you were looking for?

During the Cold War with Russia, as the space race played out in the background of my elementary school years, a Russian cosmonaut named Yuri Gagarin carefully reported back from the stratosphere that he couldn't locate heaven. The report stuck in my mind when our eighth-grade science teacher gave us the basic astronomy map of our galaxy. He got to Pluto and said, "There are other galaxies, of course, but we don't know what's out there past our own."

My best friend Val looked up at him all indignant and said, "God and all the dead people are out there!"

It's a matter of knowing where to look, and what you're looking for. The stars are as good as anything to look for, depending on what you want to find. On our third or fourth visit to the Big Island of Hawaii, a little bored with trying to find new things to do, Felix and I decided to drive up Mauna Kea to the Visitors Center at 8,000 feet to see what we could see. I think I was expecting to see a few stars, and maybe some planets, through the University of Hawaii telescopes.

It was December, about 30 degrees at six in the evening, with steady thirty- to forty-mile-an-hour winds and thin, clear air. When I finally braved the outside—who brings the right kind of clothes for *this* when they're packing for Hawaii?—the sky with its burden of stars made me choke up and nearly cry. Thousands of stars, more than I could possibly imagine, brighter than I'd ever seen, an unfamiliar sky suddenly opened up, lousy with stars. Orion's Belt appeared nearly eye level from here, we were so far up, and you could see the edges of the Milky Way. I had just become a Benedictine oblate-novice a few weeks earlier and was just beginning to learn to pray the Divine Office with its burden of psalms each day. One of them sprang to my mind right there and then:

> When I see your heavens, the work of your fingers,
>     the moon and stars that you set in place—
> What are humans that you are mindful of them,
>     mere mortals that you care for them?
> Yet you have made them little less than a god,[7]

It was so cold and lonely there, standing at the edge of heaven. I felt glad that God chose to come among us so we wouldn't have to be cold and lonely ever again, standing on the outside of heaven.

The stars blinked back, dead, unanimated things. I rushed to the car to get warm again, and we headed back down to ordinary skies. It began to snow on Mauna Kea an hour later, and I forgot all those things made manifest from watching the stars.

*Oh, come, let us adore Him.* Whether as high as I can get this side of heaven, or here, in a cold, quiet retreat chapel, it is the season to follow the star, to pay homage. And the fact is, our trek may not lead us to lofty and heavenly places after all, but to homely, unexalted ones, like the retreat chapel.

One of the younger men who lives in the bungalows at the abbey and works in the kitchen comes into the chapel while I'm studying. He kneels on the floor for a while, staring at the gold-caped Blessed Sacrament. Then he moves to the front of the little chapel and prostrates himself full length before the Sacrament. I try to stay busy and unobtrusive in my corner. I hate to be the intruder of such intimate moments.

Finally, he rises and settles in the front row with his rosary beads. This I can stay with. The click of rosary beads being prayed is a comforting sound, like the adding machine's ratta-tatta-tatta I heard each night as a kid, falling asleep to the sound of my father, the CPA, working on somebody's books in the kitchen.

Then, the young man's cell phone erupts, making us both jump. But he has manners. He leaps up, says, "I'm very sorry!" to me, bows to the Blessed Sacrament, and rushes outside the chapel and yells into his phone, "I'm in adoration, dammit!"

The Magi are the phone call that helps me remember what I was looking for: God. Like Jacob, I can't help but exclaim: "Surely the Lord is in this spot; and I did not know it!" Epiphany is the knowing and the star that leads us there in adoration.

## Step 2: Following God's Will

"Humility," says Andrew Murray in his book of that name, "the place of entire dependence on God, is, from the very nature of things, the first duty and the highest virtue of man."[8] Again! Going *up* in pursuit of lowliness, like a backwards elevator.

For Benedict, this "place of entire dependence on God" is the second rung of humility's steps—*not his own will nor [taking] pleasure in the satisfaction of his desires; rather he shall imitate by his actions that saying of God.*[9] In other words, says Benedict, replace self-will with God's will.

It doesn't seem to be an impossible step when I just read it, at least not compared to some of the others. St. Benedict isn't saying to give up free will and become a puppet to God. He's only telling me to turn over the agenda to better hands than mine.

But the step is at odds with the culture of self-reliance that we're so proud of. Alcoholics Anonymous, the original self-help group, proclaims reliance on a higher power, but in the AA universe, it's still all about us—even the higher powers that members turn to are self-defined. I think God is a pretty good sport about all the terms and conditions we impose on our relationships with him.

In his marvelous book on Benedict's steps to humility, Father Michael Casey suggests that Step Two poses the question, Who is my master? "Either I look for self-transcendence based on faith," he argues, "or I lock myself within my narrow world of experience, memory, and perception."[10]

Well, I've been in *that* world all my life, and worse than the narrowness of my experience, memory, and perception is the fact that they *move*. I change my mind. My perceptions about the rightness or wrongness of the situation rush to follow suit. And then, damned if my memory doesn't begin to rewrite the story. I lack consistency. My self-will lacks a steady focus. I'm all over the place.

One of the commentaries on the Rule offers a way out of self-will: "I find myself pointed toward God rather than my own self."[11]

To which Father Stanislaus, who now rests in peace in the growing cemetery next to the abbey church would say, "Praise God!" More than any Bible-thumping televangelist, Father Stanislaus believed and preached praise as the way to position ourselves toward God and away from our self-will and laundry list of petitions. He claimed that petition turns us away from God as we look around and tell God what to fix next—as if he doesn't see all this himself and needs our friendly reminders.

Father Stanislaus's focus caught me by surprise. I'd been visiting the monastery only a few months when he led a Day of Recollection for my parish. I thought he was dour and serious and hard to understand in church. But here he was, smiling broadly, cracking terrible jokes, happy as hell to tell us to "get out of the petition business!"

Shoot. We were all good people, trying hard to be good, deserving extra credit for all the prayers and rosaries we offered for the needs of others. We were carrying our petitions around like little crosses when along came this nutcase monk with a funny accent telling us not to bother.

"If you praise God, then God is the Father, and you are God's child," Father Stanislaus said. "If you petition God, then God becomes Santa Claus, and your focus is on me-myself-I. Right?"

He was answered by stony silence.

"Scripture says," continued Father Stanislaus, "that you should pray always, sincerely, and wholeheartedly. You should pray in secret, every place, cheerfully, faithfully, persistently, and earnestly. Yes? What type of prayer gets you all of these at once?"

I felt like we were on a game show. Drum roll, answer: Praise does! Only nobody answered, because we were all getting sulky and didn't want to be led down Father Stanislaus's strange path to holiness.

Father Stanislaus handed out pages to all of us. "Your guarantee," he said. I looked at mine. Oh dear, he'd really written up a guarantee of what praise-prayer would get me.

1. I would be always praying.
2. I would pray everywhere.
3. I would have more peace.
4. I would be able to control emotions. *(Ha!)*
5. I would have greater awareness of God.
6. I would glorify God always.
7. I would put everything into prayer.
8. I would grow in holiness AND *(drum roll)*
9. I would possibly escape Purgatory!

Now, how can you beat all that? Not once did Father Stanislaus use the word *humility*. Not once did he talk about self-will. Not once did he mention anything resembling the self. He was too busy telling us how to turn our souls to God, like flowers growing toward the sun.

We were told at his funeral that when he learned of his cancer, his response was to praise God for all the opportunities his illness provided. In his agonies, he lectured himself: "Sacrifice! Sacrifice!" For Father Stanislaus, it was all about God. That's what St. Benedict is trying to tell us in this step: maybe it's not all about you after all. Yes, it's humbling. And it's harder than it looks.

I wasn't crazy about Father Stanislaus—he was too fierce for my weak-willed nature. On the other hand, being weak-willed has the singular advantage of giving up—to God, to better ideas, even to strange dark monks with strange prayer habits—more easily than my stronger-willed comrades. Father Stanislaus handed out praise exercises for us to practice. ("Learn a favorite hymn of praise by heart and sing frequently.") He handed out a sheet answering the what-how-when aids and benefits of praying praise. "I like to compare it to swimming," he wrote at the bottom of the page. "Swimming in itself has so many benefits. It is a fun sport, and a wonderful exercise tool, etc. But the more you practice, the better you are able to compete in tournaments or go to the help of someone who is drowning. Likewise, the more you practice the prayer of praise, it will bring about its own benefits. But it can also be used to overcome negative feelings and bring you peace."

It's like hearing a voice from beyond death, rereading those notes I tucked away for safekeeping in that year's prayer journal. I think Father Stanislaus must have climbed the ladder of humility, and I think he must have had a peaceful death, facing the Divine in praise as Christ came forward to welcome him home.

I followed some of the suggestions, listening to music of praise on CDs instead of the radio while driving in my car, learning Psalm 150 by heart ("Praise God in his holy sanctuary"), and creating a praise rosary to say, with bits of praising prayer and doxologies. Although it's a difficult turn to make in a prayer life—petition just seems to be what prayer *should* be about—the good news is that self-will falls away more easily, if only because of neglect.

Plus nobody ever asks me to pray for them, so "getting out of the petition business" was easier when you were working for yourself anyway. I don't know why I never get asked to pray for others. Maybe I don't know people who believe in the effectiveness of prayer, or maybe the ones who do just don't think I'm the one who can deliver the goods. My first (and, to date, *only*) prayer request, putting me back into the petition business, came twelve years after my conversion to Catholicism, and three years after becoming a Benedictine oblate. My colleague and non-believer friend at work, Cecilia, asked me to "send some good thoughts out" for her daughter who desperately wanted to carry a baby to term and had been repeatedly unsuccessful. The daughter thought she might be pregnant again.

"You mean pray for her? But you don't believe in that stuff."

"I don't want to leave out anything that might help," said Cecilia, ever the practical, concerned mom.

"Well, sure," I replied, happy to oblige. "Catholics have a special interest in babies. Especially miracle babies."

Prayer and liturgy are the making of art to a Benedictine. If I am called, as a Benedictine oblate, to prayer, then, after three years of practicing my call, I had my first commission. What I discovered within minutes of the request: I didn't know how to pray a petition anymore, or if it works or why. I only knew I should do something because Cecilia asked, and she never asks for anything. This was important to her.

I stumbled through prayers, mostly directed to my own patron saint, Blessed Joanna Mary. Neither Joanna nor I had ever experienced childbirth, or even stillbirth, but certainly the *wanting* of new life was something we knew in other forms. And we seemed to be Cecilia's only route to God. Father Stanislaus was dead, and I didn't have anybody to ask, so I e-mailed my mother's Episcopalian priest—a woman I knew slightly, who seemed unusually gifted in discernment:

> It's a perfectly nice thing to pray for, but I'm wondering what it all means, this matter of Christian petitionary prayer. If the result is yes, did our prayer necessarily have anything to do with it? If the result is no, how do we understand that? Isn't the result going to be whatever the result is going to be no matter whether we pray for a particular outcome or not? Does our own selfhood get in there as an intercessor? I am already chomping to get in there and start working prayer to see how powerful my prayers are, like this is a test. Somehow that doesn't seem to be what this should be about. But I don't know what this *should* be about anymore.

I stumbled along, waiting for answers that didn't come. In my morning sacred reading practice, I was making my way through St. Paul's letters for the second time around, and this time I came across the phrase *the Spirit gives life*.[12] If that is so—and I've never had any reason to doubt Paul—then my thoughts turn to Cecilia's daughter and that bit of baby the doctor says is the size of a grain of rice. Is it human yet? The Spirit gives life. What was lifeless before—a tangle of threads and a blue-stamped piece of fabric—comes to life as a baby quilt because the Spirit makes it so through the work of my hands and my grumbling heart, asking Blessed Joanna Mary to keep a prayerful eye on that baby while I am stitching.

Combine egg and sperm, in the bedroom or the laboratory, to create this grain of rice, this bit of tissue. It is filled more with the hopes of a few and the prayers of another than anything else. But the Spirit can give it life and create a baby.

Or not. Humility—especially in this step—says it's not about me, or the juice my prayers have. It's about God's will in us and for us. It's about the words we pray in the Lord's Prayer: *Thy will be done* (not mine!).

I like the way Sister Joan Chittister answers the debate of my will versus God's. "The will of God for us," she says, "is what remains of a situation after we try without stint and pray without ceasing to change it."[13] I think we forgot that the outcome—whatever it is—is God's will. Our will doesn't win outcomes. It just gets in the way between God and us, interferes with our real business of praising God "always and everywhere" as Father Stanislaus put it.

I had a friend from childhood who was determined to thwart God's will. She didn't see it that way, of course. She wanted a child and was subjected to endless early, violent miscarriages. The old ones said it's not meant to be. But how could that be so? The couple was handsome, successful, in love. They would make such good parents. They adopted a beautiful baby boy at birth and everybody said how fortunate to give the baby such a nice home; especially since, unfortunately, you can't have one of your own. But my friend kept trying to have a baby of her own anyway twisting against the obvious answer, until she finally carried to term. The baby was born deaf and blind and the old ones said it wasn't meant to be.

Who knows? The Spirit gives life, even to deaf and blind babies. My friend Cecilia did what she could do: counseled her daughter on prompt medical and prenatal care, prepared both of them as much as possible for any outcome, asked somebody she knew who was a "pray-er" to pray. We who believe—even when we do not know exactly the nature of our belief—get to pray for those who do not, but our prayers and petitions do not create life. Only the Spirit does that.

The trick is to know what is and isn't God's will, and we can only test our knowledge of God's will against God's knowledge of that will in our petitions.

There was another petition-prayer, this one played out on the front pages of the newspaper: nine coal miners trapped in a flooded mine in western Pennsylvania for more than seventy-two hours. I'm sure their families and friends prayed unceasingly for their rescue— you saw the pictures of the families, with rosaries in their hands and tears streaming down their faces in the newspaper articles. But I will admit it was only a newspaper story until our summer priest, Father

Adrian, linked it to the Feast of Sts. Joachim and Ann, the parents of Mary. St. Ann is also patron of miners, said Father Adrian, and he asked our prayers for the miners' safe recovery.

They were found alive and close to being rescued that very evening. "You will shatter the jaws of all my foes," says the Psalmist.[14] For reasons we cannot know, St. Ann heard the prayers—or did not—and God shattered the jaw of the enemy of the miners—Death itself—bringing them all back after three days in the ground, as certainly as any resurrection.

I was so happy for the miners and their families. Once Father Adrian had captured our imagination, showing us the humanity of the miners' peril and the irony that it occurred on St. Ann's feast day, I waited in confidence that our prayers would be answered affirmatively.

But maybe our prayers had nothing to do with it. Maybe the miners would have been rescued without a single prayer. And maybe not. If it's in God's hands, why bother? And if the rescue is in our hands, why bother God?

It comes down to the rung of obedience to God's will, I think. "We are all connected in ways we cannot imagine, and prayer alters the relationship we have with each other and our relationship with God," wrote my mother's priest not long after the miners returned from the dead. "What it does for God no one knows. All we have for sure on that front is the fact that Jesus told people to pray. Hence, I do."

So do I, out of obedience to that command, if not to God's will. Cecilia's approach was simple: leave no stone unturned. Move both heaven and earth, and see what comes of it.

That's obedience of the best sort. Pray like hell for the friend or husband or trapped miner—because you are asked to, or because you love the one you pray for. Surrender to God and become transformed in God by your obedience. As the old abbot loves to say, the saints didn't need psychiatrists. They surrendered themselves to God and lived in humility's obedience to God. And that was the outcome—the transformation itself, not the answer to a prayer of petition with a yes or a no.

In that way, responding to God with obedience is no different than anything else you might petition of God. Move heaven and earth to see it through. See through it, to God's hand. It may be different than your desired results. Who knows why? Only God, and

God's not telling. But our responsibility is to move heaven *and* earth, and there's no purpose in trying to get off the hook since God doesn't try to get off the hook of his responsibility to us.

It is humility to do God's will and set aside our own. With Father Stanislaus's formula, guaranteed, I could turn to face God in praise and not have to think about self-will. But a beautiful prayer request from a friend also reminds me that I will pray and test God on what I think is right and just. And that it is always God's will in the end, where humility will reside.

## Epiphany

The ladies on retreat at the abbey this weekend are milling about aimlessly. It's two hours after breakfast and an hour before Mass. They walk around with heart-shaped name tags around their necks, the intensity of their retreat dissipating like the morning frost, as they begin longing for the warmth of the comfortable return home. You can see it on their faces: the desire for the quietude of the hill mingled with the desire to go back down to the world—their world.

The monks are not so torn. Their lives are here until they die and then, like Father Stanislaus, they're buried here on the hill. I'm not so torn either, only because I travel up and down the hill so much that I am nearly a visitor in both worlds.

Epiphany has that feeling. Despite the recent arrival of the Magi, the excitement is old news by now. Ordinary Time beckons—as if January weren't bad enough in itself. By tomorrow the crèches and lights and garlands will disappear, and the monastery will be as bland as January gets everywhere else.

But it is still Epiphany today. I want to watch for the stars.

Felix received a telescope for Christmas, and spent a great deal of time setting up and preparing his latest toy.

"Check it out," he said mid-afternoon, which surprised me. I thought astronomy was strictly a nighttime activity.

I peered into the eyepiece and witnessed the less-than miraculous sight of an ant crawling inside a rose. "What's so special about an ant in a rose?"

"Carol," he said in that exaggerated tone you use when somebody is really not getting it. "That rose is on the other side of the golf course!" Astronomy and its tools take far-away ordinary things and bring them into spectacular closeness. The astronomer at the Fleet Science Center in San Diego showed us all the constellations we would be able to make out with the new telescope, named them all, and then added, "Constellations are illusions, you know. The stars we tie together with a line drawing and a name are nowhere near each other. They're illusions based on where we live and our position in the galaxy."

Maybe that's the "behind story"—as Felix's Korean business partners call what happens behind the scenes—of the star that called the Magi and sent them on their way to find the child king. Maybe it's the illusion of time and space collapsed around an extraordinary moment of our human history. Whatever it is, it's not enough, even for God, to enter mankind. Something else has to happen, too: people have to find out that God has entered mankind. The ordinariness of an ant on the other side of the golf course crawling around a rose becomes spectacular when it fills our view from far away.

Who knows what will fill our view and become our life? I spend so much time planning and plotting my life, especially at this time of the year. There are New Year's resolutions, and work plans, and the coloring book of my spiritual life to fill in. There are five-year plans and retirement plans, goals and objectives, accountability measures and to-do lists.

Humility isn't on any of those lists. Neither is "submit to God's will"—not even on the spiritual growth list. There's a story in Luke's Gospel of the ten lepers near Samaria and Galilee. They must have known everything on *their* to-do list that day, but then Jesus walks into their village. Keeping their distance, the lepers raise their voices and call out, *Have pity on us!* And Jesus says, "Go show yourselves to the priests." You have to wonder why they listen, knowing their loathsomeness, their uncleanliness, knowing they would probably just get thrown out. They knew enough not to get too close to Jesus, right?

But they break ranks with what they *think* they know and submit in faith to Jesus. And before they even get to the priests, they realize they're cured—all ten of them. But only one returns to praise God. Praising wasn't any more popular with them than it was with our crowd at Father Stanislaus's day of recollection. Jesus looks around and says, "Ten were cleansed, were they not? Where are the other nine? Has none but this foreigner returned to give thanks to God?"

And while all of them are cured, Jesus pronounces a special blessing on the one who returned. "Stand up and go; your faith has saved you."[15]

It isn't about the doing—the act of running to the priest. The lepers are cured before they get there. It's about submitting in faith to the will of God. It's a big step of humility. "This tug of war between my will and God's will for me," as one writer describes it, "I will suffer because of it. Still, I strive to choose freely, again and again, God's will, and His speaking in my soul."[16]

Fittingly enough, this season closes with our annual oblate Epiphany party. Abbot Antony doesn't do much with the Christmas oblate meeting, but the Epiphany celebration has been going on, I am told, for as long as the abbey has had oblates. "There is good reason for joy and celebration!" writes the abbot in his letter to us. "A few years ago, we enjoyed listening to oblates tell of their family Christmas celebrations. For this party we would like to hear from more of the oblates about how you celebrate the birth of Christ in your homes now or when you were a child. We all have different traditions." I feel like I've exhausted my own meager supply of such memories in just decorating a Christmas tree and setting up a crèche, but I go to the party to support the other oblates and to listen.

But first, when we arrive, the old abbot declares that there is an "oblate present" for all of us, in honor of the season. The new oblate library is ready! We tour the facility, barely able to keep up with him for his excitement.

"We have over twelve hundred books for your edification, plus fifty videos!" he exclaims. "There is room here for up to ten people to study or work quietly. Please return what you borrow. We usually get them back when you die, but that's a bit late for the others."

This fine little room, with windows that open onto a quiet courtyard, tucked against the cloister as close as we can get, is a little chick, nestled against its mother. It's like the little study room of the House of Silence from so long ago, and I've waited so patiently to enter and use it. I'm flooded with warm memories of quiet places, gifts of great hospitality, libraries of my past that have welcomed me. I can hardly wait to return here to study, and to give back to the pray-ers their own house of silence in the chapel, undisturbed by my presence.

But first, we party.

From the forty or so oblates in attendance, we hear deeply moving or amusing stories of celebrations growing up in Mexico, the Philippines, Ireland, Switzerland, Argentina, Hawaii, and Viet Nam. Abbot Antony, face shining with happiness, and age-cracked voice growing firm, remembers long-ago Christmases in Indiana—eating fruitcakes soaked in rum "that made the cakes better than they really were," popping corn to string on the tree, and Christmas stockings with an orange tucked inside—a December treat in Indiana in the early 1900s. "Now, I can have them all the time, but every time I smell an orange, it takes me back to Christmas." Abbot Antony's been around a long time, but these memories are the closest to his heart.

It doesn't matter if the Epiphany story is made of fact or myth, does it? It's memory and celebration. It's old stories, lovingly retold and re-created. It's manifesting the truth again and again.

Outside the abbey as we leave, the moon hangs brightly, praising God, the largest full moon of the year, reminding us of the Star in the East so long ago that led even the wisest of men to the smallest of children. It's definitely Epiphany.

# —3—
# The Temptation

## Lent

Lent is the cruelest season—not for its sacrifices or temptations, imaginary or otherwise. Lent's cruelty is in its timing. Was it just a few weeks ago that the abbey church was filled with the fresh pine scent of the boughs from Christmas wreaths? Weren't we just practically falling over statues of stable hands and lowing cattle and mangers, and singing lusty glorias? Didn't we just prepare ourselves penitentially for the great feasts of Christmas and Epiphany?

How did we find ourselves here? With all the suddenness of the Gospel narrative, it seems. In Mark's telling, Jesus has barely been baptized by his cousin John the Baptist when, in the next couple of verses, he's off to the desert, tempted by Satan for forty days, as the angels ministered to him.[1]

In my youth, listening to the Gospel story in the King James version, I easily imagined Lent as the time of temptation, with the Devil in a red suit, sporting horns and a tail, offering Jesus the opportunity to strut his stuff and show his power. The Devil would have been pretty easy to pick out, and I didn't think Jesus had a tough time recognizing trouble and resisting this obvious rabble-rouser.

But I didn't know then what I know now: the Devil can look like the easy way out or the sly whisper in my ear telling me *exactly* what I want to believe. I didn't know that on special occasions, the Devil can even masquerade in the dress of the Church itself. I didn't know then that the Devil was in the details, or that the slippery slope of temptation could begin with just one drink, one drag on a cigarette, one iota of the substance that always welcomed you in and never let you go. The temptation to show your power—power you actually have—must be nearly irresistible. But Jesus resists.

We all taste temptation and resistance during Lent. Suddenly it's gone dark and cold again, from feast to fast in a few short weeks. As a lector at my parish church, I get a workbook to help me understand the readings and put them into the context of the liturgical seasons. My public Lenten readings are, ideally, informed by my private study. "Though we may not look forward to Lent's abstinence and severity," says the workbook on the beginning of Lent, "it's important to acknowledge our sinfulness, the sober truth of our mortality, and the need to take stock of our lives."[2]

Now *there's* an upper for walking up to the pulpit and reading from the Book of Joel, which is a downer if there ever was one. My lector workbook assures me that the congregation will be "in a receptive mood, expecting a message that will help them live up to their Lenten resolutions."

That's not exactly what I saw as I looked up from my reading that first week of Lent. It was eight o'clock on a Sunday morning that was cold for southern California, with the grass frostbitten and the everlasting sun refusing to get up, go to work, and warm things up. It was the start of the everlastingly long season of Lent, cruelly juxtaposed alongside the holiday of cheer and glorias. The faces in the pews that looked up at me wore glazed or weary expressions: here we go again.

Lent comes in the middle of the academic year, which, for a university lobbyist like me, means the heaviest travel schedule, the hardest work, the shortest days, the bleakest, darkest cold nights. It comes during that long stretch of time between the fresh hope of a new school year and the triumph of commencement. Receptive mood? Not even the lector could fake that one.

The weather in New England could have conspired to make Lent even colder, darker, and less hopeful in my childhood than in my adult life in southern California. But when I was growing up in the Episcopal churches of Rhode Island, I didn't see it that way. For one thing, time itself wasn't scrunched up like an accordion box the way it gets later, when you can barely unwrap a birthday gift before it's coming around again to bag you for another year—or decade. Time, when you're young, living in a small, forgotten state, can stretch out forever, whether you're waiting for Christmas, Easter, or the time between the two.

Back then, Lent was about giving up stuff, rather than giving in to the temptation of despair, like a few of those Sunday-morning faces reflecting back at me. For us, Lent was about the mite boxes we were given in each Sunday school class through sixth grade. I never realized they were called mite boxes to represent the story of the widow's mite, where Jesus praises the humble offering of the woman who has so little and yet gives so generously from her poverty.[3] I wish I'd made the connection then, instead of thinking—if I thought about things at all—that a mite box meant simply donations from little kids—mites.

I used to collect donations door-to-door in my neighborhood for the March of Dimes. I could never get over how it was the people in the poorest houses—the rundown, beat-up houses with trash flowing out of the buckets right outside the front doors, laundry flapping out back, and unhappy dogs barking within, the houses where I was afraid to walk up to the front door and ring the doorbell—who tended to give the most. They knew need the most. They knew poverty of spirit the best, and what it felt like to give from that place and feel rich in it. I could have understood the season of Lent a lot better if I had been able to put all that together.

But instead, I folded in the flattened sides of the mite box each Lent, punched out the slot at the top, and contributed the pennies, nickels, dimes, and occasional quarter that resulted from the Lenten sacrifice—usually candy. The goal was to have the heaviest mite box come Palm Sunday, when we followed in the procession of palms and left our mite boxes on the altar for another year. Pennies were especially good for this purpose. Those kids whose parents threw a dollar in the mite box for them to march in the parade were usually embarrassed by the lightness of their good Lenten intentions.

My father felt differently. As the church treasurer with just a few volunteer counters, he had a whole different mentality about breaking up a couple of hundred cardboard boxes so that he could manually stack and count change that probably didn't amount to two dollars per box. And since *his* giving up for Lent was usually smoking, and Palm Sunday came seven weeks into nicotine deprivation, and one week before Easter's resumption, he could get pretty crabby about mite boxes on a pretty regular basis.

By seventh grade Sunday school, we got rid of the mite boxes and joined the adults in the dime-a-day folders marking down the forty days of Lent from Ash Wednesday to the day before Maundy Thursday. At that rate, your Lenten sacrifice equaled $3.80, plus it was hoped you stuck a dollar or so in the slot left for the holy days between Maundy Thursday and Easter. But, even by mid-1960 standards, it was still a slim harvest of resisting temptation, and I think my poor father had a few choice unchristian thoughts about pulling all those dimes out of their little cardboard slots for such small total benefit.

Still, even such smallness, of giving up or giving out, seemed to last forever. Our good intentions of Lent probably lasted longer than our more secular New Year's resolutions, but eventually the focus wore off, and life returned to its pre-resolution normalcy—proof positive that an ounce of sin weighs more than an ounce of good intention.

When I converted to Catholicism and came back to church as an adult, Lent became a new set of negotiations. For one thing, there were no mite boxes, no daily signs of trudging through the season of sacrifice and penance. Some churches had meatless potlucks and the Stations of the Cross, which *sounded* pilgrim-y and penitential, but usually consisted of saying a set of prayers designed around the events of Good Friday—and I wasn't ready for that yet when Lent was just beginning. In health-conscious southern California, meatless potluck meant garden salads and eggplant Parmesan. Felix says I should consider this a fortunate happenstance of converting to a post–Vatican II Catholic Church. Otherwise I'd be getting tuna-noodle casseroles with crushed potato-chip topping.

The only daily offering of sacrifice associated with Lent seemed to be connected to fast days. I knew Catholics did this during Lent when I was growing up in the pre–Vatican II days, because the Catholic kids I knew were always so *loud* about it. I knew about the no-meat-on-Friday rule that put soggy tuna fish sandwiches in the Catholic kids' lunchboxes. But the fasting rules for Lent, once I learned them as an adult, were embarrassingly modest: on Ash Wednesday and Good Friday, you get one regular, meatless meal and two small ones, "so that together they do not equal in quantity a full meal."[4]

This is fasting? I did it the first year of my conversion mostly because I was trying so hard to *feel* Catholic that I would have done *anything*. But this was all they offered. I went to Mass on Ash Wednesday and got ashes because that was the most distinctive day for knowing who was and wasn't Catholic when I was growing up. But that wasn't enough connection to the season for someone without a personal lifetime of tradition behind me, and within two years, with my busy springtime travel schedule, I'd completely forgotten the rules. Even when I did get to church for Ash Wednesday, the priests seemed determined to remind us that it wasn't a feast day and that attendance was entirely optional. It wasn't, they told us, even the beginning of Lent, which officially kicks off the following Sunday. I went to the Franciscan mission one Ash Wednesday, and we wrote our sins on a piece of paper (my paper was too small and I had to borrow a pen), and then ushers came and took the papers and burned them in a caldron, and the same ordinary ushers blotted our foreheads from what we were told were last year's burned sins.

Now, *that* was cool. *That* was the way to ring in Lent.

The official Catholic documents seem to take the punch out of Lent and turn Lenten sacrifice into bland volunteerism. "It would bring greater glory to God and good to souls," one Catholic website reads, "if Fridays [during Lent] found our people doing volunteer work in hospitals, visiting the sick, serving the needs of the aged and lonely, instructing the young in the faith, participating as Christians in community affairs, and meeting our obligations to our families, our friends, our neighbors, and our communities."[5] I'm not saying I do this, perfectly or imperfectly, but aren't we called to better our communities by our Christian call? Isn't this what we're supposed to be doing all the time? What makes something a Lenten practice, it seems to me, is recognizing temptation and resisting it, becoming generous in our poverty of spirit. Even the mite boxes were out-of-the-ordinary attempts, no matter how ordinary their results.

I hardly expected St. Benedict to turn Lent into a meaningful time, but that's what he did. In the Rule, Benedict suggests that *the life of a monk ought to be a continuous Lent.*[6] For those monks or secular people who live their daily lives in tedium or frustration, boredom or terror, a life of Lenten sacrifice is probably one they feel they understand too well. For the rest of us, there is the season of Lent to draw us closer to sacrifice and self-denial, to remember, however slightly, "the sober truth of our mortality."

As Benedictine oblates affiliated with an abbey, we share with the monks their *bona opera*, or "good works," in addition to our ordinary, expected service. Benedict offers, as suggestions, *prayers, spiritual reading, compunction of heart,*[7] and abstinences.

I may not be a person who knows a lifetime of continuous Lent, but I have certainly felt like I've lived a life of abstinences. In my twenties, I had to get a grip on binge eating. In my thirties, I was forced to abstain from alcohol, and given my all-or-nothing tendencies, abstention was actually easier than moderation. In my forties, it was smoking and nicotine I finally abstained from. I was glad Benedict gave me the option to include good works for Lent, not just abstinence.

"Nothing needs to be too burdensome," Abbot Antony cautioned his oblates as he passed out *bona opera* forms. "All in moderation. That's the Benedictine way."

Well, it wasn't *my* way, but I had only been a candidate for oblation, an oblate-novice, for a mere three months. Plus either Abbot Antony as our oblate master or Abbot Henry as the abbot of the entire monastery had to approve and bless my *opera*. So I went moderate: fast on Ash Wednesday and the Fridays of Lent (one abstinence) and recite the Rosary on those fast days (one addition). A short time after I submitted it, Abbot Henry sent it back with the blessing, "May our Lord in his mercy deepen your joy of self-denial!"

There was no place to go but deeper, really. It didn't seem like much of a joy to begin with. After all, I wasn't doing that weenie Catholic fasting. This was bread-and-water, guts-to-glory fasting. It was a start to getting Lent, and that seemed important to me. Without the self-denial, how could I, as Benedict says, *look forward to holy Easter with joy and spiritual longing?*[8]

The next year, fully vested as an oblate, I upped the *bona opera* ante. I dropped recitation of the Rosary because I thought—incorrectly, as it turned out—that the monks didn't say the Rosary. Many do, but it is part of their private life, and was private enough for me to miss the clues at first. I upped the bread and water fasting to *every* Wednesday and Friday in Lent, throwing $5 for each fast day into my fasting envelope to give to the monastery at Easter. It was like my old mite box, only much lighter and easier to count. And I added daily reading of *The Imitation of Christ*, because even though I hated it the first time around, it was Abbot Antony's favorite book, and I had to see what I was missing.

"May our Lord grant you the wisdom and strength to follow him more closely in this Lent," wrote Abbot Henry on my *bona opera* form's return. Not catchy, but a blessing on my efforts nonetheless, for a Lent marked by rigid adherence to my *bona opera* and raging out-of-control eating, sleeping, gossiping, and *not* working out.

I have no copies of my *bona opera* for the next year, although I know I pledged the same fasting and reading of *The Imitation of Christ*. The reading was difficult enough to qualify as *bona opera*, but on a daily basis, it was at least do-able, and I still didn't like it, so it still counted as extra credit. That year, with three lines left on the *bona opera* form, I upped the ante again: I would memorize Psalm 51. I'd already painfully acquired a selection of two memorized psalms, plus the Gospel canticles of the daily office. Psalm 51, prayed in *every* Friday morning office, approaches greatest hits status for penitential psalms. And it has forty lines—far longer than anything I'd tackled to date, but perfect for Lent. With a bit of trepidation—was I taking on too much?—I sent in my form.

The reason I don't have it to refer to now is because it never came back. Abbot Antony broke his knee that Lent, and papers and blessings must have gotten backed up or forgotten, and my *bona opera* was a small casualty.

Not to me, of course. *Nothing* related to me is a small casualty. In my prayer journal on Ash Wednesday that year, I wrote, "No blessing from the abbot, which bothers me. May God bless this feeble offering." The next day, having memorized the second line of Psalm 51 and read three more chapters of *Imitation*, I wrote, "But no blessing from my abbot! Lord, be my blessing."

The next day was the same, both in terms of doing my *bona opera* duty and awaiting its belated sanction: "I am sorry I am so bothered by the lack of blessing. It is part of the Rule. I feel like I'm doing something off-line." Even four weeks into Lent, my prayer journal noted sadly, "My Lenten *bona opera* continues in its unblessedness."

It was like driving uninsured. I was being more careful than usual about *everything*, not just my stated *bona opera*. I didn't feel like I could afford an accident. And going unblessed while trying to do more for Lent definitely feels like an accident waiting to happen when you're an all-or-nothing type trying to match the extra works of Lent into a rule of moderation. That's the Benedictine way.

## Step 3: Obedience to Earthly Superiors

Having covered the absolute necessity of obedience to God and surrendering to his will, Benedict suddenly does an about-face from the sublime to the silly and tells us to submit to earthly superiors, too, while we're at it: *that a man submits to his superior in all obedience for the love of God.*[9] That's a move, in a few measly paragraphs, from obeying God to obeying my boss? How homely, how . . . *earthly* can you possibly get?

"Oh, that's very Confucian," says Felix when I complain. "You see that as part of leadership training in Korea all the time." But I am not working in Korea, as he does so often. I am not studying the Rule of St. Confucius. I am a free-for-all, me-first American, whose biggest, deepest desire is to become a hermit. But at least right now, I have to settle for Benedict's Rule, community instead of solitude. I'm none too happy about that, and then Benedict comes along and says true humility will be reached by obeying the *boss?*

One Benedictine monk, in his commentary applying the Rule for oblates, cheerfully concurs. Monastics aren't the only ones who practice obedience, he says. Ordinary people do, too. If the only step were obedience to God, we might be a bit daunted that we'd be tempted to step away and leave all that to the religious types. But we don't get off so easy, the monk reminds us: "Everybody is obedient to an employer."[10] This guy might be a monk, but he sure hasn't worked lately in a shared-governance state university.

Chittister suggests that this step "helps us face an authority outside ourselves."[11] That may be especially helpful to people like me. If I remember to even try submitting to God in obedience, I have trouble distinguishing God's tone of voice—or God's will—from my own. The added advantage of this step—at least in the upside-down, Alice-in-Wonderland world of humility that raises you up for being lowly—is the practice it offers. It takes me far more practice to obey some other lousy, flawed human being who holds rank over me than to obey somebody like, say, my beloved Abbot Antony, under whose authority I willingly place myself.

Welcome to the land of the free and the home of the brave. Humility House, here we come. Sometimes when I vote in an election, my picks don't get into office. Not only do I still have to obey the decisions made by the ones I didn't choose, but as a lobbyist, I have to work with all of them, no matter how I feel about them or their political stands.

No less an authority than Jesus himself suggested we give to Caesar what is Caesar's and to God what is God's.[12] There is obedience by choice and there is obedience due to rank. It's hard to swallow, this kind of obedience, and Benedict undoubtedly wants it done cheerfully as well. I have to cheerfully obey the boss! My jaw clutches just thinking about it.

Well, nobody in this step said that those earthly superiors have to oppress you, although they certainly can. For me, it's been easier to look at this step through the prism of another culture that I admire from afar and sometimes dip a toe into: the Hawaiian people.

My joke going out to Hawaii this last trip was that I would learn the ukulele and bring one home. I'd seen plastic ones for $20 in all the tee shirt and macadamia nut stores. I'd buy one, I announced to everybody before I left, learn Christmas carols, and play them all the way home on the plane.

"Do that, and I'll have to come home drunk," Felix complained. It was a *joke*. Can't anybody take a *joke?* And ukuleles are inherently funny. Witness the Tiny Tim jokes my threat was always met with. It never occurred to me that there were serious ukulele players out there, or that you could actually buy a ukulele in a music store like a real musical instrument, for a real musical instrument price tag. It was a *joke*.

In a moment of daring, or calling my bluff, as soon as we arrived on the Big Island, Felix pointed out that Waikoloa was offering *free* ukulele lessons (ukuleles provided) on Monday mornings. "So did you put it on your schedule?" he asked.

I did. It was still a joke, though I wasn't laughing quite as much ten minutes before class time, when I was the only person waiting and somebody said, "There's the teacher."

"Am I going to be the only one?" I asked Felix. "Let's leave. I can't be the only one."

"Oh, relax. Think of all the attention you'll get," he said—then wandered off to window shop and maybe take pictures of my great experience. A few more people materialized out of the shadows, all of them clutching ukuleles. We pulled plastic lawn chairs into a circle and somebody from the mall's facilities department dropped off a big box of plastic ukuleles and told me the lessons lasted about a half hour. I could do anything, I figured, even look like a jerk, for a half hour.

Then Auntie showed up, very much in charge. I was the only new person in the little group of local people who showed up faithfully from all over the Kona side of the Big Island on Monday mornings to submit to ukulele practice under her firm, kind rule.

"Show her a C chord," she instructed the fierce older gentleman sitting next to me. He did. I played it twice. "This is an F chord," she said. I couldn't convert her mirror image into what I needed to do. The young man on my other side showed me the F chord. I still couldn't do it, so finally he plopped his left hand over mine and hit the correct frets.

"Now, strum!" Auntie said. The six of us began strumming C–F–C, and Felix, who was nearby taking pictures, had to exit the scene before he laughed out loud and got people mad.

"It wasn't that the music was comical," he said later. "It was the sight of all those good players with their beautiful instruments, playing baby chords over and over because that's all you could do."

And that barely. My fingers hurt. I could hardly hold a chord—even an easy one—*and* strum, and I was holding everybody back from playing all the Christmas music Auntie brought to share. It was humiliating. I hated being new, especially when it forced everybody else to begin again, too.

So there I was, trying to play this stupid plastic ukulele, when I suddenly remembered my old friend Victor, who had moved from his home in Hawaii to MIT in Cambridge, Massachusetts, for graduate school. As soon as he arrived, he bought himself New England winter clothes and signed up for Tae Kwon Do. He'd been a student of Tae Kwon Do, a Korean system of self-defense, since elementary school. "You can never learn it deeply enough," he told me. "It's not just the martial arts. It's a discipline and practice in humility that you can never totally master."

"Why would somebody go to a school of discipline and humility anyway?" I asked. "Doesn't MIT offer enough of that?"

"Not as a major," Victor said, snickering at his own cleverness. He would come back to the lab after a class and I'd say, "How did it go?" And Victor would reply, "Well, a new person came today, so we started at the beginning moves again."

"*Again?* Victor, you had a new person *last* month, and the teacher made you start at the beginning, and the person left after two weeks. How do you make any progress like that?"

"I don't mind," he said quickly. "What's progress supposed to mean anyway? More moves? The important thing is for the class to stay together and get the newcomers feeling like part of the group, isn't it?"

Well, no it isn't. I thought it sounded like some horrible plot against proficiency and mastery. I thought Victor's deep study sounded more like futility. I couldn't understand his willingness to subject himself to that kind of instruction. I wondered if it involved an Eastern mindset I would never understand.

"C–F–C–F–C again," called out Auntie. She turned to me and offered encouragement. "With C and F, you can play songs already! 'You are my sunshine, my only sunshine. . . .'" The little class launched right in alongside her. I got most of it, too, although changing chords, strumming, *and* singing—all at the same time—was beyond me.

Poor Felix hung around forever, taking pictures and trying not to get too bored. We played for two hours. "What happened to a thirty-minute lesson?" I asked one of the regulars.

"That was the part going over the chords. That took about a half hour. After that, we play until Auntie gets tired."

It took Auntie two hours to get tired. By that time I had dents in my fingers from the strings and a headache from playing the C and F chords whenever they came up in the avalanche of Christmas music we waded through.

Auntie leaned back and said, "Thank you, everyone," as if we had been *her* teachers, and the class began taking down the chairs.

"Where can I buy myself a good uke?" I asked.

"Well, mine cost $1,800. You'll never play well enough to buy one like that." Auntie directed me to a music store in Waimea that had never done her wrong. "Buy used," she said. "You don't play well enough for new yet. You may never need to get a new one."

It was a lot like Victor's class, I realized, but now it was me voluntarily submitting to a superior. Felix and I drove to Waimea and checked out the stock. We drove clear around the enormous island, three hours each way, to check out ukes in Hilo, the only real city on the Island of Hawaii. Then we came back and bought the uke in Waimea.

"You have come back and you have brought an ook-a-lele!" Auntie cried the following Monday morning when the regulars and I shuffled in. Her eyes grew wide when she saw what I was carrying. "Let me see your new ook-a-lele."

"It's used," I muttered. "I got him in Waimea like you said. His name is L'uke." L'uke the Uke had to be a he—it was a tenor ukulele that fit my small size like a little guitar instead of a Tiny Tim toy. It was made of spruce wood, made in Brazil, and I was quite smitten with the thing. "How do I tune it?"

"When you leave here, go back to Waimea and buy a pitch pipe," she said. "When you are here, you will tune to my instrument."

What a surprise.

But there were real surprises, for the class as well as the teacher. Some were surprised the mainlander showed up again at all, and I had to pass L'uke around to everybody like a new baby admired by the extended family members. We did a rousing rendition of "You Are My Sunshine," but then I launched into "Christmas Island" with the best of them. I knew the G7 and C7 chords from last week. I knew I couldn't make my fingers do a D7 no matter how hard I tried.

Auntie showed me the "ladies' way" of doing the D7 that sounds the same but didn't hurt. "You've been practicing!" she exclaimed. Daily, in fact. My new Christmas music, distributed just the week before, was lousy with practice marks and coffee rings. I was having fun. I even e-mailed home and discovered that there was a ukulele group right in Lake San Marcos, California—who would ever imagine?—and that my house sitter was not only a member of the group, but had invited them to my house that week.

The mall group thought it was great that I would have a group at home to learn from. "That's how it's done," explained the young man. "You don't buy videos or instruction tapes and learn alone. You sit in a group, listen, keep your hands busy, and try things out."

"Are you here next week?" asked Auntie.

"No." Suddenly a chill descended on my sunny Hawaiian life, so recently enriched and expanded. "I'm going to Kauai next."

Auntie nodded. "Beautiful Kauai!" she called out. And they were off singing, playing: "There is an island across the sea, beautiful Kauai, beautiful Kauai. . . ." I thought I heard a C chord. I plunked sporadically.

"Where in Kauai?" Auntie asked.

"Hanalei," I said mournfully at what, just weeks ago, I thought would be the best part of the trip.

"Hanohano Hanalei!" she said, and the group leaped into the next song: "The glory of Hanalei is its heavy rain—slippery seaweed of Manu'akepa . . ."

I was gently being strummed out of the corps I had only just joined. When Auntie grew tired, it was time to go. There were hugs from all the group, and I tried not to cry. Felix took pictures of me with Auntie's arm around me while I stood clutching L'uke. Then we departed like so much sand tossed ashore by the sea and reclaimed by the outgoing waves.

When had I ever been so completely claimed by a group before, or so willingly obedient to the authority that governed it? On Kauai between rainstorms ("the glory of Hanalei is its heavy rain . . ."), I plunked out "Christmas Island" and searched for a group to play with. There were none, and we came home shortly afterwards, with me lugging L'uke in my backpack and feeling as though I was leaving something very special.

"L'uke's going to get homesick," I kept saying on the flight home—where I did not play Christmas carols on my uke. "He's an island uke. He needs an island."

"Fine," said Felix. "We're island people. You're from Rhode Island. I'm from Long Island. He'll do just fine."

My ukulele group was my experience of community and obedience on the islands, and it gave me a taste of what Benedict teaches about submitting to authority. No less an authority than St. Paul urges the same thing: "Let every person be subordinate to the higher authorities," he writes, "for there is no authority except from God, and those that exist have been established by God."[13] But that means more than just crowd control. It is good practice for obedience to God. There can be no spiritual wild child for God, I guess, out there on her own, making it up, beholden to no one. Even hermits nowadays require the approval of their bishop before they go off to their caves. We're bound together in the love of Christ and in obedience to temporal authorities. Otherwise we become little gods of our own making.

Drat.

Do I have to accept this step? Of course not. Will I? Probably. I returned home with L'uke, a fistful of Christmas music, and a picture of Auntie and me that I promptly framed and sat next to a picture of the only other person I'd ever joyfully obeyed: Abbot Antony. I joined up with the local group the following Saturday. The Lake San Marcos group my house sitter introduced me to was hosting a much larger ukulele group from Orange County. They took over the repertoire like foreign plants choking out native growth, and everybody galloped off with it. I didn't have the music or the expertise, so I tried a few chords before quickly getting lost. Somebody suggested I could play better if I had a new instrument. I was not only *not* having fun, but L'uke was getting insulted!

"I know you all like to play fast, but here's a slow song I like," said a young man whose mother was visiting him from Hilo. The group politely fingered through Hanalei Hula before racing into another number chosen by a louder voice.

I grew tired and went home to play "Christmas Island" and "You Are My Sunshine," to think about how somewhere maybe Auntie would be facing a new player on Monday morning and marshalling her students around the new person into a rendition of "You Are My Sunshine."

It wasn't the same feeling in the group here as with the group in Hawaii. The difference was Auntie and the obedience she demanded. Here, the group was all wild child soloists.

The thing about obedience to earthly superiors, especially as I'm looking at it during Lent, is that it's all about practice. Since his retirement, Abbot Antony practices obedience to God by practicing obedience to the new abbot, some thirty years his junior. Lent helps us practice resisting little temptations so we can resist the major stuff—evil—that could otherwise keep us on the other side of the joy of Easter.

I was gathered up by Abbot Antony and given a Rule to live by. I thought I was giving it my best shot, but I was missing a lot of the basics. I want to pick the superiors I obey, like Abbot Antony or Auntie. I don't want to obey just for the sake of obeying.

But obeying is good practice for humility. And, as one Benedictine monk writes, "Humility joins us with the rest of the human race. It is pride which causes us to believe we are not like others. . . ."[14]

The monks know this. They live the Rule more deeply than I do, so they know when obedience to others supercedes obedience even to a *bona opera*, or other good Lenten practices, blessed or unblessed.

But for now, in this ukulele group without obedience to an earthly superior, I cannot work on the steps of humility, and only practice chords.

## Lent

This morning the air is full of chattering birds, but the retreatants at the abbey are quiet. They're either getting their last session or making up their beds to get ready to go home. I have no idea what the monks do in the time slot post-Vigils, Lauds and breakfast, and pre-Mass. I assume they read, since that seems to be what Benedict prescribes for monkish down time. If it were me, I'd be sleeping, but nobody ever said I'd make a good monk—or even a good oblate—except Abbot Antony.

The quiet of the abbey reminds me of childhood Sundays. The quiet muffles my ears to the cynicism and sarcasm developed over time, like scar tissue to cover the rawness of innocence. I am filled with images of a mother, father, sister, of Sunday comics, pot roast and brown potatoes, of Sunday services and choir music, of Daddy counting the collection in the back rooms afterwards while the rest of us tried (not too hard) not to spoil Sunday dinner with too many cookies at the collation that followed the service. In Lent, the prayers were longer and the collation minus the cookies because it was about temptation after all, and Easter coming up, and you don't spoil Easter with too many cookies in Lent.

Now my sister has moved on, my mother is in Florida rehearsing for the Spring Follies at her mobile park, my father is dead, and nobody I know eats pot roast (or cookies) anymore.

It's *bona opera* time again. I have a long memory for the hurtful silence of an unblessed *opera*, but I also have a strong desire to follow the Rule to the best of my ability. I took my form this year and, unimaginatively, listed the same three resolutions: to read the *Imitation of Christ* again, to do my hard-core fasting on Wednesdays and Fridays, and to memorize Psalm 51.

Abbot Antony returned my form to me a few days later with his blessing. He carefully circled the line drawing of Christ crucified on the cross, which appeared at the top of the page as a sort of letterhead—and which I'd never taken notice of before. Underneath, in the flawless handwriting of the old generation where penmanship mattered, undeterred by the hand of a gentleman in his nineties, he wrote, "What more could I do for him who loved me so much?"

He has truly captured the spirit of this season.

Psalm 51 begins, "Have mercy on me, God, in your goodness."[15] I recognize my weak, sinful nature in this opening line. I can do nothing to make God come to me. I can only stand here like the sinner in the Gospel[16] and say, "be merciful to me a sinner." That's what this psalm opens me to. The praising psalms open head up, with a song. The cursing psalms open mouth wide, flaring curses. But these penitential psalms begin with the head bowed down in sorrow. The singers of these psalms are victims of nothing except their own sinful behavior. Recognizing that, they ask God to enter in and "heal the sin-sick soul." This psalm is an oblation, an offering, as I am an oblate, an offering. It is a prayer of penance.

"In your abundant compassion blot out my offense."[17] God as tissue, as mop, as housecleaner. Blot it out! To do that with a stain, you take something bigger than the stain, moisten it, and press firmly and repeatedly until the stain is lifted up. Maybe that's what this prayer is about: we're pressed down by the weight of our sins, only to be lifted up in their removal.

"Wash away all my guilt. . . ."[18] We can't wash it away ourselves. The Lord must be our partner. Some partnership! We sin. He forgives. We try. He helps. We fail. He picks us up. We charge off saying, Lookie, lookie, I've saved myself—and everybody else nearby—again!

And the Lord smiles at our vanity and shortsightedness. Or sighs and walks off the set of our lives to grab a sandwich and wait for us to start screaming for help again. Which we will.

"That you are just in your sentence."[19] Well, God is justified in sentencing me because I keep giving him all the evidence he needs. This is God's idea of justice: I sin. God forgives. It could far more understandably be: I sin. God condemns.

"Wash me, make me whiter than snow."[20] First, I think of a bad ad for detergent, and then I think of the Transfiguration. We read that story in church during Lent, of all weird times, but it's about glimpsing the glory that's still to come. Whenever I hear it I think of the old abbot. His face shone like the sun on the day of his seventieth jubilee, as his cracked old voice repeated the vows of his youth on the Feast of the Transfiguration. I could see the transfiguration taking place before me: seventy years of trying to please God daily, and as he spoke his vows, you could see he was ready to really *try* to get to the good stuff, to do it better for the next seventy years.

"Do not drive me from your presence. . . ."[21] I have felt cast away from God's presence many times—mostly here in California, for some reason. I may have screwed up and been screwed over and definitely been screwy in New England, but there were always angels picking me up, brushing me off, or rushing around like lunatics to keep me from falling at all.

My angels didn't make the move here when I did.

Where do you go when God himself seems to be giving you the old heave-ho?

"Restore my joy in your salvation. . . ."[22] I continue the daily struggle to memorize this. It is a good *bona opera* in many ways. It forces me to think along the lines of sin, especially mine, and that is such a slippery slope of thought. It works my mind—this difficult task of memorizing—as hard as my heart, and heart and mind work together on the treadmill each night.

And because, like Lent, it has forty lines, if I slow down or skip, I'd fall off!

Here, deep into Lent, the season of self-denial, Brother Nicholas is cutting a slice from a magnificent cake set out for all of us to share in the retreat cafeteria. Who eats cake in Lent? Aren't we all supposed to be practicing virtue and resisting temptation? But an elderly lady on retreat brought the cake to celebrate her son's birthday. "I'm here and my son's in heaven," she says.

Brother Nicholas cuts himself a big slab of that cake and sits down to celebrate with her, here in Lent.

# Interlude

## *The Passing of our Blessed Father Benedict (Solemnity)*

At the abbey, an "oratory of oblates" (my name for our multitudes) gathers for the eleven o'clock mass and then lunches together afterwards with Abbot Antony. Father Prior Vincent, in his homily, talks about death and our preparedness for it. He tells us again how St. Benedict yielded himself in glorious death, arms raised up to heaven, a holy offering.

*Oblate* means "offering," and while I haven't exactly been offering myself in holy death this Lent, I have spent the last nine days praying a novena to St. Benedict. I'm not particularly the novena type—this is one of the first times I've tried this spiritual practice—and I suspect that many Catholic converts like me who entered the modern post–Vatican II Church are in the same boat. We don't exactly get the point of a nine-day act of devotion. There's nothing magical about nine days, or so I am told, but *novena* literally means "nine," and this kind of devotion is nearly always done over nine days. It's clunky enough that I have to backtrack from St. Benedict's day in my Palm Pilot to figure out which day the novena starts. What's so magical or mystical about starting an act of devotion on March 12? It's definitely the kind of thing I need to calendar if I'm going to do it at all.

And why do a novena, anyway, in the deepest part of Lent? "Isn't enough enough?" I can practically hear Felix saying, although he'd never really say it out loud. The twice-weekly fasting, the daily reading of devotional literature that even Abbot Antony would approve, the memorizing of psalms—when do you get to live the life of balance the Benedictines *tell* me is found in the Rule?

Thank goodness for Lent, I think. At least the small practices I commit to with my annual *bona opera*—and my dismal failure with them—show me how easily my self-discipline and selflessness tip over into self-will and selfishness.

And thank God for the opportunity the old prayer custom of novena gives. Though I read a portion of the Rule daily, and though I've mired myself in his steps of humility this liturgical year, I still tend to forget Benedict when I set the table for "communion of saints" company at Mass. Benedict is a shadowy presence at my personal table of favorite saints. I don't even seat him there out of preference, but more out of obligation. This novena allows me to think about him and our relationship over the course of nine days.

Benedict died on March 21, which pretty much guaranteed him a remembrance during Lent, when feasts and commemorations are muted affairs. That would have pleased Benedict in his humility. On the other hand, because of the timing of his death, another feast on July 11 honors Benedict as the Patriarch of Western Monks. I am not sure being granted two feasts instead of one would have pleased him at all.

Doing a novena now, smack in the middle of Lent, is another extra. Not accounted for in my *bona opera*, it's part of the battle to balance the reluctant checkbook of my soul.

The antiphon that opens the novena praises Benedict simply, in storybook beginnings: "There was a man, Benedict, who was revered, for the holiness of his life, blessed by God both in grace and in name."[1]

Who would think about what's in a name, beyond parents of newborns? The monks do, and each of them is given a new name when he moves from his candidacy to his first vows. I hadn't particularly thought it through before, but *Benedict* is the old Latin form of *Benedictus*, or *Blessed*. Surely with the name Blessed, there would be times when you'd want to go home, shut the door behind you, and kick the cat. I know that poor Felix is doubly cursed with good cheer—his first name means felicity or happiness, and his family name is Latin for good man. He says the only reason he didn't want to go home, shut the door, and kick the cat was because he didn't know he was doubly cursed with happy until adulthood.

My own first name is Old French for "song," which I thought was pretty funny when I went to major in voice performance in college. But give me points for consistency. In Camp Fire Girls, when we got to pick bogus American Indian names, I picked *Yakani*, "I sing."

The first thing you do as a professed oblate, following the custom of the monks, is take a saint's name, preferably a Benedictine saint, as your protector, guide, and mentor. The monks are allowed to make suggestions for their new name, but their abbot makes the final choice. Nobody, including the monk and his family, knows what that name is until it's spoken at the altar during the most breathlessly awaited part of the ceremony. Oblates, on the other hand, have a more democratic system and get to pick their own names.

I wanted to follow the model of the monks, so I submitted three names to Abbot Antony as oblate master. Would he choose Paula, the female equivalent of my beloved St. Paul? Theresa of the Little Flower, who I loved for her existential darkness? Or Blessed Joanna Mary, who he found in an obscure martyrology and claimed as my relative because her last name matched my husband's? I wrote out my choices, and my reasons for them, and sent them to the abbot. I lobbied hard for Paul. The old abbot didn't answer me, which bothered me until I realized he'd already chosen Blessed Joanna Mary. What's to answer again?

Ah, Humility, we hardly heard your voice, even when we requested your song! Joanna Mary, the Blessed is as much my blessing "both in grace and by name" as Benedict was for him.

Through the days of saying this novena, I realized if I want to see this blessed man, Benedict, more clearly, I can see him best reflected in the Rule he wrote. Like this novena, there's nothing magical in the Rule of St. Benedict. When I used to go on frequent retreats to the Franciscan mission nearby, the friars would cheerfully offer up a full buffet of prayer practices. You could sample a rosary or centering prayer. You could experiment with collage art or reflect on the Sacred Heart. The Franciscans were the first to show me Adoration of the Blessed Sacrament, which, more widely practiced before Vatican II, was off my newly arrived radar.

And of this sumptuous buffet of practices, the Franciscans said simply, all are ways to God. None are wrong, none are better. Take and see what works for you. It was all about *my* choices, *my* preferences, *my* way to God. And like a buffet, I seemed to always take too much and get confused by the choices.

The Benedictines, on the other hand, invited me to a sit-down meal, serving me the Rule of their founder, the man named Benedict. My invitation to the banquet, like the name I received at oblation, didn't have anything to do with my own personal preferences. It was all about my participation—and my obedience—as a Benedictine. God isn't a bouncer, with the club rules and practices in hand, checking admission. But since I'm part of *this* club, *this* way of Benedict's, I'm bound to its Rule, its obedience, as metaphor of how I've chosen to bind myself to Christ.

Benedict is not only a man of God, *by grace and in name*, but a teacher and coach. He called his training program *a little rule for God's service*, and I'm already pledged, as an oblate named Carol Joanna Mary, to follow it.

In a letter St. Paul wrote to Timothy, he says, "Train yourself for devotion."[2] What does such a life look like? How would you train for it, and how would you know what it looks like once you're trained?

Benedict laid it all out for me: the rules of the Office I pray every day and the rules of Lenten observance, the holy reading, group behaviors, and punishments, the rules on eating, drinking, clothing, and prayer, and most of all the rules of obedience, humility, and stability. He incorporated it all, together with the biblical antecedents, and handed it all to me through the aged, respectful hands of Abbot Antony as my training guide for a life of piety, a way of life.

This Benedict, a shadowy figure, emerges in his Rule as a teacher. Life as a student of Benedict's Rule is a life in training, like an athlete. We are spiritual athletes to Benedict, and I am never going to graduate from this school of the Lord's service. This race ain't over 'til it's over.

I can spend a lifetime reading Benedict's Rule, but I won't get it unless I am also living it. The Rule embodies the commands of Christ, and thus embodies me as his follower. It's more than pithy phrases or tiresome administrative details. It's a school, where Benedict teaches and I am a student.

"Then you will be pleased with proper sacrifice. . . ."[3] I'm finishing memorizing Psalm 51, winding down to the last lines. Lent itself wears down into the last days of self-denial. The psalm has made a good road to follow through Lent. I'm not sure who followed whom. I memorized it on planes to Washington D.C. and Sacramento, on road trips and treadmills. I said it every day in the car on the way to work: four stanzas per finger. Eventually it began to breathe with me, into an awareness of my sins that I hadn't noticed before. That's what the Rule itself is meant to do. That's why we read it, piece by piece, every day of our lives.

I would love to slide into Easter now—home plate, jellybeans, bunny rabbits, and smiley faces. But first, I think, I need to ask more questions before I can get to the answers.

What more could I do for him who has loved me so much?

# —4—
# The Passion

## Holy Thursday

The abbey seems hurried and harried this morning. Until lunch, it's still the place where monks pray the Office, and the Retreat Center still holds the last of its Lenten retreatants in penitential thrall. But around two in the afternoon the liturgical year begins to tilt and then tumble into the Triduum, the three days of high drama upon which all Christianity turns: Holy Thursday, Good Friday, Holy Saturday.

For now, the last dregs of Lent are poured out in an ordinary penitential quiet. Shortly the place will be filled with the heightened awareness of an unspeakable sacrifice. The monastery will be filled with the on-lookers and witnesses to the Passion. I would rather not look.

I have a particular knack for not seeing. Others—artists, saints, and the sensitive, who see Christ in the eyes of the suffering—see clearly, and suffer painfully for what they sometimes see. Me, I don't look. Or I look and don't see. It isn't necessarily a talent, but it's certainly something I've developed into a high art over the years.

"Did you read this article on the front page about the terrorist attack in Jerusalem?" Felix will say, looking up from the morning paper, his eyes sick with the horror of inhumanity.

"No. Missed it. What page is it on?"

"*Front* page!"

"Oh."

A little later, a different tone. "See how there's a sale on bedroom furniture? We might want to check it out."

"Oh? No, I didn't see."

"Carol, it's a two-page color spread!"

"Oh."

Silence, then he says politely and carefully, "What exactly *are* you seeing this morning?" Poor man—he looks at me, and I *seem* interested, *seem* to be reading, seem to be here. So how am I missing a front-page headline and a two-page color advertisement of something I've been talking incessantly about buying?

Answer: selective vision. I don't see what I don't want to see. I don't want to see human ugliness in action, and I really don't want to see myself spending big chunks of money. I spend big chunks of money, of course, but I hate being premeditative about it.

Once, this quality of my not-seeing resulted in a vivid dream, my Dream of Not Seeing, as I called it. I was standing in front of a monster TV screen that was supposed to be my computer monitor. This was in the early 1980s, when it was a rare soul outside of financial institution mainframe users who even saw computers, but I was working in a research lab at MIT. I inputted, processed, witnessed, and interacted with a nearly monastically hidden virtual community all day every day.

On this oversized screen in my dream, images poured across the surface, broken bits, vividly colored with everything I refused to see in daily life: starving children in African villages, willful cruelty to animals, burning, bombed-out cities, and toppling rain forests—one image after the other, all the awfulness and horror inescapable—until I woke up and said, "Wow! Too much caffeine late at night!" I wrote it down in a dream diary to discuss at the following week's therapy session, and went on with My Life as I Filtered It.

I don't think I ever did discuss it with my therapist, much as I loved dream work with audience participation. True to character, I buried it in a diary and probably forgot about it—or conjured up a more meaningful dream later in the week and talked about that one at therapy instead.

I only remembered that dream fragment now, some twenty-five years later, when I was buying books in my favorite Washington, D.C. bookstore at the beginning of Lent. The quest was simple. I was on a legislative visit to D.C., taking advantage of airfare discounts for a Saturday night stopover, and I ran out of things I wanted to do. I was also running out of things to read and had many hours on the plane and in airports before returning to San Diego. I spent two hours and three lattes in the bookstore before I emerged with three spirituality books. Two were collections of short pieces I was dying to get at, and one was a series of meditations on the Passion that looked edifying to my spiritual growth, to use Abbot Antony's favorite expression, but a little on the grim side.

"I'd rather not see that one now," I thought. I mean, meditations on the Passion as reading for a plane trip? No one would blame me for saving edification until I got home, or even for a retreat.

But the suggestion to not-see triggered the dream memory, and this time, so many years later, I wondered: exactly what is it you wish to avoid seeing, O delicate one?

One answer, at least one of the most important of many answers, came from the very book I dutifully plowed into on the Dulles–Los Angeles flight. Father Richard John Neuhaus knows why his book is the last I might want to read, and it's nothing personal. "It is easy to understand why people might want to avoid the cross altogether," he writes in his meditations on the Passion.[1]

Well, yes. As a kid, I could slide past all the goriness of Good Friday as the capstone dreariness of a long gray Lent, and hurry on to Easter Sunday without too much effort. The drugstores helped by setting out chocolate Easter bunnies weeks ahead, and the media cranked out stories of Easter egg hunts on the White House lawn. By now, so heartily sick of Lent—and winter, since they always went hand in hand in unending dreary gray of New England—I'd welcome any promise, any crocus popping up through the snow, any chocolate bunny rabbit as a sign to be done with it.

But the Passion deserves its time in our spiritual journey. The Passion is not the end of Lent, nor is it Easter weekend. The Passion is itself, its own time, where all is gathered up and broken apart, and we must see it and witness it with our eyes and our hearts. We can't get from the temptations of Lent to the joy of Easter alone. We have to be led to where we don't want to go. We have to see what we want to avoid.

Catholic writer Sister Lavinia Byrne says that the word itself, *passion*, carried the double meaning of pain and pleasure. "To come this close to another person is to make oneself vulnerable and open and to reveal the depths of one's desire."[2] Who is it I might become close to, this Passion, if I can make myself vulnerable and open?

What is the desire of my deepest heart that is hidden and obscured by my not-seeing?

Neuhaus, my airport reading, reminds me that if passion in our culture is associated with heavy-breathing romance and expensive perfumes, how quickly we will be pulled up short by the reminder during these intense three days "that to love is to suffer, and the suffering is not always sweet."[3]

Perhaps it's not always sweet, but suffering can have a ragged beauty about it, if we're willing to see the kind of beauty that still has its tags and rough unfinished edges showing. I figured that out when my stepson left for a year as an exchange student in Germany. He was just sixteen, barely in possession of a driver's license and a girlfriend, when he left all he knew to live abroad with a strange family and unfamiliar language because it seemed to be the right road right then. What bravery in somebody so young! He'd already said goodbye to his dog, his bedroom, and his stuff. At the airport were the high school friends, the sweetheart, the parents and sister, and, awkwardly, at the edges, the stepmother.

I felt badly for him because people were making his goodbyes more difficult with all their crying. I tried to think about it from his perspective. "Have a great adventure," I said, sticking out my hand.

"I will," he said, ignoring the hand and giving me a hug instead. For once, I didn't resist the hug. "Write lots," he said. "You like writing letters." And with that, he was gone. I gave Felix all my tissues and drove him home.

When we got home and I saw Petie, my pet parakeet, there was something wrong. With birds, especially the smaller ones who squawk instead of talk, you really have to pay attention. You have to sense the subtle changes to know when they're wrong.

"Not now!" I howled at Felix. "There's something wrong with Petie."

"How can you tell?" he asked. To him, Petie was just a dumb bird who sat on his perch all the time, just as he was doing now.

"I just *know*." It's in what you see and don't see.

I cried all night. I cried until my eyelids turned purple and puffy and looked as if they would burst any minute. I cried until I couldn't breathe, and then kept crying until my lips cracked from gasping for air through my mouth. I cried myself to sleep. I woke up crying. At some point, a surprised little voice in my head said, "Surely this is not *all* about Petie the parakeet?" But I didn't know. I was dumb in my grief. I didn't know love could hurt your insides so much. I didn't even know until then that I loved my stepchildren. But I was starting to get suspicious.

Petie died the next morning of diarrhea, which can kill you when your weight is measured in a few grams. Felix did the body removal. I was afraid to look at Petie. I was afraid I'd see him still breathing. I was afraid he'd see how helpless I was to stop his suffering. I couldn't look anymore, but I could look back, at least, and see for the first time how beautiful suffering could be—if it was for love.

Holy Thursday is not the end of Lent, nor the beginning of Easter. It is the first day of Passion, of love and suffering. The big liturgy today begins in community, the rite of the Lord's Last Supper. Jesus' followers are fresh with the triumph of their entry into Jerusalem, and now they join together for their Passover Meal. It's a good time, a good feast, and we are all together celebrating, yes?

At St. Peter's, a beautiful Episcopal church just blocks from the Pacific Ocean, I joined the parish one year for the Lord's Last Supper celebration. Growing up Episcopalian, I barely remembered anything about what we called Maundy Thursday except that it might have been a communion service on a Thursday night, waiting for Easter.

Returning after a long absence, I was struck by the change in liturgy and how those changes made for a different understanding of all that was taking place. We went through the communion service, which seemed suddenly rich in its story telling. And when we approached the rail, there were gobs of communion wafers for all of us. It was like a fire sale on communion wafers. I had to chew and swallow well past any sense of delicacy. We were sweeping the place clean, Father Corey told us. There would be no vestiges of Jesus left behind when we were through.

I got caught up in the drama of it—not because of the chewing or sweeping clean, but because of what happened next. The Altar Guild came forward—those ladies you never saw except for their meeting notices in the bulletin. You couldn't join them like a club; you had to be invited in—it was like a Call. And it always seemed, to an outsider like me, that there was a fussy, old-lady quality about Altar Guild.

But not this night.

The ladies came forward from their scattered seats about the congregation where they had been wives, mothers, and grandmothers, anonymous in their pews, sitting with their families. Now they rose up and came forward together, carefully dressed and groomed with the heart-breaking care you see in little girls making First Communion. These were all older women, fastidiously dressed for Christ. They came forward like a collective bride, and they began to fold up and remove the altar linens.

I have since seen this done in other churches, all Catholic. It has never affected me the way this one did. I have seen huffing, grunting ushers dismantling everything in sight, and I have seen tidy priests efficiently sterilize their surroundings. But here, by the Pacific Ocean, the Episcopalian ladies of the Altar Guild rose as one, made their way to the altar, and proceeded to remove everything with the most loving hands you could imagine.

These ladies *knew* how to fold clothes. They knew their furniture and linens like the back of their aged, shaking hands. It was a lifetime of women's work, and here it was performed as the best prayer, like a lyrical psalm, with the greatest tenderness and respect.

When it comes to the language of mysticism, as Sister Lavinia Byrne points out, "it is not by chance that it relies so heavily on bridal imagery."[4] At first, that's what I was seeing before me—a mystical, multiple bridehead coming forward to greet the groom and do a little housework as well.

But as they quietly returned to their seats and their anonymity, I looked again at their handiwork. The gorgeous red cedar wood gleamed in the fractured light of early dusk settling through stained glass. It was painstakingly bare, like the simple statement of the Station of the Cross: Jesus is Stripped of his Garments. They're not even preparing the body for burial yet, I thought. That comes later. They're preparing him for death.

It's a pretty awful task. Who else but the anonymous old ones will do it so well, so lovingly? They're the ones who've been around, the ones who know Death and all his kindred cousins of aging and loss, the ones no longer afraid to see, to touch, to be touched in all of Passion's meanings.

We left the church, having emptied it of Christ, and retired to the Parish Hall on the second story level of the library building. It was advertised as a Seder special and I didn't know what that meant. Father Corey said it meant fish, which I hate. But I wanted to be part of things, especially this night that opens in community before the dark abandonment ahead.

The plates of fish were passed around with bread and maybe something else. All I remember is that everything on my plate was white, and the plate itself was white, so nothing had any edges, which made the food a lot easier going down. It was a silent meal. We ate and clanked silverware in nervous silence. When even the clanking stopped, a member of the choir began quietly, without accompaniment:

Were you there when they crucified my Lord?
Were you there when they crucified my Lord?

It's probably one of the only hymns whose verses I know by heart. You can sing it right out of the place in your heart you didn't know Jesus lived until now, when he's leaving and going someplace that you don't want to follow. I closed my eyes and added soprano to the dusky alto start:

. . . sometimes it causes me to
tremble,
tremble,
tremble.
Were you there . . .

"Were you there . . . ?" As Episcopalians, we stripped the altar bare and consumed every last bit of the Host and removed Christ from us. We recognized his departure from us through our most sacred symbols.

As Catholics, we take a more literal turn, since Christ is present in the Host, and the Blessed Sacrament is always present in Catholic Churches, continually worthy of respect and veneration. All those months of studying in the Retreat Center have not been months of being alone. I have hidden myself away in a little House of Silence with the Blessed Sacrament, with Christ hidden beneath the beautiful gold cloth at the altar. But on Holy Thursday, the Sacrament is removed from the altar of the Retreat Chapel, and the doors of its hiding place are flung open, as if theft has taken place. It feels that way. It feels alone suddenly, time to pick up and move over to the Oblate Library. The Oblate Library is unoccupied, too, hence alone, but it has never intended to be otherwise when Oblates are absent from it.

"Libraries are a lot like churches anyway, aren't they?" asks my friend, Richard, when I explain how in the long ago of memory, the House of Silence contained both library and chapel. "Cool, smelling of parchment, quiet, and honoring dead people."

The Oblate Library is waiting for someone to come in and make it a place of study. The Chapel is waiting for us to recognize our loss. "It is so sad," Adelle says about these days. Adelle comes to the abbey every Saturday to pray along the prayer walk and adore the Christ Hidden in the Chapel. "Even though he is hidden, you know he is right with you. And then suddenly he is gone away."

"Were you there?"

When I opened my eyes at the end of the song of the Seder meal above the Pacific Ocean, half the people at my table were weeping. Beyond us all, the sun held itself together just a moment more before disbursing along the ocean's edge.

I didn't know where I had been, but I had a better idea of where I was about to go.

## Step 4: Perseverance

To reach our goal of achieving humility, we must never give up or give in, says Benedict, regardless of how difficult, unfavorable, or unjust our circumstances. We must embrace suffering and endure it without seeking escape. Quoting the Gospel writers, Benedict says: *Anyone who perseveres to the end will be saved.*[5]

When I first read this step, I wasn't sure whether Benedict was telling me to endure or to persevere. Some of the different translations of the Rule seemed to share my confusion, too. I wasn't even sure that there was any difference in persevering or enduring.

*Endure* comes from the Latin, *indurare*, which is to harden and make lasting. I imagine it is to resist the pull of outside forces aligned against you. *Persevere* has much the same connotation of strength in adversity. Derived from the Latin *perseverare* (meaning "very strict"), *persevere* means to persist in anything you start, maintaining your purpose in spite of difficulty—more reaching out and beyond than pulling in and putting up. But that was all semantics to me until I went out to watch and support the university's fledgling golf team.

The five men playing for our golf team are young. For the second year in a row, the golf coach is working with first-years, straight out of high school, baby faced and untried in anything beyond high school meets, now struggling with unexpectedly high demands in the classroom and on the golf course. The reason Fred got all freshmen two years in a row was because *none* of his men's team from the previous year stuck it out beyond the first season.

"They didn't have what it takes, even though they were all excellent golfers," he told me as he began a new year with another new team.

I went to San Luis Rey on the second day of their invitational to watch them play. Grouped in threesomes with other teams from similar-sized campuses, they played their way through the course. Of twenty teams, our guys were in eighteenth place. Our best golfer had his score disqualified when he submitted an incorrect scorecard.

They endured. I'll give them endurance. Nobody stopped playing or threw a club or claimed a sprained back. They had a job to do—eighteen holes of competitive golf—and they ground it out. But it wasn't persevering. The team had given up. You could see it in the dead-eyed expressions and too-relaxed body postures. You could hear it in the lack of camaraderie or support for good shots or bad. You could feel it in the lack of energy, the lifeless game of motions they were going through.

"So now I know the difference between persevering and enduring," I told Fred afterwards. "Enduring is sticking it out. Persevering is not giving up. They gave up."

"Exactly!" said Fred, who is patient with my religious metaphors if it will help me understand team sports and athletic training. "And you know what? They don't understand that. They think if they're still playing, they haven't given up."

Now I know what Benedict wants us to do to climb the rungs of humility: To persevere. Merely enduring will never advance us in our spiritual school. Persevering means doing something over and over until you're successful. Endurance isn't about taking up a challenge, but about staying *with* something you're already in, like those poor baby golfer team members.

Or, as they say in the best tradition of bumper-sticker philosophy: failure is the path of least persistence.

Different spiritual traditions and probably different practitioners focus on different aspects of the spiritual journey. When I traveled briefly with the Franciscans, they urged discernment and offered exercises in centering prayer to help you get to the place of knowing

God's voice and will. The Benedictines, on the other hand, use the first word of the Rule (*Listen . . .*) as their operative until I'm nearly ready to howl. For St. Benedict, perseverance as a step to humility is grounded in Scripture, not only in the words of Jesus, but in the songs of David: "You led us into a snare;/ you bound us at the waist as captives./ You let captors set foot on our neck;/ we went through fire and water. . . ."[6] The golf team suffered the snare until the game was over. That's endurance and fortitude. Had they persevered, they would have been chewing their shoe spikes off the snare to break out. It's not humility in itself, but without perseverance you *won't* get to humility either. As the speechwriter sound bite puts it: Success is getting up one more time than you fell down.

Perseverance comes to my acquaintance through Abbot Antony. His namesake was a desert hermit of the early centuries after Christ who lived to be 106. Abbot Antony might just beat him. He is ninety-three, a testament to perseverance in itself—and partly bionic. He's had surgery to fix his eyes and replace an assortment of worn-out hips and heart valves.

But beyond a strong constitution and physical perseverance is his mental perseverance. His handwriting is as unwaveringly beautiful as a well-schooled middle-aged lady of letters. He reads and prays the same schedule as the youngest monks and, since his retirement as the monastery's abbot at the age of eighty-five, has served as oblate master. He's completely unafraid of death, and yet at his age, he sees absolutely no excuse to stop in his perseverance towards his goal of reaching the New Jerusalem. He also clearly plans to bring along as many oblates as he can on his journey.

Last year during Holy Week, I was horrified to see him zipping around in Brother Robert's motorized seat. My travels had kept me away from the abbey, so I didn't know his kneecap had shattered. "I took one step and then a second, and then I felt it let go," he told me at breakfast.

"You didn't break it from praying too much?" I asked indignantly.

"Well, I'm sure that caused *some* of the fracture," he said, unperturbed by my tartness. When I'd seen him zoom in for Mass, my heart sank. It's the beginning of the end for him, I thought. He certainly gave it a good run.

And indeed he did. Brother Robert had died the year before, so his motorized chair was available, and Abbot Antony zipped around in it like a pro. My retreat cell that year was the ickiest, most remote room in the entire facility, the farthest from the cloister, the chapel, the church, the prayer walk, the cafeteria, but conveniently located alongside a parking lot where trucks rumbled up the hill in the very early morning hours to make deliveries. But that didn't hold back Abbot Antony. He made the motorized journey Easter morning to my remote, icky room to deliver books he thought I should be reading. The only thing he couldn't do was surprise me with his arrival. Even with surgically replaced hips, the abbot walked on little cat feet. With a busted knee and motorized cart, at least, I could hear him coming.

I guess he didn't know it was the beginning of the end like I did. I guess he knew perseverance where I only knew, on my best days, endurance. Four weeks later, I came back to see if he was still alive or in the cemetery with his fellow monks, all younger than he. As certain as the San Diego sun, Abbot Antony marched in and out of Mass with the rest of the monks. He sat down and got up when the service called for it—slowly, but unassisted.

"Your knee is doing really well," I said at lunch when he returned from getting *my* coffee.

"The doctors said eight weeks for recovery," he said. "It's been seven weeks since I broke it." If pride weren't a sin, I believe he would have indulged at that moment.

The old desert fathers, like his namesake, were always subject to fresh no-nothing upstarts like me or the more earnest seekers of truth, all turning to them for a mantra, a story, a bit of wisdom, a thought, or perhaps a single word they could then take back with them from the desert to meditate and ponder on. It's what we don't admit to doing with our horoscopes in the morning papers. Indeed, my favorite such word, lovingly typed into my Palm Pilot so I can read it when I'm going crazy with scheduling, is what Abba Moses gave a fellow monk of the early desert hermit times: "Stay in your cell, and your cell will teach you everything."[7]

I am aware, of course, that Abbot Antony knows the old desert traditions and stories, too. "If you were an old desert father and I came to you and asked for a word, I know what you'd say," I announce.

"And what would that be?" he asked, setting down his coffee cup, eyes alert, ready to play my silly game.

"Perseverance."

"That is *right*," he says with great delight. "For if we cannot persevere, all our other steps are taken in vain." And then Abbot Antony adds, "This is good. When you're old, you can talk about these things that the younger ones don't understand."

Certainly he must have experienced pain when his kneecap let go. And since then, I've seen him nearly fall twice, but Brother Maurius, with the quick hands of the magician he once was, caught him before he hit the ground. The agony of the moment turned the abbot's face deep red, and drops appeared on his face, frighteningly like I'd imagined Jesus in the garden of Gethsemane, where "his sweat became like drops of blood falling on the ground."[8] But the abbot's fierceness was such that he shook off anything beyond immediate rescue and continued in his work of prayer.

"There remains the need to grit one's teeth and survive,"[9] writes Father Michael Casey in his marvelous work on humility. A few pages later, he ties this step of humility into this season of Passion: "Instead of diagnosing each element and seeking to neutralize it, one begins to give assent to the Cross of Christ and in its embrace discovers a love which makes hard times tolerable. . . . Our task is to wait in hope."[10]

Life is full of hard things that are not impossible or immoral, suggests Sister Joan Chittister. And that, she says, is what this step of humility is all about: "Sometimes in the spiritual life we have to stop running away from the things that aggravate us so we can see what it is that is being demanded of us that we are refusing to give."[11]

And what might that be for me? Of all the vices I have known and loved too well, of all the addictions that have spread their clammy claws around my life, one in particular stretched out and snagged my soul as well: smoking.

It's pretty modest, as vices go. It used to be socially sanctioned, although the moral pendulum had already turned by the time I took it up at the grand age of twenty-eight. I'm just a late bloomer in vice *and* virtue. Although I wanted to be Catholic ever since I was eight years old, playing nun—much to my English, Episcopalian grandmother's displeasure—I wasn't willing to brave any potential wrath and sign up for convert class until I was thirty-eight years old. And though I'd always wanted to smoke—less for its glamour than for its existential, artistic angst—it took me until I was twenty-eight to brave my first puff. I was pretty sure it would hurt to inhale. All my growing up years, my mother said that it would hurt to inhale smoke, and I had no reason to doubt her. So when I finally started, I started light with the wimpiest cigarette I could find and worked my lungs up to Marlboros slowly, three packs a day. No pain, dubious gain.

"You're nuts," my father said when he saw me smoking. After smoking since his early teens and numerous, awful quits, he celebrated one year smoke free as I was lighting up my first. "And you look like an amateur," he added.

I worked on the amateur part as hard as I worked on the inhale part. Nobody ever said persistence was always a good thing. I persisted until I could claim the identity of smoker for myself. Little did I know the depths of smoking's claims on *me*—until I decided to quit.

For all my persistence in *becoming* a smoker, I had surprisingly little perseverance in *staying* one. Within weeks, I decided it was too expensive to smoke, and I should quit. It was quite a surprise to try willpower and find out what a flabby, unused muscle it was. Smoking sucked. But abstinence was worse, as a book called *Smoking: The Artificial Passion* describes it:

> [T]he intermittent tug on the sleeve, the feeling in the chest, the whisper in the ear saying how good it would be to have just one cigarette. But one cigarette . . . [so] they get to carry on unhindered for only 40 minutes at a time, at which point they have to return to Mother Nicotine to receive permission to remain themselves. . . .[12]

Smoking became *me*. I became smoking. Once in a while I'd test the quit waters, but abstinence got ugly fast. When people say, "Quitting smoking was the hardest thing I've ever done," *believe them*. It undoubtedly was.

But for fifteen years, many of them bouncing between quitting and relapsing, I had no idea of what they were talking about. The relapses into smoking were the returning to self. The quitting was hell and always smelled of failure that was worse than any stale cigarette smoke. If I wanted lessons in humility, all I had to do was quit smoking. Again.

THE PASSION • 79

The wild bells begin ringing. The faithful gather in. As Jesus said at a similar point in time, "I tell you, from now on I shall not drink this fruit of the vine until the day when I drink it with you new in the kingdom of my Father."[13] So, too, we will not hear those bells again until Easter morning.

## Good Friday

It is cloudy, overcast, and cold on the cliffs above the Pacific. The Passion comes particularly early this year, raw March early. Count back the five weeks from that and you've practically got mistletoe in your Ash Wednesday ashes.

The weather is appropriate for Good Friday. It shouldn't be too spring-like—not yet anyway. Good Friday is not the sort of day you backlight in pink and purple cellophane, like the Easter baskets full of goodies. It isn't that time yet.

As a kid, I focused on Easter. Who wouldn't? Besides marshmallow chicks and chocolate bunnies and coconut-filled Easter eggs to contemplate on our post-Lenten, no-candy mortification, there were also new outfits to consider, and the performance of all that hard-practiced new music from choir rehearsals.

But first, there's Good Friday. Our fifth-grade Sunday school teacher, Mr. Moran, really went into the details that year to explain to us in no uncertain terms how awful a Roman flogging and crucifixion could be. I'm not sure what his lesson plan was pointing to, but these were the pale days of the pre-revolutionary late sixties, and war and violence was still far away—no nightly news, no slasher movies for rent. We just didn't know yet how bad the world could be to its own, so Mr. Moran introduced us to it, using Jesus as our first example.

I suppose it's not the worst introduction to the subject of man's inhumanity to man, but we were a little young, just two grades past singing "Jesus Loves Me This I Know, For the Bible Tells Me So," and just a year away from the doctrinal terrors of getting ready for confirmation.

Some of the girls cried when Mr. Moran talked about a body torn open by whips, bled by thorns, and pierced by nails and finally a sword. He assured us how, awful as all this was, it still didn't kill—suffocation did. He was long on physical details, short on the amazing agony of who this body broken was, or how it voluntarily came to this horror.

While some of the girls cried, the boys, who were just as upset, taunted the girls who cried to distract from their own discomfort. The irony of that behavior was lost on Mr. Moran that morning. Me, I wasn't going to cry, especially since it would set me up for ridicule. The Passion, so told, quickly turned to a tiny drama about fifth grade boy-girl dynamics, and it was all about us in the least noble of terms. I turned the whole thing off in my mind like a light switch and mentally blanked out. By the time I dreamed the Dream of Not Seeing so many years later, I was a master of selective sight. My training began with a fifth grade Passion Sunday school lesson.

When it came to the Passion of Christ, I never turned the light switch in my mind back on. I got the message the way a horrified, grossed-out fifth grader can, and let it stay mummified in that state of knowing and not-seeing.

People seem to need to show the Passion of Christ in graphic representations well beyond Mr. Moran's gory descriptions. *The Greatest Story Ever Told* did it, for one generation of moviegoers. *The Last Temptation of Christ* caused enough controversy to ensure good sales in another generation. In my freshman year of college, *Jesus Christ, Superstar* hit the stage and airwaves. The music alone was compelling and horrifying enough for me to know a bit of a crucifixion's horror. At the Bible college I attended, there were earnest panel discussions about the musical's depiction of Jesus: was it all-human, not-enough-divine, like a cake improperly baked? half and half? historically accurate? Bible college professors thrive on discussing this kind of stuff. But to me, it was all about the music. The music reached the places the logic of professors would never find.

Now the passion of Jesus seems like old stuff. You can't make this kind of torture and death any worse than what we read in the morning newspaper while we eat our breakfast, or what we see displayed in any movie.

The problem for us is that we modern types caught up with the Romans long ago. We've devised near-deaths and tortures that blend a cocktail of physical agony and anticipatory horror beyond what even crucifixions managed, and we can splay them across big screens that force everyone to see these unspeakable depths. While I refuse to look at all, others look until they become numbed. Still others look and enjoy the view; deadened to pain, they glory in it as entertainment, like gladiator sport revivals.

It has to be the man this Passion is about, the part Mr. Moran left out of his story. It is, after all, Jesus' story, and he wants it told. He wants my witness. "It was Jesus himself, risen from the dead, who initiated the retelling of the story of his passion and death and he changed its meaning forever," writes Father Victor Hoagland, on a website devoted to the meaning of the Passion.[14] He notes that, left to their own devices, the apostles would have skipped the dreadful failure that the Passion represented to them. Historians of the time found Jesus too insignificant to mention. And unlike our era, lived under a microscope, reported on TV, and bared before a web cam, crucifixions were too grisly and barbaric for any public discussion or exposure, except for derision.

As Mr. Moran proved to me in the fifth grade, a Passion without the Man at its center is both insignificant and barbaric. What helps me live the whole story are the Stations of the Cross as meditations artfully designed to employ all your senses and bring you into the story interlocking human suffering and divine will. Although the lovely cedar wood Episcopal church on the Pacific has small stations fastened on its walls, for the most part I only see them in Catholic churches. And, for the most part, I've responded best to the experiences of the Stations outside the church building. They bring me where I do not wish to go and help me see what I must see.

My church does the Stations every Friday during Lent. Though I wanted to resist blurring the lines of Lent and Passion, I also wanted to see how these indoor figurines nailed haphazardly on the columns and walls of our beautiful church could serve us in sharing the Passion. I wondered if we would march around the church aisles clutching our rosaries.

Well, you can't do that because, like most Catholic churches in southern California, our membership is a cast of thousands, the church seats about 1,800, and—heartening in its crowded way—we can turn out hundreds of people for just about anything, even the fourth week of Lenten Stations of the Cross.

So Father Don comes out alone dressed like a martyr in white with a blood red sash, and he alone walks the jagged road from station to station, kneeling at each. We respond from our pews, using our response sheet, craning our necks (me at least) to see where he's going *next*.

In a way, it's embarrassing and too close to the real thing. Father Don is singled out, set apart to represent Jesus, as we, the crowd, stay comfortably in our pews, following our scripts. It reminds me of the way the liturgy involves us now in reading the Passion on Palm Sunday, where we get to stand at our pews and say, "Crucify him" and understand crowd sin, but not the aloneness of the stand-alone parts, pre-assigned and rehearsed.

In Tucson, Los Dorados regularly gathers the faithful in and throws them into the middle of things. My sister-in-law Blanche told me about the group—she'd only seen them on television—and when I knew we would be in Tucson for the whole holiday the next year, I suggested we take part.

"Great!" said Blanche. "We can carry our rosaries, and I'll get us some water bottles. Wear good walking shoes. It takes a couple of hours. And bring a jacket. It gets cold at the top."

The top? I didn't realize this wasn't a park setting with statues like they have at the mission in San Diego. These crazy people were going to *climb a mountain*, meditating on the Stations of the Cross (all fourteen of them) *and* saying the rosary (all five decades of the Sorrowful Mysteries), *and* carrying an oversized wooden cross.

Well, it wasn't a meditation I could do in solitude, so I brought comfortable shoes and bottled water and prepared to become part of the crowd.

Blanche and I got there as the Mexicans were lifting the cross out of the back of a truck. Much bigger than a man, it was a white coffin with crossbar, edged in gold paint. All of the members of Los Dorados wore identical tee shirts. The men lugged the cross into position, while the women decorated it with flowers and distributed response booklets with half the Stations in Spanish, half in English. People poured out of trucks and cars, half of them Mexican, half Anglo, and assembled behind the cross. The Diocese of Tucson has two bishops, one Anglo, one Mexican, and when the Hispanic bishop arrived with *his* entourage, half the crowd collapsed prostrate at his feet.

"He's a sweetheart," Blanche explained. "They love him."

Behind me a little girl asked her mother, "Is that God?"

"No," her mother answered. "But close. God's in the box. We're bringing him home now."

Wow. The bishop's assistant held an umbrella up to protect the master from the rapidly warming desert sun, and the bishop began: *"Te adoramos oh Christo y te adoramos."* And some of us responded, *"Porque por Tue Santa Cruz has redimido al mundo."*[15]

*Jesus is condemned to death.* He did nothing wrong! When was the last time I caved in and pointed fingers because it was the easiest way out of having fingers point at me? *Jesus is made to carry his cross.* And after what he's already been through. These are the littlest things I cannot even bear to bear. *Jesus falls the first time.* Under the weight of what he willingly took on. And still he gets up; he is not finished. *Jesus meets his mother.* Would it be easier to bear if he did not have to be seen by someone whose heart is torn out with grief?

On and on, up the mountain on its twisting, tortuous dirty pathway. After a certain amount of walking—I didn't know how the stops are determined—the cross was lowered, although not put down completely, and the bishop prayed. We all prayed. The mariachi band burst into music. It was probably sad music, but to my Anglo ears, mariachis always sound like margaritas and good times, even when I hear them at funerals. Then the men hoisted the cross to shoulder level, the women fingered their rosaries, and we continued up the mountain.

"They share carrying the cross," said Blanche, "but the men lift it up and put it down because it's so heavy." Indeed, people were crowded in especially close at the cross as they took turns with the load. At first it was just the ones with the matching tee shirts, then others from the crowd. A few of the younger women took a turn.

Station Five: *Jesus is helped to carry his cross.* I was pressed forward by the crowd. Before I could think, I had one hand under the cross. "Lift!" a heavyset man in front said urgently. We lifted.

What goes through your head at a crazy time like that? It's not as heavy as it looks because so many people are carrying it. I guess that's the message I was supposed to get. Can I let somebody else do it now? They're carrying it too high, I'm too short, my shoulder's starting to hurt. The rosary sounds so beautiful when it's murmured like that. The Spanish and English are like a gorgeous two-part harmony when they're laid next to each other. I can't carry this anymore. I can hardly move. I'm walking sideways, for crying out loud. I wonder where Blanche is. Are we there yet?

We reached the next Station of the Cross. I should be praying, but I lost my folder with the words. I'm glad I peeked at the English version this morning or I'd have no idea what they're saying now. It must be hell for Spanish-speaking natives here in Tucson not to know what's going on most of the time. Is that the message I'm supposed to get? Will this parade ever stop? That woman stepped on my foot again. . . .

At the next stop, *Jesus Falls the Second Time*, I was pressed away from the cross in the same hands-free way I was pressed in. I was suddenly just one of the ladies bringing up the rear. The mariachi band blared on. I looked for Blanche. "Lift!" the heavy-set man ordered. They lift, including Blanche this time.

When she was rotated out, she looked as radiant as a bride. "They let me carry the cross!" she said. "I will remember this day for the rest of my life!"

And I, of course, will remember: Were you there when they crucified my lord? And how my answer will be: Well, I was sorta there. I had a shoulder problem, and they were all taller than me . . . and the Passion will be about me again.

When we reached the top, we saw Tucson in panorama with its silky purple mountains on three sides. The men hoisted the cross one last time and stuck it into the ground where they had already prepared a hole. The flowers were laid in front of it with great tenderness. The mariachis played a closing lament. It was 3:00 P.M., and Jesus said finally: *"It is finished."* The little, loved bishop was driven down the mountain, and most of the rest of us walked. A few of the ones with the matching tee shirts would stay with their provisions and sleeping bags at that cold, lonely place until Sunday morning, because they would not let Jesus be lonely even in death, because they would be the first to know the truth when the sun rose over those darkened mountains on Sunday morning.

The following year, I didn't climb the mountain with the group, although Blanche would have liked to do it again. My father was dying in Rhode Island, but I had to be in Tucson on Good Friday. The only Passion I was thinking about had become very personal. My misery centered on what was happening—and would happen—in Rhode Island, and it hung over the Passion in Tucson as I waited for the call to come back east. *Daddy! Are we there yet?*

One of the most spiritual places in Tucson is its Franciscan mission, San Xavier, lying like a wounded dove on the floor of the Santa Cruz valley, engulfed by the Tohono O'odham Indian Reservation. It's not a sophisticated, born-again, built-again mission like those in California. It is a working Indian mission that resists gentrifying, although it seems perpetually in the throes of yet another facelift. Although it looks like a sweet dove on the outside, with its white-washed façade, inside it's a gaudy, heartfelt nightmare of colors and images of the style More Is Better. There are side chapels braced with candles you buy in the mission shop, smokeless so as not to mess up the murals and the wooden statue of St. Francis lying in death at another side chapel that the Indians and Mexicans especially like to touch, thump his head, and kiss.

And that's the official part of the Mission. There's also a stand-alone Indian chapel, an Indian cemetery next to it, and a thriving fry bread stand in front.

None of it is pretentious, and after you've been to Mass here once, you know that the pale, hardworking Franciscan friars with names like Patrick and William and their store-bought Spanish phrases are not in charge. They are just the priests. It's the Indians' mission, their school, their kids, their neighborhood, their lands, their fry bread.

It was Good Friday again. I took my two-dollar, smokeless candle and looked around the mission for a place for us. The Indian Chapel was appealing. The candles there filled the altar and every available nook and cranny and weren't the smokeless, identical two-dollar kind you got from the mission store. They were the 69-cent kind from the grocery store with luridly colored pictures of obscure saints and apparitions. The rows of them, in all their varieties, made a beautiful sight. Some of the candles had family pictures propped against them; others had little letters—prayer requests, perhaps, shoved dangerously close to lighted candles. Still others were draped with plastic rosary beads or decorated scapulars. The statues, too, dripped with beads, scapulars, flowers, and photos, a nearly-breathing reminder that these prayers were for people who were loved and missed, that the faith of the people was a tangible, living thing.

A large dog with even larger feet lay stretched out on the cool stone in front of the altar. But there was no place for a human to sit or kneel, so I took my candle and went to the furthest corner of the side altar to Mary, inside the Mission proper.

It was noon, and the three-hour Good Friday service was beginning. A woman sitting next to me in the grotto began to weep. I was already crying by then, so I shared my package of tissues, which she accepted. As the Good Friday service of remembering continued with the priests and mariachi chorus at the main altar, my little grotto carried on its own private devotions. The weeping woman was replaced by an earnest young couple going back and forth with the rosary in their glorious Spanish: *Santa Maria!*

Why was I weeping? It was my father's Passion far away this Good Friday, not mine. And yet I could not bear to place the candle I bought for him alongside the dozens of identical ones already at the altar. I'd already said goodbye to him once, at Christmas. I'd have to say goodbye again at his funeral, soon. To put this candle with the others was somehow a way of diminishing his individual light.

I quickly became attached to that singular candle of mine, set alone at a corner of Mary's altar, away from the others. There were two Good Friday services going on in tandem, the way the prayers of Spanish and English were continuing together and yet also separate. There was the public recognition of Jesus' time on the cross. There was my private recognition of a small minute of human suffering in my immediate family. The two services began to intertwine in my mind as I watched my candle through teary, unfocussed eyes.

Alone, my candle set up a fragile, flickering light against the cavernous old walls of the church. The Masses of candles in the middle made up in glow and glory what they lacked in individuality. My little candle, like the little father it was lit for, would extinguish its light soon enough after I departed. Did the light have to go out alone, just because I was afraid of putting it with the others?

I finally moved my candle to the middle with the others, weeping as I did so. I tried to memorize its position, wondering if I could find it—*my* candle, *my* daddy—when I returned from a fresh air break. To leave it was like the tearing of flesh, but I'd been sitting there for two hours, and my body had its needs.

A half hour later, I'd stretched my legs, had a coffee, gotten my face back together, and returned to spend the last half hour of the Good Friday service in my position at the side altar. But in my absence, the little altar had been swept clean of all the candles. They were all flanked around the statue of Mary. Daddy had joined the heavenly chorus.

But it was a comfort, for those last few minutes, to sit in my little corner banked with candle souls, knowing he was there, knowing he was not alone, knowing the greatness of the Passion in knowing a small love and in knowing pain.

## Step 4: Perseverance (continued)

In her book on Benedict and wisdom, Norvene Vest devotes a long chapter to Benedict's steps of humility and the virtue of committing to the *practice* of humility. You train your heart, she says, by removing its focus on thoughts and feelings and emphasizing persistence of action. Those who have ever quit smoking, she points out, (or used AA programs to quit drinking, I would add) know about this substitution of action for emotion. "Perhaps the 'thought' of a cigarette will return from time to time over many years," she suggests, "but habits of mind have been created to deal with the thoughts. It is no shame to receive the initial impulse, but we seek not to let it linger."[16]

Or, as the old-timers in AA called it, stop the "stinking thinking." Your thoughts wouldn't get you drunk, but keep it up, and they'd reintroduce you to what *could*. Norvene Vest knows what she's talking about: the training over time gives you the tools to deal with the odd, stray thought and wrestle it down. I have a great example of where this training can save you. Ten years after my last drink, I was in graduate school, carpooling to another campus. When we left our night classes and walked to the parking structure at ten at night, my car wasn't there. Had we miscalculated the floor we were on? We checked above and below. There were many cars, but none were mine. "I think we have to call campus police and report a stolen car," my carpooler said.

And in my mind, clear as a bell, desperate to be heard, a voice said, "Can I drink now?" If I'd heard that voice eight or nine years earlier, which I frequently had, I'd have had to jump up, call a sponsor, ask for help (our secular euphemism for "pray like hell!"), or get to a meeting. Maybe I'd have had to do all of the above. You didn't argue with little voices or big ones saying those things early in the struggle because the odds were that you would lose.

But ten years later? I was surprised at *that* rusty old voice surfacing, amused at how loudly it spoke. And then, mentally, I said, "Oh, just drop dead." And I went to call the cops.

Smoking was harder. For one thing, it's still more permissible to step outside for a smoke than to walk inside rip roaring drunk in the middle of the day. Maybe smoking had a different voice, "the whisper in the ear saying how good it would be. . . ." I committed to the practice of quitting smoking a hundred times. I got permission from Mother Nicotine to return to myself 101 times.

I tried prayer, mysticism, Nicotine Anonymous, and twelve steps. I quit cold turkey just once and was amazed at how bad early abstinence—withdrawal, in fact—could *hurt*. I tapered down. I drew images of myself as a happy, smiling, nonsmoker in my diary. I went through acupuncture treatment, which removed smoking as surgically from my body and soul as if I'd never been a smoker. When the treatments stopped, however, I was suddenly a smoker who wasn't smoking, and I fixed that hole in my psyche as fast as my little legs could get me to a convenience store.

I became a regular at my HMO's smoking cessation program, cheerily called Positive Choice. Over time with research and experience backing them up, they made changes to the program, but it always included journaling (a word I hated), attitude adjustment (*really* hated that one), group support (hated group, hated everybody when I wasn't smoking), and lectures on low-fat eating and exercise to give you those action items as substitutes.

They offered focus smoking as an option, which is a cute expression for aversion therapy. The first time I did it was very dramatic. I experienced tingling halfway through the first cigarette. By the second one, I had a pounding heart and clammy skin; I was drenched in sweat and beginning to get nauseated. And *then* I smoked two more cigarettes as fast as I could because there was still time on the clock, even though big, beefy men were stumbling out the door to throw up.

I did okay until I hit the fresh air outside afterwards. I sat down on the parking lot and discovered I might not have much willpower when it came to quitting cigarettes, but I sure *could* keep myself from throwing up when my body wants to—which it really *did* want to, twice.

As I sat on the pavement, bracing myself against the building, sweat running down my face and onto my once-beautiful silk dress, I thought to myself, "Smoking sure is very glamorous."

At the following night's aversion therapy, I mostly developed aversion to Evelyn, who hyperventilated, cried, and carried on until they stopped the entire thing. This was my aversion therapy, too, dammit, one of my last nights to smoke! The final night was undramatic. The first cigarette wasn't any fun, the second got boring, and I wanted it to be over. My feet tingled, my mouth went numb, my hands went clammy, and a voice in my head said, politely, "This just doesn't fit who you are anymore." I left the room before time was up.

But I was back smoking within three months. I used all the leftover nicotine gum from my prescription even when I went back to smoking because it gave you a kick that would blow your head off.

I continued to quit, continued to quit quitting. My father-in-law had advanced emphysema. He would use up an entire large tank of oxygen in four hours—more than two liters of oxygen per minute, and it wasn't enough. If he bent over, he became completely breathless and couldn't speak. He'd wheel his oxygen tank outside to smoke.

I couldn't bear to watch his suddenly skinny frame—he'd always been a stocky man—heaving to find air. I couldn't comprehend the panic that must accompany a slow suffocation.

"I've got to quit smoking," I said to Felix after watching his father in the advanced stages of the disease. "I'll never succeed, but I've got to try."

"Well," Felix said carefully, "the fact that you've admitted helplessness is the first step."

"Stop that. I taught you that!"

Back to Positive Choice. Hi, Janet. Hi, Carol. Are you ready for us this time?

I sure was. I journaled even while I was in focus smoking. "Cigarettes numb me. Numb is dumb." I did my feelings. I used my nicotine patches, since we were no longer doing gum. I shared. I remembered the names in my group. I called them up, even if I didn't need to or want to because maybe *they* needed or wanted to call somebody and couldn't. I took up walking, then jogging. I counted fat grams. I ate strange, green, leafy things. On graduation night, I said, "Thank you for your patience with me. I had to keep quitting until I could quit. This time has been really different, and I'm so grateful for the difference." Janet surprised me with a special certificate that everybody in the class signed because I'd been so open this time, so honest, so scared, so ready to do it, and I brought everybody along on my journey.

Nine months later, for no apparent reason except that I was ready to blow my brains out, I began screaming. My pet cockatiels freaked out and flew around the kitchen right after I'd finished cleaning it. They did this nearly once a day, but this time, I started screaming, full throttle. "You stupid birds! You miserable, stupid birds!"

The birds got back to the cage, as they usually did after an unscheduled fly-by, and huddled together in the farthest corner while I kept screaming. Then I started crying. What was wrong? I didn't know. I'd either go crazy or die.

"Can I smoke now?" a voice whispered.

Correction: I'd either go crazy or die or smoke . . . at which point they have to return to Mother Nicotine to receive permission to remain themselves.

I only smoked for three months after the screaming attack. Between dermatology and gynecology appointments at the HMO one day, I went outside to smoke. A car drove up to the building to discharge a woman who obviously couldn't walk from the parking lot to the entrance. She could, however, walk to the smoking area from the curb. As she made her painful, wheezing way over, I prayed hard: "Please don't. Please don't do that. Please don't come here. I hate it when people in the smoking section are half dead and still smoking. They ruin it for everyone else." She lit up and began to rage about how they treat smokers. I started to answer, but caught a coughing jag. The cold Felix had lasted three days. Mine was in its third week and beginning to branch out into bronchitis. "Oh, Bonomo, you're as stupid and as desperate as all of them. You're doing the same thing as your poor father-in-law and his oxygen tank."

But even my poor father-in-law eventually had to quit smoking because the exertion of drawing in a cigarette was too much for his perforated lungs. I was furious on his behalf. If you're going to make a pact with the devil, the devil should at least play fair. After all my father-in-law went through to keep smoking, he ended up quitting smoking anyway.

So the hell with it.

"Hi, Janet."

"Hi, Carol. I'm glad you came back."

I have not failed 10,000 times, Thomas Edison is reported to have said. "I have successfully found 10,000 ways that will not work."

And Lavinia Byrne writes, "You can't win a battle by simply running away. You need patience and humility if you want to rise superior to all your enemies."[17]

I successfully knew 10,000 ways that would not work. I knew the only way that would. I had to persevere in quitting, no matter how stupid or weak *that* made me look.

"I quit smoking," I announced to my mother, no longer with pride, but as the fact of today.

"So, did you go back again?" she asked carefully. Nobody knew where I was anymore in this revolving door; everybody knew I was a loser.

There were no special certificates this time around in Positive Choice. "It's important that the group support each other," Janet chirped. "Going around the room now, Carol, do you know everybody's name?"

"No. And I don't particularly care." I never spoke through the six-week program, except once when Janet said, "Can I tell you all what next week's class is about?"

"Sure," I said. "The evils of fat grams. The virtues of green, leafy things."

"You don't *have* to come next week if you don't want to," Janet said.

Good. I didn't. I didn't show up for graduation either. I sat there dumb in absolute defeat and surrender to the demons who ruled me. I alternated that with the rage I had on my poor father-in-law's behalf.

The devil doesn't play fair. And mentally I finally said, well then, the devil can just drop dead. Or I will. There wasn't room for both of us anymore.

Smoking was my best friend, my next breath, the substance that gave me permission to be myself. But it was a false friend, a devil's toy, and I was now the devil's toy, too. Furious resignation ended the game, gave me the perseverance to get up one more time than I fell down.

I had been an ex-smoker nearly four years when I went back east to see my father in the hospice before he died. Wild Bill shared my father's room. When I arrived, Wild Bill had been there two weeks, dying of lung cancer, too, cursing the air blue when he was awake, no longer eating, making big, gulping snores when he slept.

The day before my father died, Wild Bill woke up and demanded corn flakes for lunch. Then he ate the fish being served to everybody else. Then he talked a hospice worker into wheeling his entire bed outside—he had way too many hook-ups to transfer him to a wheel chair—so he could smoke a cigarette, which the hospice volunteer was going to have to liberate from another patient.

"You really shouldn't do this," said the volunteer as he went off to poach a cigarette.

"It's too late for that!" yelled Wild Bill after him. For a moment, he looked sad, but suddenly he brightened up. "It's *damned* late. Bring back two." You can't stop persevering. The words don't string together. "Persevere to the end," Brother Benet says simply of this step of humility.[18] And in a homily on the Gospels we read in the Divine Office, Gregory the Great reminds us: "And so it happened that the woman who stayed behind to seek Christ was the only one to see him. For perseverance is essential to any good deed, as the voice of truth tells us: Whoever perseveres to the end is saved."[19]

It is a cold and quiet Good Friday at the abbey. I approach the Prayer Walk with my little book of meditations by St. Alphonso Liguori that Abbot Antony gave me several Christmases ago, prepared to walk the path of sorrows alone, prepared to really see the suffering, know my guilt.

Yesterday when I walked it, a large, extended Filipino family was a few stations ahead of me, praying at each stop. Two men were carrying the babies, while an older woman led the recitations in softly accented English.

They are back again today, just beginning the Stations as I approach. The teenage boys in their imitation gangbanger gear whisper, "Pray for us now and at the hour, . . ." and one baby is smiling off the teenage boy's shoulder, fascinated by my blond hair.

A woman toward the back of the group gestures me in and hands me a wildflower to place at the Station. "Pray for us now, and at the hour of our death," we say together.

Somewhere, once upon a time, everywhere and every year since, Jesus breathes his last and utters, *"It is finished."*

## Holy Saturday of Our Lord's Rest

It is so damned quiet on Holy Saturday. If I were down the hill, it might be an ordinary Saturday, dimmed by overcast, cold weather, and energized by the beginning of college Spring Break.

But I am at the abbey, where things like the Lord's resting are taken quite seriously, and making trips to Palm Springs or Rosarita, Mexico, for a week of hearty party seems insignificant in comparison.

Of course, my own priorities have changed with age. Despite the creepy crawly of middle age clutching more and more of my years, while releasing more and more of my waistline, I'm one of the youngest of the regular Triduum retreat crowd. Part of that is the gift of an understanding, unbelieving husband, and no other family within 500 miles wishing to spend "Easter" together.

But taking it all seriously *should* be a priority, whatever our circumstances. In *Death on a Friday Afternoon*, Fr. Richard John Neuhaus writes:

> By these three days all the world is called to attention. Everything that is and ever was and ever will be, the macro and the micro . . . everything is mysteriously entangled with what happened, with what happens, in these days.[20]

It's relatively easy to know what happened the last two days, and the liturgy re-enacts it for us in case we forget. Enter the Last Supper. (Think da Vinci painting.) *"This is my body. Do. Remember. One of you will betray me."* And as Jesus is dragged off for one trial after another—all sham, all rigged, all fingers pointing blame and claim and counterclaim—we bundle ourselves off to bed after—maybe—an hour of watch. *"Will you not stay awake with me, even one hour?"*

Good Friday we know. Whether we embrace it with eyes wide open, or peek out from under the covers, we *know*. The sham trials are over, the orders given, the killing begun, like the terrible things we read about in the papers from bad regions of the world even today: the whips, the thorns, the mockery, the stripping, the staggering out into the streets under the weight of the instrument of death.

"If he was God, why did he do this?" I asked my father, fearful and skeptical, a horrified little kid still in shock from Mr. Moran's Sunday school class.

"That's the point," Daddy said. "He didn't have to. He could have turned them all into ants and walked away free and clear."

"Well then, why *didn't* he?" How dumb could God be, really?

"Because his heart said that this was the right thing to do."

I was crestfallen. It showed.

"I know you'd prefer he turned everybody into ants, but he didn't. You should be glad. We'd all still be ants today if that's the way it turned out."

Which is pretty good theology when you're an ordinary parent trying to explain the unexplainable in fifth-grader terms.

I didn't want to be an ant—too easy to get stepped on. I let him die.

The silence of Good Friday, the Death on a Friday Afternoon, still has the sounds of life interwoven, however awful the sound of nails being pounded into human flesh, the agonized moans, the gasps for breath, the muffled weeping of women. *I thirst.*

And in the quiet of Good Friday evening, you know what's happening, and it's a relief. It's over. He isn't suffering any more. His secret, silent friends have emerged from the shadows, faced the civil authorities, and removed and buried the body. The women prepare it; the men serve as pallbearers. They do their work secretly, hurriedly, placing him in a tomb. Out of sight, out of mind.

But what about today? What's happening now?

At the oblate meeting a few weeks ago, Abbot Antony spoke to us with unusual directness and earnestness about Psalm 90, which the monks pray every night at Compline before they go to bed.

> Truly we are consumed by your anger,
>> filled with terror by your wrath.
> You have kept our faults before you,
>> our hidden sins exposed to your sight. . . .
> Teach us to count our days aright,
>> that we may gain wisdom of heart.
> Relent, O LORD! How long?
>> Have pity on your servants![21]

"Our dear Lord died of a broken heart," said the abbot. "Not from the sword in his side, but from his love for us, which we scorned."

*Return, O Lord! How long?* We've done it now, really gone and done it, and now we're sorry, okay? We said it, we're really, really sorry.

As my pet cockatiel, Sonny, would respond in his best, one-word vocabulary: *Uh-oh.*

"Christ cannot suffer anymore," Abbot Antony continued. "It is the Church that suffers. Unite with those in pain. Ask that in suffering, you may be united with Christ in his."

The natives began to grow restless. Oblates can be a squirmy lot, and usually the abbot's monthly message to us isn't nearly so intense.

"It is *not enough* to have nice thoughts," Abbot Antony insisted, as if seeing our resistance in squirming body parts and lack of eye contact. "It is not enough. We need to know the sufferings, too. We can humble ourselves in our small sufferings."

Is he saying that the Passion goes on in our lives forever? Is he saying the curtain doesn't close when the next act—Easter—takes center stage?

Oh dear. *Uh-oh.*

I hear words roll around the edges of the old hymns and older prayers about the Church Triumphant and Universal Church. I've spent and misspent an enormous amount of energy investigating churches and making comparisons of their look and feel versus my needs. I like dark wood. I don't like stained glass. I like lots of candles. I am not fond of distracting sunlight. It's quite a shopping list. But in all my search, I haven't really considered the church as a living, breathing entity, as the ongoing body of Christ in the world today, and certainly not as the suffering Christ. It is one thing to know these things in creeds and hymns. It is quite another to see them in the face of the person at eight o'clock Mass who loves to sing and does it loudly, off-pitch with bad breath.

But the abbot, with an intensity so unusual in that kind-hearted soul of his, handed us the suffering church, united in Christ's suffering, and gave us a share of the Passion to take home with us.

The Church suffers. We, the Church, mingle and merge, like the candles I so resisted joining mine, becoming simply the corporate body of Christ in the world, living, breathing, suffering, dying. The corporate body of Christ is being broken by prosperity, commercialism, secularism, violence, indifference, scandal, and despair as certainly as the single, human body of Christ was, once upon a time. And the Resurrection becomes as unsure and unimaginable as it ever must have been the first time. Despair and indifference may very well succeed where nails and whips failed.

What does *our* heart, our corporate heart, tell us to do about suffering? What are we not seeing today? This is the problem of the Holy Saturday of Our Lord's Rest. This is what's happening today. We're thinking and remembering, and nothing's happening to distract us, and we really don't like what we see. So we set up the chairs early, prepare the Easter baskets, set up and practice for an elaborate Vigil Mass because *we want to get on with it.* We're pushing the heavy stones away as early and as fast as we can so we don't have to "rest" in the knowledge of what we've done and who we are and how we suffer in each other's suffering.

A week after the abbot thunderbolted us, I went to Mass in a strange church in a different city. Going to a strange Mass can show you how you have retired from the corporate body of Christ. After shopping around, I've found a regular church. I've flittered through the Masses and settled on that one that works best for me. I have a nodding acquaintance with a few familiar faces, and the longer I go, the more layers of familiarity and comfort I add to the whole process of going to church.

Then I go somewhere else—which happens frequently in the months my travel schedule piles up or vacation intrudes, especially given my absolute rule that I *will* attend Mass once a week no matter what my schedule or where I am. Now I'm in someone else's neighborhood, so I take what I can get, and my consolation on the bad Masses is that it's just once. You can suffer even a folk Mass with guitars just once.

This latest strange church was oppressively gloomy, but by the time Mass began, the place was mobbed. I guess I should be pleased at the robustness of the faith, but instead I'm always cranky at the sheer size and numbers wherever you go in southern California. Church is no exception. I'd already been scrunched into half a seat to make room for a large family, and the baby was already screaming itself purple and needing a diaper change. Behind me, a sharp-faced older couple was bickering non-stop. "Please introduce yourselves to those around you," said the lector before Mass began.

"You never listen!" the woman was hissing behind me. "If, for once, you would just try to listen when I'm telling you something—"

"Would you just shut up?" he interrupted. He had a hearing aid, and his whisper was loud enough to qualify for regular speech. "We're in *church* for Chrissakes, so would you just shut up?"

And in front of me, the mentally handicapped Mexican girl alternated between grunting and turning to stare at me. Her mother was standing at the altar of Our Lady of Guadalupe, head in her arms, resting on the altar, oblivious to her daughter or to any of the Mass.

It was going to be one of *those* Masses. My attendance record for Mass is a minimum of once a week, but my record for *staying* until Mass is complete is unmentionable. I not only don't persevere, I can't even seem to muster up endurance when I'm annoyed or bored.

But sometimes you get gifts at the most unexpected times, like that day, in that unfamiliar church. A gift of the Passion? *Really* . . .

But there it was, surrounding me. The suffering church, sharing in the suffering of Christ, including me in the misery of my arrogance and avoidance. For a moment, all of us, the row behind me, the row in front of me, and the row with me—we looked like so many broken splinters of an old wooden cross. And the only way to wholeness is to unite those painful slivers into one cross, one suffering.

I stayed the whole Mass. It didn't kill me to stay.

There's an ancient homily for this day that you can find on the web or in the Office of Readings for Holy Saturday. It's the first thing I read today in my little retreat room at the abbey, right after the birds twittered me awake, but before the sun tried to break open over the mountains. Its origins are lost in the mists and violence and passion of the earliest church of Christ.

> Something strange is happening—there is a great silence on earth today, a great silence and stillness. The whole earth keeps silence because the King is asleep. The earth trembled and is still because God has fallen asleep in the flesh. . . .
>
> See on my face the spittle I received in order to restore to you the life I once breathed into you. See there the marks of the blows I received in order to refashion your warped nature in my image. On my back see the marks of the scourging I endured to remove the burden of sin that weighs upon your back. See my hands, nailed firmly to a tree, for you who once wickedly stretched out your hand to a tree.
>
> I slept on the cross. . . .[22]

The prayer walk at the abbey is deserted this afternoon. The Stations of the Cross are deserted but for a host of jumpy baby bunnies and a few geckos.

*Are we there yet?*

# —5—
# The Morning

## Easter

Easter—despite what I believed as a kid and ignored as an adult—is not a one-shot deal, stuck at the end of Lent as reward for Lenten austerities. Easter Day, despite its glorious message, despite the new outfits and Easter baskets and chocolate bunnies, is only the beginning, the first day of the longest season of liturgical celebration. A book wonderfully named *The Great Fifty Days: Savoring the Resurrection* tells us what the Easter season is about:

> In this time the newly baptized pray and reflect upon the new life they have received in the Sacrament of Initiation. The whole church joins them in celebrating the new life of love that the Lord has given to us through his death and resurrection received in the Easter sacraments.[1]

We do?

In 1990, at the great Easter vigil, I received something—I still don't know what it was—that permitted me full access to the sacraments of the Roman Catholic Church. Some of my group were called catechumens, brought into the Church through the Rite of Christian Initiation (RCIA) and the Sacrament of Baptism. The rest of us were candidates, baptized in another Christian church and preparing, through RCIA, to be confirmed as Catholics. It was like an adult First Communion, without the pretty white dresses.

Or perhaps it was like the culmination of Confirmation class when I was in seventh-grade Sunday school. Instead of the Bible stories and filmstrips we got in the earlier classes, we listened to Mr. Snower read the Holy Communion service word for word and talk about what he thought each word meant. Our reward for endurance was, one late-spring Sunday, the arrival of the bishop, who laid his hands on our heads and offered us the opportunity to partake of Holy Communion for the first time. The girls got to wear white dresses and a few of the boys fainted from nerves or the early, unaccustomed summer heat.

That was all my confirmation meant to me in the Episcopal Church when I was twelve, my first go-around. The second go-around, when I turned Roman Catholic at the age of thirty-eight, actually meant even less, although I wanted desperately for it to mean so much more. There was no white dress. The preparation was negligent in the accidental hands of well-meaning and untrained parishioners. And somehow I missed—or ignored—the fact that the Catholic Church doesn't let you receive communion if you're not fully reconciled with the Church even though it was printed clearly enough on the back of the missalette. I'd been taking communion unreconciled since I'd walked into the Catholic Church a year earlier, and I knew no more about its meaning as an insider than I did as an unwitting outsider. But at least I was now a legitimate Catholic.

I rushed back at seven-thirty Easter morning, after being received into the Church just ten hours earlier, to a comfortably full church. Father Thomas, the young and handsome priest, looked around almost mournfully. "I've missed you," he said. "I want you to be the first to know we're open *every* Sunday, not just Easter."

My RCIA class had scattered after the Easter Vigil like the disciples after the crucifixion, and there was no gathering up to pray and reflect on this mysterious new life we'd undertaken. But the good news of Easter is its yearly reminder of a new beginning. We all get to celebrate this new life as we all gather—even the once-a-year-flock—at the great gathering that begins at Easter.

"Remember that on Easter, it gets crowded here," Father Don reminds us at St. Elizabeth Seton Church, where I'm a regular eight o'clock type. "It gets *very* crowded," he adds for emphasis, looking around at all of us. "Come early if you want a seat. Come very early if you want your regular seat. And if your regular seat is filled, don't glare at those strangers who took your seat. Find another seat. Be nice to the strangers. Exchange the peace with them, even if they're not the regulars, and *especially* if they don't act like they know what the peace is. And don't excuse yourself from being kind by saying, 'But they only come once a year.' Jesus came and died and rose from the dead to save all of us, not just the ones who come to church every week."

Ha, ha. We all look grumpy at that. He's not supposed to know how the regulars feel about getting pushed out of their seats by the superstitious one-timers-plus-Easter-brunch crowd. In *The Great Fifty Days*, Francis X. Gaeta meditates on Easter Sunday, saying:

> [O]ur churches are packed with believers today—Jesus is risen from the dead. The throngs of people that are present do believe. Even if many don't come to church during the year, there is that seed of faith in their hearts waiting for the right moment, right place, right moisture to break into life. . . .[2]

"I've missed you."

Ironically, this glorious season of joy and germinating faith gets rushed on one end and terminated prematurely on the other. Even at the abbey, the preparation for Easter crowds into the silence of Holy Saturday. Barely dinnertime on Saturday, the Retreat Center's recreation area was a rush of activity to set up for refreshments after the Vigil. The unlit prayer walk was unsuitable for a last few moments of reflection, and a few monks outside the church were preparing the set-up for lighting the Paschal candle later.

"Marshmallows tonight?" I asked as I walked by.

"It's the *Easter* fire!" the novice monk hissed, shocked.

"Okay, okay, I know it is." Inside the church, Brother Andres was vacuuming with great vigor everywhere. It was no use. It might still be Holy Saturday on the calendar, but here the feeling was pre-Easter—and the women long ago and far away were still *hours* from making their way to that empty tomb. I retreated back to my cell to await the Easter dawn.

And as soon as the Easter Mass ends, everybody goes home—or out for Easter brunch in new finery with family. But not only is the Easter season fifty days long, the Feast of Easter itself lasts for eight days. I found the reality of the Octave of Easter when I left the abbey and returned to my ordinary parish's weekday Mass.

It's Easter Monday, regular 8:30 daily Mass at St. Elizabeth Seton—or so the regular daily Mass goers think. But the adorable little day chapel is locked, and the regulars find themselves huddled in the front pews of the main church. The day chapel fits 120 and is comfortably full on Monday mornings. The church seats nearly a thousand people and resembles the empty tomb with just 100 people huddled together. The flowers, at least, are gorgeous.

The *really* early regulars get there a half hour earlier to pray the rosary, and they jump right into their regular Monday set of mysteries—the Sorrowful Mysteries. The first sorrowful mystery—The Agony in the Garden—is jarring in its retracing the way of the cross so soon. The women who found the empty tomb are still trying to find all the disciples to tell them the amazing news!

At the end of Mass, Father Don explains his decision to hold daily Mass this week in the main church. "The Octave of Easter—eight days beginning Easter Sunday and lasting through the next Sunday—all of these days are Solemnities," he says. Solemnities are the most important days in the Church's life, more significant than even feast days, Sundays, or memorials. The Easter triduum is the most significant Solemnity of them all. Second would be Christmas, Epiphany, Ascension, Pentecost, Holy Week, and the Octave of Easter.

"So it seemed appropriate to continue these most solemn days of Easter here in the main church," he continued. I liked the reverence he allowed us all to share this way, savoring Easter into its full season. "Besides, if you knew what these Easter flowers *cost* . . . I want us all to get our money's worth."

I love Father Don as my pastor and priest because he can take the most serious things in this world and the next and enjoy them with a sense of humor. Even his solemnities have humor in them. Plus he owns a dog and a smoking habit, which makes him more like me than like God. I like that in priests. And the flowers *are* beautiful, especially the day after, when most of the crowds have melted away. It feels really holy to celebrate now. It feels like we are those few people who stayed and remembered the whole story.

St. Paul has an interesting way of opening my eyes to the Easter story as a beginning rather than an end, when he writes to his followers in Colossae. Pay attention to the "higher realms," he suggests, to things above rather than things of earth. "After all, you have died!"

he writes bluntly. "For you have died, and your life is hidden with Christ in God. When Christ your life appears, then you too will appear with him in glory."[3]

Ahem. Usually there is a little bit of separation between Christ's actions and mine—a separation that I am more than happy to crawl into and make wide. Christ died *for you* we are told in liturgy and the word. Christ died *for you* and for *your sins*.

Not so fast, Paul responds. *You died, too.* You did it again that night, that long Easter vigil night in 1990 when you stepped up and said, "Me, too. I'm with him." And whether you knew what it meant or not, you signed the death warrant for your old self, and put on a new self in Christ.

Dear Paul's all-inclusive understanding is still a bit of a shock. Here is the one time when it is all about me, but it's also the *one* time I say, "Oh, you go first . . ." And he *did* go first, in his choice to die and his glory to return, and I am scared, running off like so many of his disciples, like my catechumate class did before the blessing finished echoing in the church.

*After all, you have died!* I can almost hear a peevish Abbot Antony talking to us oblates in Paul's words to his pupils. Abbot Antony is the kindliest person I will ever know, but the tenets of his faith are absolutely unshakable for him, and for anybody within his reach. When my little group of three oblate novices was preparing for our vows, Gregory kept asking if there wasn't perhaps anything more he could do as an oblate. "You must follow the promise of your baptism!" Abbot Antony responded, with a near-testiness, as if to say, "Isn't that enough to do in one lifetime?" It's the kind of testiness you hear that in Paul's words: *After all, you have died!* What more do you need to do before you dismount from your misguided vision of the things of the world rather than the things of heaven?

And here I am, afraid of death, and it has already happened? That means I have nothing to fear. It doesn't mean to live each day as if it were my last—which implies cramming it full of earthly, calorie-laden goodies—but as if it were my *first* day, filled with the newness of life everlasting. I don't have to fill it—it is already full, and of such goodness.

*After all, you have already died!* Imagine dying to yourself. The long and painful part is over and behind you and done. You face each day as if it were your first, as if you already know its ending—because you do. You are transparent with the light of the sun, reflected from the face of Christ. And someday you will be allowed to stay in that light, like the flicker of so many candles sitting together on a humble altar in the middle of the desert.

This is all such big stuff, and we poor humans grapple with it all through the half-closed eyes of faith. But I got a glimpse of what it means, when endings are mere beginnings, during a long car trip I made immediately after my father died.

It was only a simple matter of logistics. I bought a one-way airline ticket from San Diego to Providence, and I would drive my father's car back to San Diego when it was over—the polite way of saying "after he dies." The trip out was a personal experience of witnessing the final suffering and death of my father. A parent had died and I'd moved one notch up in the queue. The return trip was the road beyond, the beginning of a new life beyond childhood and adolescence.

I'd never driven more than 300 miles by myself. The road beyond was, according to my cheerful AAA Triptik, approximately 3,200 miles long. Off we went, me and a beanie baby tiger named Francis, and my father's 1996 Toyota Avalon with its Florida plates, Episcopal Church sticker in the rear window, and one faded Garfield cat stuck to the other side of the back window minus one suction cup.

I let the road beyond take me where it had to: Pennsylvania Dutch country; Columbus, Ohio; Indianapolis, Indiana; St. Louis, Missouri; Tulsa, Oklahoma (the halfway point). Through Amarillo, Texas, to Defiance, Arizona, across the Mohave Desert and finally to San Diego. There was the long companionship of Route 66, crossing and merging with highways, then hightailing off in an opposite direction like a scared jackrabbit. There were hours of silence across the Texas panhandle between radio stations and civilization. There were pat-the-buffalo photo stops, and there was the man walking his horse on a leash in Edgewood, New Mexico. There were ads for body wraps and aromatic therapy in Santa Fe, New Mexico, and fry bread at the gas stations on Indian reservations. There was the Painted Desert and Crystal Forest, where I cried for two hours and couldn't keep driving because my mind suddenly shouted, "Daddy, where *are* you?" But there was no answer in return.

It was, in the beauty that comes alongside tragedy sometimes, a watershed trip, a wonderful journey, a great adventure, at least for the first 3,000 miles.

The last 200 miles, however, sucked—high winds, a chewed-up interstate, nasty truck drivers barreling up and around both sides of the Toyota at death-defying speeds in blinding, lashing, can't-see rain. Driving a brutish interstate on water-soaked roads that made a car think it was a hydroplane, seventy miles an hour and being honked and fingered at on either side by trucks trying to slow down was a living, driving, California nightmare. For three hours, I gripped the wheel afraid to stop, terrified to move forward. Welcome to real endings, I thought, not the made-up, epiphanic, meaningful endings you get in books and movies.

And *that* was the meaning, I realized, pulling the car into my own driveway, in my own sweet Lake San Marcos. There was the metaphor I needed for my father's cruel death. Yes, the last 200 miles were hell. But, ah, the 3,000 miles before that. And all the miles beyond. Don't judge a book by its cover. Don't judge a journey by those last 200 miles. Look at the road that got you to the sorrow. Look at the road beyond it, the road that leads to the New Jerusalem. The lessons of a whole life are contained in Easter. Don't rush the Passion. But don't stop there either.

"The cross is not the dark side of which the resurrection is the bright side," writes Richard John Neuhaus at the end of his meditations of that death on a Friday afternoon. "The glory is in having seen it through to the end."[4]

My father, his family, and perhaps, most importantly, his church community and priest, kept the faith throughout his suffering. Unlike the Gospel narratives, nobody abandoned Daddy to his suffering, nobody left the foot of his cross when he went into the hospital after he suffered a stroke and started the last dark steps home. He spent the days before his sixty-sixth birthday someplace closer to the next world than to this one, and the group of family, friends and church members continued to pray—whether anybody knew what exactly to pray for or not. I'm sure some of us prayed for recovery and some for a merciful death. His priest prayed over him and laid her hands on him for healing, and the glory of seeing it through to the end shone around him.

And on his sixty-sixth birthday, he opened his eyes and seemed both pleased and surprised by all the fuss. He marveled at all the presents—"This is for me, too?"—as though it were a child's first Christmas. For a long time, he held on to the bookmark I'd stitched for him. He couldn't read that it said "Daddy" because the cancer had invaded his brain, but he knew his daughter made it, and that was enough.

When the presents were done and the fuss quieted, he said clearly and quietly, "I think I had a religious experience."

We don't use words like that in my family. We're all practical, plain people, my father probably the most so. My mother was the only one who heard him. "What was it like?" she asked.

"Like a touch," he answered.

Three days later, he was released from the hospital. It was not his end after all. Perhaps that was his beginning. As Neuhaus continues, "We, too, know how the story turns out, yet we neither rush to Easter nor, when we come to Easter, do we put Good Friday behind us as though it were a nightmare past."[5]

What an experience of Easter my father's parish must have had when he showed up on Palm Sunday after coming out of the coma. We were all touched by his touch, humbled in our arrogance for thinking we knew the beginnings and endings of things. On the phone with me just a week after his birthday, he was sharp, funny, angry, and confused—the full range of his humanity. He was returned to us, and we learned who chooses our death. But he was also gone from us in a way I can't quite explain. Jesus after the Resurrection is not the same as before. You know he has come back, and yet you do not know him in the flesh. My father was back among the living but clearly he no longer lived among us this time and was just gently visiting.

Three weeks later, he returned to the hospital. He looked at my mother from his latest hospital bed and said, "There's so much I still want to do." But his dying took precedence on the to-do list this time. Out of the silence he was returning to, he looked at my mother a few days later and asked, "Will you be buried with me?" The next day, dutiful son-in-law that he had been in life, he asked my mother, "Is it time to pick up your mother?" My grandmother had died seven years earlier. Perhaps the answer was yes by then. He never spoke again; the cancer moved into his brain and finally his bones, and he waited patiently in silence until I reached his bedside and he could say with his eyes alone, "Take care of your mother." And then he continued on his journey.

Who among us can say when his dying ended or his life anew began? I only know, like a little congregation in Pawtucket, Rhode

Island, did, that the messages of Easter were laid out with a heavier hand than usual that year, and that the messages lasted far longer than a one-hour Easter Day service.

## Step 5: Self-Disclosure

The fifth step of humility, according to Benedict, is self-disclosure, what Sister Joan Chittister calls the "most American" of the steps.[6] She's right. We love the confessional—especially if we are eavesdropping on other people. Sitting in an airport terminal for six hours waiting to get unstuck from Providence to Chicago one long, dreary winter morning, listening to talk show guests on the force-fed TV sets in the lounge, I felt as if I were like entering the Land of True Confessions.

"I think they are professional actors," confided the young Chinese man sitting next to me. "Nobody else would say such things publicly."

I wished he were right as we continued to watch a detailed discussion, periodically interrupted with applause, of older women, their much-younger male partners in tow, discussing their sexual needs. It wasn't a great moment for American culture. To an outsider, like my Chinese fellow-traveler, we looked like a hang-loose, tell-all crowd.

Telling all seems to backtrack away from humility. It glorifies the tellers and justifies their actions. It generates sensationalism, mild controversy, and sustainable ratings.

Benedict, however, has something different in mind: the quiet, heartfelt, disturbing disclosure of sinful thoughts and wrongful acts. In the Catholic sacramental tradition, it's called confession, or in the newer language of Vatican II, reconciliation. It's the way we reconcile ourselves with God.

In the secular, self-help tradition, self-disclosure is also Step 5 in AA's twelve steps of sobriety. Only at Step 5 do these sacred and secular steps intersect, at the point of disclosure, a step Esther de Waal calls pivotal because it moves us from an inner world to an outer one.[7]

In AA, Step 5 says that we confess to God, to ourselves, and to another person "the exact nature of our wrongs."[8] It follows the step of self-examination, which AA calls taking an inventory of our actions and their consequences. Armed with this self-inventory, we tell God, ourselves, and another what we were up to when we were up to no good.

It was never a favorite step for AA members, not the way the first ("admitting powerlessness") or twelfth ("trying to help others") were. For one thing, it's full of ambiguities, and the how-to is left too much to the imagination. Just make sure, AA directs you, to have your fifth step heard by the right person. Spouses and employers are off-limits. Priests and ministers are okay, but only if they understand AA and its fifth step. Your social worker or other professional counselor usually doesn't want to do this one with you. Your AA sponsor is considered best.

Determined to complete the twelve steps and get on to something else, I asked my sponsor Joanie to come to dinner and hear a fifth. I did the best I could, I suppose. I spent most of the time justifying my badness, and Joanie kept coming to my defense, saying that none of it was that bad, after all. We were both confused as to whether this was about all my badness or just my drinking badness (AA was unclear on this point), and whether when you cease drinking, you cease your badness.

But we did it. In my AA Big Book the next morning, I made a check mark next to Step 5, dated it, and wrote in the margins:

> Result: while I didn't act like a responsible adult all the time, my sins aren't so terrible that I have to spend my life in atonement for them. If I invested in a self-image of badness, I'd better switch investments. I didn't do all that good in being bad.

And then I moved on. The language I used was interesting. I was in between belief gigs then. It had been fifteen years since I was confirmed Episcopalian and it would be ten years before I would be confirmed Catholic. But here in the nether regions of self-help movements, I used words like sin and atonement? They sure weren't the words of the Big Book.

The "who you tell" matters a great deal, to Benedict as well as to AA. Several fine commentators on the Rule suggest that this self-disclosure be done to a wise one.[9] In other words, TV and radio talk shows don't cut it. Sometimes embarrassed AA sponsors—who may or may not have embraced a fifth step themselves—don't cut it either. During my four-year tenure in AA, the dinner with Joanie was my only venture in doing a fifth step, and I was never asked to hear one. That came much later, after I embraced Catholicism and was on a

New Year's retreat at a Franciscan mission. I must have mentioned AA in a session, although I don't remember doing so or why the subject would come up all those years later. During a silent time in our rooms, a woman banged on my door. When I opened it, she said, "I've been doing my inventory. Will you hear a fifth step?"

Shoot. There is no preparation anywhere for *hearing* a fifth step, although I presumed that listening uncritically and maybe helping see patterns of behavior would be a start. It didn't matter. Within minutes, my bed was covered with yellow pages scribbled all over in pencil, and Roberta was using them as reminders as she talked non-stop for 30 minutes. Patterns of behavior? Ha, ha. If there were any, neither she nor I would ever find them. Her motives, her actions, her starts and stops, like those damned notes, were all over the place. Uncritical? I hate messy notes and a messy bed and being invaded by determined strangers on a mission to take me hostage. The good news is that she never looked up to see my own confusion or—I'm sure it showed—growing irritation. Nor did she take a breath that might have indicated it was my turn to speak.

Finally, she flipped over one last yellow sheet, looked at me full of expectation and said, "Well?"

Well, what I am I supposed to say to this poor, tortured person, showing up at my door, huh, God? *Tell me.*

I looked at my notes, neatly documenting the retreat session we'd just attended, and a biblical reference appropriate to New Year caught my eye.

"Colossians 3:13," I said.

"Huh?"

"You need to listen to God and maybe talk to a priest. But in the meantime, Paul writes to people just like us, and in Colossians 3:13, he says, 'bearing with one another and forgiving one another, if one has a grievance against another; as the Lord has forgiven you, so must you also do.'"

There was a moment of silence in the little room, the first such moment since Roberta's entry. Then she grabbed her pencil and began to scribble on the back of one of the sheets. "It's 3:13?" she asked. "How do you spell *Colossians?* This was great! Better than most of my fifths! Thanks a million!"

"Better than most of my . . ." Poor Roberta. She didn't need a fifth step AA. She was seeking absolution. And that wasn't mine to give.

I am grateful to have moved on to a sacramental fifth, the Rite of Reconciliation, although, like a lot of Catholics, I don't go rushing to the confessional on a regular basis: it's just not any fun. And that's because it's a step into humility, and who wants to be in that place if they have a choice? St. Francis de Sales talks about confession in his classic text *Introduction to the Devout Life:*

Confession . . . not only absolves venial sins but also strengthens you to avoid falling into the same sins again, enlightens you to recognize them more clearly and repairs the damage that they may have caused. You will be practicing humility, obedience, simplicity, and charity, in fact more virtues than in any other single act.[10]

Oh great. My first sacramental confession came about six months after confirmation. Preparation for the Rites of Christian Initiation is supposed to include a first confession before confirmation, but my makeshift instructors forgot, and we didn't know to remind them. Thinking that I'd missed a beat somewhere, and still being the type who likes to cross *everything* off the list—dated, and marked done—I called Father William and asked for an appointment and a study guide to use for preparation.

"I'm not sure what constitutes a sin," I explained cheerfully. "Got anything I can read?"

In retrospect, poor Father William must have had some of the feelings I did when I was invaded by a fifth, but he gave me an appointment and left me an examination of conscience set of questions that I had great fun filling out. I loved having Catholic homework to do.

When I got to the church, a wedding was being set up. How bizarre. I couldn't imagine confessions while a wedding was going on outside the confessional. The bride was stomping around doing photos, eyeing me with great curiosity. You could see her thinking, "What side of the family came to the wedding really early and wearing stretch pants and a Billy Joel Bridge Tour sweatshirt?" I peeked to see if the Reconciliation Room available light was on. It wasn't. I finally went to the music director and then to the priest doing the wedding. "Seen Father William?" Nobody had.

"I was supposed to meet him here," I said, afraid they would ask why. "Confession" sounded funny in a church filling up with people ready to celebrate. I drove away feeling ashamed, as if I'd done something wrong, missed another beat.

There was a message on my phone when I got home. Father William didn't realize there was a wedding when he made the appointment, but, he said, "I wasn't there at 10:45 anyway, so I probably missed you. I'll be in touch to set up another time."

*Probably* missed me? By the time he called again, four days later, I was rip-snorting mad, not embarrassed at all.

"So, shall we set another appointment?" he asked agreeably.

I guess I thought he'd start with an apology. I guess I guessed wrong. "Go to hell," I said—and hung up, severing a connection from the Church I'd entered barely a year earlier.

St. Paul, in a letter to the Ephesians, says, "Be angry but do not sin; do not let the sun set on your anger."[11] I can't think how many suns went down on my wrath, or how I took that anger at being stood up and nurtured it into many sins over many years. Every time I attempted confession when I finally returned to church-going five years later, my words were choked by not knowing what to do, or what was a venial sin or a mortal sin, or how to wrap the whole thing up with an act of contrition. Every stumbling mess compounded the original embarrassment, which was starting to become my Original Sin.

A mere ten years later, preparing for Easter, my church did its semi-annual Rite of Reconciliation, traveling circus style. Various priests gather up and go from church to church during Lent and Advent and hear confessions. It's very important to go to a confessor who doesn't know you, everybody says. Father Don introduced the traveling show, and they all smiled brightly when their name was called. ("Pick me! Pick me!") We did an examination of conscience together, some people making little notes after questions like, "Have I been unwilling to share my earthly goods with others?" "Have I been harsh and demanding of my family?"

And then Father Don sent the traveling show forth—to the confessionals, the bride room, the cry room (!), his office, and all the odd corners of the church. We all scattered like crazy to find a priest we liked, or, more importantly, didn't know. The Franciscans always get the longest lines. Rumor has it they're the most liberal. The shortest line formed for Father William—older than the others, fierce looking, conservative, probably not too tolerant.

I made a beeline from one end of that big church to the other to get into his line. "Bless me, Father, for I have sinned. I have been bad-mouthing you publicly for ten years."

He didn't look surprised. He didn't look like he recognized me. He looked old and tired and kind. "Continue," he said.

And I did. It was a night where the word *reconciliation* meant something, where it's what happens after confession of all our stupid sins. And yet it was still harder to do than it should have been. In this year's Rite of Reconciliation traveling priestly circus I stood behind a lady who kept saying, "I don't know why I have to tell a priest my sins. I tell God every night. I say an Act of Contrition every day."

"So you've done the hard part already," I said, trying to be encouraging. Nobody in the line laughed.

"Maybe the other lines are shorter," her friend said. "This one's moving slowly. That's a bad sign."

"Take it from me," I said. "Based on my past experience, you'll be at the *end* of the line if you go somewhere else. Here you're not at the end of the line. *Plus*, you'll have to confess to the sin of impatience if you change lines."

Nobody laughed. Standing in line for confession is a lousy place for humor. Nobody wants this step of humility—not us, not even the priests who hear us. On the feast day for St. John Vianney, patron of parish priests, Father Don reminded us that St. John Vianney's special charism was in hearing confessions, frequently up to sixteen hours a day. "And for that alone, he deserves sainthood," Father Don sighed. "I'll never get there."

It's a hard step, a pivotal step, a step in Benedict's ladder that brings you from the inner world of obedience, submission, and perseverance to the outer world, beginning with self-disclosure to that wise other. For Benedict, the wise other is always the abbot of the monastery. For most of us, it's a parish priest, preferably one we don't know. For me, sometimes, it's the abbot.

The first time I did a retreat with my fellow oblates, I'd looked forward to walking, contemplating, keeping a spiritual journal. But I'd barely arrived when Abbot Antony banged a sign on the oblate meeting door:

Confessions: 4:00 P.M.

At least half of my mind was immediately distracted into an examination of conscience while the rest of me tried to listen and take notes during the conferences. Dang. How this catches me unaware, I don't know—I've been to a few other retreats, and confession is *always* one of the offerings, and am I just hoping this time they'll *forget?* But I've left my little dummy guide to confession at home. I have no help in conjuring up sins. I know I do wrong; I just don't have names for all the wrongness—and no hope of saying an act of contrition from memory.

Dang!

At four o'clock there's a raggedy line between the two Retreat Center confessionals. There are no priests in the confessionals, however. The lights are off; we've been abandoned.

"Don't take it personally," I counsel, becoming an expert in such things. "We didn't want to do this anyway." I go back to my room to read, now that examination of conscience is no longer necessary.

"We do not find God when the going is good," I read in Michael Casey's examination of Benedict's steps of humility. "Elation (being high) blocks us from God."[12] But the psalmist finds God in humility and trust:

> "LORD, my heart is not proud;
>    nor are my eyes haughty.
> I do not busy myself with great matters,
>    with things too sublime for me.
> Rather, I have stilled my soul,
>    hushed it like a weaned child."[13]

Well, I thought I was done with examining my conscience, but here it is again, my edgy, prideful energy (I call it) that fills me up and reduces my competitors (everybody else in the universe) to anthood. My sin even has a name—*elation*. Thank goodness confession was a no-show, or I'd have something else to confess.

At dinner, Abbot Antony apologizes for the communications glitch and announces that he'll be in the confessional from now until Compline, undoubtedly missing dinner in his effort to make amends.

My worst fear is having him as my confessor. I'm okay around priests I know or don't know because I hardly know any and so it doesn't matter. But I want Abbot Antony to think I'm better than I am. Still, I am first in line when he opens for business with a purple sash on his shoulders and the light carefully turned on.

Elation is a very old demon, he tells me in his very old voice. My penance—"but it really isn't," he hastens to add—is to place myself in the Presence of the Blessed Sacrament and to *listen*.

The little chapel fills quickly with penitents in the Presence. Elation's power is quickly broken. Why is it so hard, this little step? Unlike AA's fifth, the confession, the rite of reconciliation, is sacramental. As the Church reminds those of us who slept through the definitions, a *sacrament* is an outward, visible sign of an inward, invisible grace. This Sacrament of Confession as part of humility's ladder pivots us the other way: from inward grace to outward sign. It needs the external witness, the visible reminder through Peter's heirs, of the saving salve of Christ. It takes humility. It gives back a blessing, as Benedict does in his Rule, as the Psalmist in his song:

> Happy the sinner whose fault is removed,
> whose sin is forgiven.
> Happy those to whom the LORD imputes no guilt,
> in whose spirit is no deceit. . . .[14]

## Easter

Easter is the end of the story that began in Passion, the end of our own deaths into sin. Or else it's the beginning. If there's one thing I learned from my father's experience, death and life don't have clean cut, on-off switches.

At the abbey, Easter morning is the end of one thing and the beginning of another. I thought I would get up early, wait at the large cross at the edge of the bluff—wait for the sun to rise over the mountains as a token of that other day long ago. It was on that other day long ago that those fearful, sorrowing women went where no men dared to go, to visit their beloved Lord, dead.

But he wasn't dead at all, not anymore. He had burst through death's stranglehold, and returned to show what he'd always promised. And maybe the men who were his apostles stayed behind and never witnessed that awful moment of discovery because they were still in Passion, still in agony.

I peeked out of my little room at 5:10 A.M., after preparing myself the night before for a solitary sunrise service. But the clouds hung low on the barely visible horizon, and I had no hope of a sunrise, so went back to bed. "We look not to what is seen but to what is unseen," says Paul. "What is seen is transitory, but what is unseen is eternal."[15] Well, I not only didn't see the sunrise, I saw no potential for it, so I no longer even desired it. As a disciple, I'm last in, first out.

But Paul says also that grace, even today—maybe *especially* today—will get me there. Grace will make me an heir, confer the family name, bring me the wealth and reputation of eternal life. Whatever it takes, ok? Because we're talking quite the prize, eternal life, which is also eternal happiness.

Think of those moments of the most spellbound peace and happiness. For me, those moments are when I've become fully absorbed in something like walking or writing, stitching, or whacking on my ukulele. And suddenly there's the flash of happiness, of being perfectly blended—without edges—into the thing I'm doing. As soon as the awareness hits, the happiness separates a bit, and the edgeless blend is no longer perfect.

Now live in the moment before the flash of awareness. Only it is Christ you are blended into, along with everybody you ever loved, everybody who ever loved you—and suddenly that is *everybody*—along with those saints who put in a few good words for you, a few prayers and loving shoves and nudges, a mother who wept for you—all of that blended into Christ, forever.

It is an unimaginable beauty, this prize. And if there was no sunrise this morning, and I knew it, and didn't care to witness the empty cave, well, I am still capable of becoming heir, through hope, of eternal life.

The bells at the abbey suddenly burst out of their silence of these last days, clanging as if their stone hearts would break the dawn with joy. The monks and most of the retreatants were celebrating Lauds when I took my rosary, my cheat sheet of the Glorious Mysteries, and a candle I'd had in my little makeshift oratory in my retreat cell all weekend, and headed to the bluff where the white cross stood.

I lit the candle and set it next to the flowers placed there over the past days and settled into a ruined, rusted beach chair with my rosary to pray the Glorious Mysteries for the first of fifty days of Easter. It wasn't particularly quiet: the cars below the bluff on the highway, even at six-thirty on a Sunday morning, roared and rumbled through the canyons. The view wasn't exactly serene: below were junkyards, an abandoned drive-in-turned-flea market, and houses like identical soldiers, elbow-to-elbow marching down the once-deserted hills.

The First Glorious Mystery: the Resurrection of Jesus—and what a glorious mystery it is. Scientists discussing the Shroud of Turin talk about perhaps a burst of energy, like atomic power, breaking loose and leaving the scars on the burial cloth. Can it be?

The Second Glorious Mystery: the Ascension of Jesus into Heaven. So soon, too soon—you are barely back. Your Resurrection was such a miraculous thing, the fantasy we all wish for when our beloved die, though we settle for the dreams and occasional sense of nearness. But Mother Mary, you got the whole thing, beyond a heart's imagining, Mary, Maris Stella, Brightest Star of the Ocean. And all too soon, just forty days later, he is gone, with only a new promise, of a comforter, a paraclete, to keep us warm on our own death's dark night.

A few bunnies nibbled grass in the grim musty dawn, a dawn without a sunrise. But the sunrise will come. He promised. And I will be there, waiting in joyful hope, an hour later than I planned.

Better late than never.

*Take care of your Mother*. He said it from the cross and I hear it across the centuries, this Easter blessing: *take care of your Mother*.

At breakfast, Abbot Antony arrives bearing gifts. He hands me a copy of a postcard he has kept now for forty years. "It was such a fine postcard, I couldn't get over it," he says.

It's an artist's representation of Jesus greeting his mother after the Resurrection. The blue-toned 5x7 print is full of singing, pious angels, a crown, and a shroud tossed in one corner, a kneeling, adoring mother, a Jesus filled with heart-breaking gladness: *Mother, I'm back!*

"I think he must have gone to see her first," says Abbot Antony confidently. Of course, he saw the women who came to the tomb as Scripture tells us, he adds hastily. "But he was on his way to his mother. I'm sure of it! And they probably sat and had coffee together. He had no other place to go, after all."

The old abbot, whose mother died when he was just a teenager, and a middle-aged oblate, who will fly cross country in a few days to be with her mother during surgery, wipe their eyes and drink a little coffee together. They have no other place to go at the moment either.

It is Easter, fully. They're pouring up the hill, the cars and even taxis, to bring the carefully dressed faithful and once-a-year regulars to Easter Mass. I make one last walk out to the bluff to catch one last hope of a sun. My single, solitary candle has blown out.

# —6—
# The Comfort

## Pentecost

Pentecost is good theater. Some of the great stories of the Christian faith are best told in the quiet of a living room, with family gathered around, a fire crackling in the fireplace, and the hushed, respectful tones of the narrator as counterpoint. "For today in the city of David a savior has been born for you who is Messiah and Lord."[1] I read out loud in Felix's presence. He knows this story well—Linus reads it aloud in the Charlie Brown Christmas Special every year. It is a good, quiet story. But it is not theater.

And then there's Pentecost, which starts in a quiet room, too. But the hush is one of fear as much as anticipation, of what is to come and when. For these poor, fearful, excited followers of Jesus have been through an emotional upheaval these last few months. Imagine their joy on Palm Sunday when the recognition seems finally to be rolling in for the man they've left everything to follow. Shouts of triumph and joy were still ringing in their ears when that terrible night of betrayal and trial began, culminating in torture and an agonizing death.

Still in shock and dismay at the abruptness and awfulness of it all, these same poor, confused followers are greeted just a few short days later with a reality even harder to accept: Jesus is back. Jesus won. Jesus is everything he said he was. And now that we know what the phrase "Son of God" really means—now that we know what the Son of God looks like—can anything ever be the same again?

In a word, *no*. Imagine the deepest desire come true: our beloved comes back from death, and we have the chance to say all the things we should say in life and get too busy or preoccupied to do: I love you. I missed you. I can't live without you. Please don't ever leave me again. The poor disciples got the chance we all desire more than anything and Simon Peter even got to declare his love for Jesus three times, atoning for his three-time denial.

And then he is gone! Again—although this time he is *lifted up, and a cloud took him from their sight,*[2] which leaves a far better aftertaste than blood and suffocation from hanging on a tree. But you promised. You promised never to leave me again.

The stage is set. It is empty of everything but painful hope. You promised! They're together, the ones who followed Jesus, afraid to be apart, afraid to break *their* promise to stay in Jerusalem together and wait for what Jesus has promised them— baptism in spirit instead of water. Who knows what *this* promise will look like when it comes? Who knows when will it come? And who knows how to recognize it when it does? After all, we've been wrong before. We didn't know the Son of God would bring a heavenly kingdom. We were picturing more earthly ambitions, a more ordinary man—somebody like David, who would help us sweep the Romans out so we could run our own affairs like we did in David's time. How wrong we were. How wrong we could be again. And so we wait for what we do not know. We wait for something we might have missed or failed to recognize.

That's the setting for Act II. There's a light in an upper room where you guess the characters are off-stage. But the stage itself is still empty, and everybody is restless with waiting, fifty days after that really strange Passover.

Act II: Pentecost. From out of nowhere, a wind rushes across the naked set and rattles the windows of that upper room as though it were shaking the poor disciples by the shoulders and saying, *Listen to me!* Bits and pieces of fire follow the wind and alight on each person in the room. Suddenly the stage is filled, as the disciples pour out of hiding, the crowds gather to catch the latest, and the fire-tongues begin to dance and speak.

This is Pentecost, what I learned in Sunday school was officially the Church's birthday. It was probably the only birthday party where I was glad to see no birthday cake sparked with candles. Enough already!

Those poor fearful people who followed Jesus in their ignorance and through their personal agendas and despite their disgustingly human limitations are suddenly babbling away in the town square to hundreds of people from all over: Parthians, Medes, Elamites, people from Mesopotamia, Judea, Cappadocia, Pontus, Asia, Phrygia, Pamphylia, Egypt, Cyrene, and even Rome, Crete, Arabia.

If I wasn't careful, the same thing might happen to me. And I didn't want that—the response the poor apostles got to their big stage-grabbing scene was hardly encouraging. A few of the crowd remarked with a sneer, *They have had too much new wine.*[3]

Good stuff, great theater, even if I'd rather be a spectator than a participant most of the time. It's definitely Act II stuff, where all that has gone before in Act I is poured out into the weakest vessels around—faulty, cranky, ordinary people like me, to continue the story of salvation. Writer Phyllis Tickle frames the meaning of Act II/Pentecost when she writes of the compelling story that it is:

> Christ is gone, removed, triumphantly absent. Now life—human, humdrum, secular life—must end its mourning, hang up its miracles, question its memories. And History would have done all those things . . . would have life to erode its one truth . . . except for Pentecost.[4]

Time is the ultimate Judas, the final betrayer of memories, miracles, and even grief. It is such a shock to witness, four years after my father's death, that life goes on and memory fades the mind's pictures, and the sharp-edged knife of grief that twisted along so industriously in the very core of my being has lost some of its edginess. It feels like betrayal, what time does to us, but it is life itself continuing, even as we think it should have stopped forever in our personal sorrow.

And what Tickle says is that, yes, this too, the "greatest story ever told," to quote the movie marquee, this story of God who loved us so much that he joined us, died for us, came back from death like an unfinished ghost, only this time in flesh and blood for us—even this story would have faded into time like Greek myths and Roman legends have. But this story had a different ending. It had an ending that began with a roaring wind and tongues of flame that have not yet been extinguished.

As a kid, I was a little afraid of Pentecost, afraid it was something I might catch that would subsequently force me to march around the neighborhood, ringing doorbells, and saying as Peter did, center stage, "Let the whole house of Israel know for certain that God has made him both Lord and Messiah, this Jesus whom you crucified."⁵

It was hard enough to ring doorbells and ask for spare change for the March of Dimes. I didn't want anything harder, thank you.

But the part about Pentecost I liked were the tongues of flame. To me it was hilarious that the apostles got little tongues of flame above their heads and then rushed outside and talked in foreign tongues. Share and share alike, I figured. But I also saw that piece of the story very literally. All those people from all those parts of the world—countries that I'd never heard of, since I skipped anything resembling geography in the fifth grade—*were confused because each one heard them speaking in his own language.*⁶ It never occurred to me that the disciples might not have been speaking English before the flames arrived, so now I imagined them suddenly speaking French, German, Italian, and Spanish. Inheriting foreign tongues without studying! What a great gift!

It wasn't an idea I revisited as an adult. In my RCIA class there were lots of opportunities to look again at the stories I'd understood in the literal way of my childhood and see them with the fresh eyes of spiritual maturity. I might remember Jesus literally causing a blind man to see. But now I could understand the metaphor: All of us stumble along in spiritual blindness until Christ steps down before us, spits on the mud in our ordinary pathway, and clears our eyes so we can truly find our way. With such stories, I came to realize the Bible wasn't locked in a literal, one-time history; it was open for all to take part in.

Unfortunately, the convert class graduates on Easter Vigil and starts with the school start around Labor Day. So during my year as a Catholic-in-training I never revisited the story of Pentecost. When I finally did, it was accidental. Shortly after Easter one year my parish's evening prayer group held a one-day prayer meeting.

I wasn't sure what it was, but it sounded like a nice way to meet others in the big parish that I'd just joined. Besides, the church is in a gorgeous neighborhood that I wish I could afford to live in, and lunch was free.

The morning session was ordinary enough to feel comfortable with, the sing-song, hand-clapping folk that's supposed to make you feel uplifted but nearly always makes me feel like going home and putting on Mozart's Requiem—or anything else I couldn't clap along with. There was a homily by Father Don, some readings, and some sharing.

After lunch, we divided into little groups, each led by a member of the evening prayer group. We were asked to be open to—and pray for—the gift of tongues. It dawned on me that this stuff was Pentecostal—what other people might call Spirit-filled but what I'd call emotional and maybe a little weird. That's probably because I don't have—and have never asked for—the gift of tongues. Actually, it's the last gift I'd look for under my Christmas tree.

To show us what she meant, our leader closed her eyes and seemed to retreat in spirit, beginning to speak a gentle rainfall of sung syllables that touched my ears pleasantly, uncomprehendingly.

"That's what it is?" I remember thinking. It was hardly French or German, or anything resembling language as I knew it. It was too musical for baby babbles, and too self-contained for the drunken rambling that the apostles were accused of.

When I was much younger, a confirmed drinker of spirits, rather than a speaker of the Spirit, and I would hold court for hours, talking in French. Backed up by high school conversational French and aided by large amounts of homemade wine with whiskey thrown in—terrible tasting stuff you drank fast to get past the taste and into the kick—I could carry on extensive conversations with the French-Canadians in the room. They rarely understood me, although they felt they almost could. It depended on how far along they were with their own kick. I, of course, *knew* I was speaking French and knew just what I meant.

That was what this experience of tongues reminded me of. I wasn't frightened, as I thought I would be, but I was disappointed. As a child I'd imagined Pentecost as a wind that opened up the world to receive the truth of Christ, the burning embers scattering outward. Instead, the tongues seemed to turn inward, unintelligible, like a secret code no one would ever break.

I learned that what I heard was prayer in tongues, described as "a personal gift used to praise and glorify the Lord in community prayer settings, and also in private prayer."[7] We prayed to receive the gift of tongues, and then we were offered the opportunity to be baptized into the Holy Spirit. I was learning things I'd never known, since I understood baptism as a once-in-a-lifetime opportunity. Indeed, I'd been rather envious of my RCIA classmates who were going to be baptized first before we were all confirmed. They, at least, knew what was happening and could maybe appreciate it in a way a two-month-old baby could not.

But another chance? Unknown to me, it was rooted in those earliest moments after the wind and the fire gave birth to the Spirit in the disciples:

> Now when the apostles in Jerusalem heard that Samaria had accepted the word of God, they sent them Peter and John, who went down and prayed for them, that they might receive the holy Spirit, for it had not yet fallen upon any of them; they had only been baptized in the name of the Lord Jesus. Then they laid hands on them and they received the holy Spirit.[8]

And that's what we did at the gorgeous blonde church on a wonderfully springy Saturday afternoon. The prayer group prayed over us for the stirring of the gifts of the Spirit, with a particular appeal for the gift of tongues. They laid hands on us. Nobody fell over—though we were warned that this sometimes happens. But nobody who came without tongues left with them, and I wondered how heavy the power of suggestion might be, and why even that didn't work when I was willing to be suggestible.

Two weeks later, I called the Benedictine monastery and asked for whoever was in charge of the program for people like me. Two months later, I made beginner vows as an oblate.

Were the events related? I didn't think so, since the baptism of fire, as I called the first event, seemed so focused on the private, lovely babble called tongues. But the prayers weren't *just* for that, but for the gifts of the Spirit in general. In his first letter to the Corinthians, Paul spells out *the manifestation of the Spirit*—gifts given for the common good. Paul lists these gifts as wisdom, knowledge, faith, healing, miraculous powers, prophesy, distinguishing between spirits, speaking in tongues, and interpretation of tongues.[9]

Sorry if I seem ungrateful, but if you wrapped up any of these and placed it under my Christmas tree, I'd be thinking about exchanging it for something I *really* wanted. These are glorious gifts, of course, but far too grand for the likes of me and my ordinary life. And so, maybe—just *maybe*—the Spirit gave a few Benedictines up the hill the wisdom to grab me and pull me in before I hurt myself as a random, spiritual soloist.

Perhaps the Pentecostal flame encroached even on my solitary, unwilling heart, guided by others similarly blessed with the Spirit of Pentecost. It certainly is too mysterious and foreign a path for me to have found any other way.

## Step 6: Acceptance

When I met Felix and we went out on our first date—or whatever you call the getting-acquainted, going-out, beginning-relationships of people older than high school—he looked at me with great energy and interest and said, "So what's your five-year plan?"

I felt like I was being interviewed for a job. And maybe in a way, I was: Prospective wife sought. Must have good sense of humor, enjoy outdoor activity, and possess five-year action plan. Actually, Felix said later, it was just his way of getting me to talk about myself, my plans, and my general ideas about my life's purpose. He got quite an earful in response, because I didn't have any plan or sense of direction and didn't particularly like being reminded of it.

And it *did* remind me of the worst job interview I'd ever had, when I was asked, "Where do you see yourself in five years? How does this job help you get there?"

"It's just a job," I wanted to answer. "Like the job I've got now, only yours pays more." Somehow a series of jobs unfolding to higher and higher paychecks—and presumably more and more responsibility—didn't seem like the kind of answer anyone with a job opening would want to hear. So I answered, "It's your job I want in five years. This one will teach me all your secrets because I'm going to take on as much of your job as fast as I possibly can."

He was a cognitive scientist at MIT, running a research lab devoted to solving esoteric mysteries of how we think that I would never understand in a lifetime. I was applying for the job of administrative assistant. My answer made no sense, but he liked my attitude, hired me, worked my brains off, taught me everything he possibly could, and when he couldn't teach me anything more, pushed me out with great recommendations to interview for jobs that paid even more.

He was probably one of my best bosses, and one of the best teachers I ever had. But we were at MIT, one of the best research institutions in the world. As a teacher, St. Benedict subscribes to a different school entirely—*a school for God's service*, as he describes it in the prologue to his Rule.[10] And while he hopes that *nothing harsh or oppressive* will be demanded of the student, in laying out the steps to humility, he certainly doesn't have successful job interviews in mind either.

Step 6 on Benedict's ladder of humility is an ego-killer: *acceptance*. It says that we reach this level of humility *content with the lowest and most menial treatment . . . a poor and worthless workman in whatever task he is given*.[11] It is a hard step to swallow, and when you do you taste more fully what humility represents in a world like mine that thinks more about getting more than about having enough.[12]

Getting more and getting ahead is the heart-and-soul of having a career. It's the by-product of a five-year plan and the heart and soul of a consumer economy that urges us to spend as a cure. It's the treatment for everything from low self-esteem to bad breath, the personal response to terrorist attacks, and the solution to the heartbreak of unrequited love. Shopping is considered a hobby in America, like bowling or sewing, and ranks higher in the polls of what we do with our leisure time.

And if I seem too quick to point an accusatory finger—since I hate shopping in malls, but amazon.com is different!—I have the extra curse of getting more that used to flare up in drinking and smoking. Now I can see addiction's face and fuel in chocolate or collecting books. As a recovering addict explains it:

> Today I don't see myself as an alcohol addict or as a drug addict, a sex addict, a love addict, a food addict, or whatever. Although I am all those things. I like to look at myself as an addict. My drug of choice is *more*.[13]

It seems to be a peculiarity of the American mentality and bounty, this more-ness. Look at my friends—non-addicts in substances like alcohol or tobacco—who have a house overrun with collections of basset hounds, dolls, cut glass, or books. Look at my first homemade attempt to streak my hair blonde: if *some* bleach was good, *more* was much better. And if the instructions told me to poke my hair through every third hole in the cap, wouldn't poking my hair through *every* hole really do it right? Subtlety isn't mine to call. (My streaked blonde hair came out white with brown undercoating.) This drive for more doesn't shake loose easily. Newly sober, I was taught the Serenity Prayer. But I wasn't buying it.

"When is accepting the things I cannot change just settling for less?" I snarled at the first AA meeting I ever went to. "And why would changing what you already know can be changed need courage, and how come wisdom comes last, after you've obviously already mucked around and refused to settle for less *or* change the unchangeable, huh?"

I think everybody reached out for another donut at that point. It was five minutes into a 7:30 A.M. meeting, and the old-timers knew they were going to need sugar this morning.

Acceptance won't get you the job of your dreams, either, or the salary you deserve, *or* the changes in your life you know you've got to make. When you don't get the job no matter how badly you wanted it, or the salary you deserve no matter how hard you worked for it, there's always acceptance, building our step to humility. Come to think of it, that was Benedict's idea of the way to live, not yours.

There's an old desert story of how some monks of Scetia came to visit Amma Sarah. She offered them a basket of fruit and they left the good and ate the bad. At that, Amma Sarah approved, saying, "You are the true monks of Scetis."[14] It's hard to get to this place of humility, hard to stay there. This step really glares at me and says, "So are you serious in this school of St. Benedict, or what?"

"Contentment is the key word," suggests one writer. "God does not want an ambitious and competitive person, but one who is content even in the lowliest of occupations."[15] How countercultural can you get? Even the hippies I so admired in the late 1960s for turning their faces away from corporate ladders and media-defined success grew out of it and became Yuppies, fueled on Starbucks, stock options, and handheld computers. In the discontent, the writer goes on to say, they're relying on externals for their satisfaction, churning up more competition.

Another writer on things Benedictine re-enforces and expands on this viewpoint. "We like embossed business cards, monogrammed leather briefcases and invitations to public events," she writes.[16] Well, *I* sure do, and the Levenger catalogue can send me into spasms of lust—even though in my wildest imaginations I have no need for the monogrammed leather briefcase I want so badly. I just want to be the kind of *person* who requires one. I want to be the one important enough in the world's eyes to warrant such handsome accessories.

There are dangers beyond financial limitations to not accepting what is. A professor at the university who grew up in China during the Cultural Revolution told me the story of a decree by Mao Tse Tung that left a deep impression on him. Mao was determined to increase the yield of the crops the farmers produced, but the farmers complained of birds eating a portion of their crops before they could be harvested. So Mao came up with the idea to have the peasants turn out to the fields and bang pots and pans together to scare the birds away.

The peasants banged their pots and pans for three days and three nights without stopping. The low-tech solution worked: the swallows dropped dead from the skies, dead of exhaustion because the noise frightened them and kept them from landing.

But a great famine followed, and millions of peasants died. The swallows had, indeed, consumed some of the grain, but they had also eaten the pests that would otherwise have destroyed the grain. Without the swallows, the grain was overrun by pests and withered, and the peasants died of hunger.

Higher food production is a good thing, but sometimes, accepting a little bit less can also be a good thing—the lesser of two evils perhaps. The trick is discernment, the ability to know what we can and should change versus what we cannot or should not mess with. It's that cursed Serenity Prayer again, tricked out in humility.

Humility is not an action, Father Michael Casey believes, "nor a sequence of actions, nor a habit formed by the repetition of actions. It is, rather, a receptivity, or passivity; a matter of being acted upon. . . ."[17] I find this hard going, and would like to blame the multitude of teachers, family, friends, bosses and would-be bosses, together with various psychologists, social workers, self-help books, and daytime talk-show ladies for demanding I take charge, get a life, make one, and get on with it. Wasn't Mao after just a little more grain for people to eat? "Where do you see yourself in five years?"

Mr. Kim Bok, who worked with Felix years ago on a project in Asia, knew acceptance and lived it probably in Benedict's best sense of humility-building. Mr. Kim had been a college friend of the owner of the company. The college friends went off to make their way in the world, one staying in Korea and one finding his way into textile manufacturing in the American Southwest. Ironically, the Korean-based businessman succeeded wildly in the post-war economic build-up, and the American-based businessman lost his business due to competition overseas.

Mr. Kim returned to Korea where he was hired by his college friend to manage a production line. Things went smoothly for years until the friend died and the son took over the business. Times were changing, and the son was looking to move the business into new areas. Mr. Kim was never in danger of losing his job, although all his expertise and contacts were in the old industries. The son would never do the disrespect to his father of terminating the college friend. But there was no work for Mr. Kim, who represented the old guard in a time of change.

An American business would likely have let Mr. Kim go anyway, respect or not, to help the company save money and move ahead. An American businessman in Mr. Kim's predicament might have used the transition time to update his resume and move on to another firm where he'd feel important—or at least useful—again.

But Mr. Kim picked up the leaves.

As he looked around to see what needed doing, he noticed that the front of the building was untidy, so he picked up leaves until new product lines were developed and he moved into their operations. But in between, he allowed himself to be acted upon and accepted the role that he found. It never occurred to him to abandon the company of his childhood friend. Like St. Francis, who took the call to "build my church" literally, pushing the stones around the hills of Assisi until new clarity was offered to him, the only thing that occurred to Mr. Kim was to accept the role he found himself in.

One of the definitions of humility I especially like comes from Benedictine oblate and writer Norvene Vest. She writes that humility is "facing the truth about our human condition, accepting our limitations, and cheerfully depending on God."[18] Maybe it's the quantum leap from humility to cheerfulness, all in the same breath that I like. Such cheerfulness indicates a wonderful sense of acceptance that I don't see in the you-go-girl daytime television audiences that encourage self-esteem and personal power instead of acceptance. If it was working, would these audience ladies be sitting in a television studio talking you-go-girl or would they be busy doing what they could? Even in AA, where we could learn to accept our condition—

even cheerfully—or we could die of it, acceptance and cheerfulness didn't necessarily go hand in hand.

It's hard for me to see where acceptance could reside in my life, since it clearly isn't something I'm comfortable with. Finally, I thought to look at my discretionary spending, on the off-chance that I might be trying to buy what I didn't already possess.

I began to write everything down to see where my consumerist demons were having their day. Hawaiian music CDs were right up there, and crafty things are always on my radar screen. Does that mean I'm not content? I don't lust for the big stuff Felix does—cars, gadgets, trips—but on the other hand, (a) he isn't actually *buying* those things, and (b) I *am* buying my stuff, siphoning off the discontent and making it more bearable. What if I stopped my little treasure hunting and made myself content with what I have, like Benedict proposes?

Well, first of all, I'd have to *make* myself be content. It wouldn't just happen. We live in a contentious, consuming culture. And even as I ponder being content, a little voice in my head whispers, "Sure. As soon as you get those last two Hawaiian CDs you wanted!"

Sometimes it isn't good to listen, no matter what Benedict says. What that stubborn little acquisitional voice is saying is that I never think I have enough, never make do with what I have, that I keep desperately seeking the kind of identity and happiness that money *can* buy.

Interestingly, I had to see that money can't buy humility. Spending on non-needs is the antithesis of acceptance. I have no acceptance. And until I do, I'll keep reaching for what is not because I don't recognize it in what is. Jacob had his dreams and their blessings, and only when he woke up could he know and exclaim, "Truly, the LORD is in this spot, although I did not know it!"[19] Me, I was too busy shopping for proof of my identity or trying to construct new ones I'd like better. God was calling, and all the lines were busy. Couldn't I begin to be content in what I have, and therefore come to know it again?

## Pentecost

I was busy trying to catch Pentecost by making diagrams and trying to keep everything straight. A tidy Pentecost or no Pentecost, that's my rule. Okay, there are gifts of the Holy Spirit and fruits of the Holy Spirit, and which, if any, would you like, dearie? Could the Holy Spirit descend on me this year?

When I sat with the prayer group in our church that time, I felt bad because tongues seemed the only gift officially worth having from the Holy Spirit, and I didn't have it. And for the ones who did have it, all it got them was a splinter group where they could meet and play tongues together. It was a gift that closed people out instead of bringing them in from the cold to the warmth of those flames.

Down the hill, the Franciscan Mission was putting on a twilight retreat called "What Really Happened at Pentecost?" It promised to look at the time between Easter and Pentecost "and how that time continues to creep into the life of the church today." I'm more interested in what happened in the time *after* Pentecost, but this is my best offer, plus dinner and Mass, all for ten dollars.

I remember when the Mission first began its monthly twilight retreats. I went to many of them, mostly for the joy of being able to go to Mass at the old mission, which is usually locked up tight and considered too small and too badly laid out for Sunday Masses. There were usually one or two people I'd recognize from my regular retreats, and we'd all explore a prayer practice new to me—Jesus prayer, centering prayer, Adoration, and so on. I hadn't been back since I'd become a Benedictine, and I was curious to see what twilight retreats were up to these days.

By the evening of the retreat, I was too tired to go, but forced myself to drive there, convincing myself I could rest and retreat in the strength of others. Sometimes I lead, sometimes I'm part of the choir, sometimes I'm soloist, and sometimes I need to be carried home. This was a carry-me-home night.

It was a tiny group—maybe five or six people—waiting to go inside from the suddenly sharp spring weather. Everybody knew each other, and I was the outsider. "You're dressed wrong for the weather," one of them barked at me.

"Indeed I am," I answered, "still in last week's weather report."

"What's *that* supposed to mean?" she asked her friend, not me. I pulled out my hand-held digital assistant computer and began to check e-mail while we waited for the Mission to get unlocked.

"What are you doing?" another woman asked.

"My e-mail."

"Oh. I could never be bothered learning that," she said—to the woman next to her. I was getting bad vibes, but maybe I was just overreacting? It's Pentecost. I want to learn what it means and go to

Mass and eat dinner, and maybe pray and remember things. Father Rusty once stood there at a twilight retreat, practically dancing in his joyousness over a wooden painting of a gilded horse that looked exactly like the image of the Holy Spirit he was praying to find. I was looking to be inspired, even if I had to rest in the prayers of my fellow twilight retreatants and even if they seemed a bit cranky.

"Do you all know each other?" I asked one woman as we began filing into the church.

"I don't," she said. "It's my first time to one of these."

"Oh, how nice. Maybe we can sit together then?"

Her name was Madge, she said when we sat down. She was interested in doing more things like this now that she was a widow.

"And how long have you been a widow?" I asked.

"Oh, nearly a month," she said cheerfully. "I need to get out and do things more." Her jaw trembled with the effort of cheerfulness.

Oh dear. My mother had become a trained grief counselor working with the recently widowed after becoming a widow herself. Could I remember *anything* about what she'd told me about the recent widows of her experience? Madge was terribly polite in her neediness, too numb perhaps to be broken with grief. I needed to become the attentive daughter instead of resting in others. I got us settled into Mass, and then through the food line in the cafeteria. She found a table with one empty seat and took it, clearly uncomfortable at being new and not fitting in. I'm used to it, which was good, because I ended up eating alone.

"Come, Holy Spirit, Come"—well, maybe not tonight, but the invitation is open-ended. The Mass itself was dispirited as we huddled together like strangers in a bus stop instead of witnesses in Christ. The food was dark and desultory, and the weather outside was edging into nasty. Maybe God is everywhere, but I couldn't recognize him in this lifeless, tired experience. I left before the talk began, feeling no Spirit and all failure.

There is a story told of Rabbi Zusya, who said to his followers, "In the world to come, I shall not be asked, Why were you not Moses? No, instead I will be asked, Why were you not Zusya?"[20]

My identity is a fragile thing, changing and permuting with moods, wants, and desires. I want to be an Episcopalian when the Catholic Church irritates me, which it does with great frequency. I want to be a secular, color-loving artist when the Episcopal Church ignores me, which it also does with great frequency. I like thinking about returning to the Secular Franciscans when the Benedictine monks step on my feet in my spiritual pathway, and I wonder where the escape hatch is when it doesn't work with the Franciscans, like at this Pentecost twilight retreat. I want to be me, as the song goes, and all these stupid people are getting in my way. St. Paul says, "If we live in the Spirit, let us also follow the Spirit. Let us not be conceited, provoking one another, envious of one another."[21]

I need to know what the Spirit of Pentecost looks like to find it. When my mother and father came to visit us in San Diego one year, they found a greatly reduced airfare by flying through Phoenix on America West. That was the good news. The bad news was that they arrived in San Diego at 2:00 A.M.

"Don't worry about it," my mother said. "I called and confirmed that the shuttle bus will pick us up and bring us to the Lake. If you just remember to leave the door unlocked, we can get in without bothering you."

We agreed to that plan, but at the last minute, Felix and I decided it wasn't hospitable. So we napped in the early evening, and when it got late, we drove the nearly silent streets to the airport, tee-heeing at how surprised and pleased they'd be to see us there.

In fact, they got off the plane and walked right past us without any recognition at all, until I said in exasperation, "Ma, it's *me*, Carol."

I think the Spirit of Pentecost, the Holy Spirit of the Trinity, is like that. You've got to know to look. You've got to bring a few expectations to the table. Revelation of the Father is wonderfully illuminated in the older scriptures, especially the psalms. The Son was known in teachings and events of the Gospels. The Spirit was individual flame that sparked together into a conflagration that continues today. If I don't want or don't receive the gifts of that Spirit, I can still know it by its fruit: love, joy, peace, patient endurance, kindness, generosity, faith, mildness, and chastity. Where the fruit is, the Spirit has been and probably still is.

At a Sunday Mass, Father Kelly talked of the year he had a condo in a small town in Japan where he was stationed as a Navy chaplain. His parents came to visit, and while they were visiting, the plumbing needed repair. Father Kelly's dad offered to take care of it while his son went to the ship by day.

"Okay," said Father Kelly. "What you do is go downstairs to the little glass office where the building superintendent is. He doesn't speak much English, so you keep pointing to the phone and keep repeating, 'Mrs. Wantanabe.' He'll understand and call Mrs. Wantanabe and give the phone to you. She speaks English. You tell her what's wrong with the plumbing and then give the phone back to the super. She'll tell him what's wrong, and he'll send somebody to fix it. I know it sounds complicated, but I've done it, and it works."

That night when he got home, Kelly asked his dad how it went.

"It went fine," his father answered. "It went exactly like you said— although the super *does* speak a little English."

"Really? What did he say?"

"I came downstairs and kept pointing to the phone and saying, 'Mrs. Wantanabe,' like you said, and he was staring and staring at me, and finally he said to me, 'Kelly-san get old.'"

Like Father, like Son. "Whoever has seen me has seen the Father," Jesus said.[22] What's in a name anyway?

The Spirit carries many names, and "Spirit" is probably my least favorite, even when first-name "Holy" is appended. It's too loosey-goosie for my taste, treads too close to the edge of New Age trendiness. When I was a kid just before the big language changes to the Book of Common Prayer, it was the Holy Ghost. I heard that the language change would help us little kids because ghosts are scary. Hasn't anybody heard of Casper, the Friendly? Ghosts weren't scary—not as much as mysterious spirits could be. Pentecost can be a lot scarier than Halloween if you let yourself think about it. Pentecost comes to *you*, and you don't get to pick the costume.

"What do *you* think the Holy Ghost looks like?" asked a non-Christian friend rather abruptly on the phone one night. Her husband of sixty years was dying quietly and with great dignity at home, and all of her considerable energy, intelligence, and resourcefulness seemed locked into his caretaking. Well, maybe not *all*. There were a few questions she seemed to be tackling on the side. "I've heard of a Holy Ghost, but I don't know. What do you think?"

Would knowledge of the official liturgical name change from Ghost to Spirit have helped? I doubted it. She was looking for a face, and Casper the Friendly wouldn't do.

"When I see Felix's grandson and watch him with his father, the love is so intense," I said. "The thing in the middle, that's what I think is the Holy Ghost."

"I *knew* it," she said, triumphantly, as if I'd settled a bet in her favor. Maybe I had.

*Love* is not one of the official names of the Spirit, which is probably a good thing given how sentimental and sloppy that word has become. The Spirit is called the Paraclete, the Advocate, the Comforter. Advocate sounds like what lobbyists do, as in, "She was a child advocate in the court system"—good works, but a little too earnest. *Paraclete* is literally "the one called in to help," which sounds like the Red Cross in a disaster. And then there's Comforter.

That has to be one of the best words in the English language. Babies cry for it, and adults yearn for it. The world will leave you cold and defenseless on any given day, or in any unfortunate life. The Comforter is God's gift to us, through Christ—the gift that keeps on giving.

Comfort wraps around you like a handmade quilt. It isn't just the batting in the middle that makes a handmade quilt so warm and comforting. It's the love that stitched it together

My parents would have been married fifty years. Fifty years is fifty years, in my book, even if they couldn't be together for all fifty of them. Sometimes my father's work separated them, and then his death did. But it was still fifty years and worthy of celebration.

I made a comfort quilt for my mother that year. The front of it had carefully faded photos of her with her brothers and parents when everybody was young and alive with promise, solo photos of the skinny teenager in the Air Force she married, the wedding picture, the children, the grandchildren.

"You wrap it around yourself when you need comforting," I explained. Time, distance, illness, or age will pick us off, one by one, but here we all are together and young and skinny and happy. Wrap yourself in that comfort.

It was a very warm quilt.

I didn't need one for myself, I decided, although I looked hers over for a long time before I wrapped it up to give her. Besides, where would I find the photos of my comfort—Felix, Abbot Antony, Mom, Daddy, sure, but teddy bears, blankies, bread, mashed potatoes, gravy, and—oh, yes—God?

So I settled for a candle to light the way when I pray the Office each day.

The fruits of the Spirit—love, joy, peace, patient endurance, kindness, generosity, faith, mildness, and chastity—seem to be fruit sparked by people together, not one person alone. St. Benedict—and

Abbot Antony—may be on to something. My flame and your flame together kindle kindness, whereas my flame alone, on a cold dark hill at Easter, is quickly extinguished. I didn't know this when the candle I lit for my dad that Passion got swept up with all the others, but I'm glad I know what a light we make when we come together.

Such comfort.

# —7—
# The Whole

## Trinity

In the old days, Memorial Day weekend was about remembering. Every little New England town fluttered their flags and honored their war veterans and put flowers on gravestones whether those remembered had fought in the wars or not.

I spent the first Memorial Day after I moved to a small town west of Boston watching the town's one remaining World War I veteran being driven down the main drag in an open convertible, followed by the WWII vets bursting out of old moth-balled uniforms, and the determined Gold Star Mothers who had lost and still remembered their sons of war. Then followed the Boy Scout Troop, the Girl Scouts, the junior high school's marching band getting a little practice in before next year's football season, a few defensive Viet Nam vets who still weren't sure if what they'd been through was appreciated, and finally another marching band—this time high schoolers, a little less ragged, a little more secure in their footing.

My stepdaughter played flute in the junior high marching band, so we stood along the route and swatted May flies while the band kids all processed behind the drum major and twirlers, making their way to the old cemetery on the hillside near the town center. Stow was an old town, celebrating its tercentennial during 1983 when the entire country itself had only recently celebrated its bicentennial. The cemetery—if those crumbling stone heads with nearly invisible and now forgotten names could speak—was full of memories. A devoted townsperson had used the occasion of three hundred years to gather what stories could be found and created a little book of history on our little town.

My stepkids laughed when I bought a copy of the book. They had been raised in Stow. They *knew* nothing ever happened there except when we got our first stop light at the main intersection. Buying such a book just revealed my newcomer status.

The stones in the cemetery didn't speak, but a planning commissioner said a few words lost to those of us at the back of the assembly. The color guard raised their flags solemnly and the drum rolled once. My stepdaughter and the rest of the flute section struggled through Taps. The World War I veteran, left behind at the road behind us in the car, along with Felix standing next to me, cried in memory.

Felix always got the significance of civic memory more than anybody I knew. Putting geraniums on graves is fine, but more appropriate to All Soul's Day if you're religious, to Mother's or Father's Day if you aren't. For him, Memorial Day was remembering the wars, the veterans, the ones who died. On the fiftieth anniversary year of the invasion of Normandy, Felix called his brother-in-law, who'd been an eighteen-year-old kid on those killing beaches, and said, "Thank you for what you did." Mickey was surprised and pleased. He'd never heard a thank you in those fifty years.

Memories fade and change in time. Despite more recent conflicts and more public support for them, despite San Diego's long-standing military culture, Memorial Day is more about the first three-day weekend that bookends summer than anything else. And besides, we're all from somewhere else, and couldn't even decorate a family grave without cashing in those frequent flyer miles.

"I've got a good project for you for the long weekend," Felix offered. We'd been cleaning the garage out, piece by piece, and there were two large, crumbling storage boxes full of paper to go through, destroy, or consolidate.

"Sure, I'll do it," I said. With Sonny the cockatiel checking my progress and leaving a few calling cards on the scattered papers, and the radio playing the top 500 songs of all time for background memorabilia, I tackled the memory of life folder by folder.

I don't consider myself particularly sentimental. I thought I'd find a few legal papers and tax returns to keep, and a few odds and ends to toss out.

But there was more life and memory stuffed into every folder that I went through than I could have imagined. There were the bad junior high report cards my father had saved and then turned over to me—God knows why—and a story I wrote when I was eight years old ("The Easter Egg's Dream") from my mother's collection. Then the timeline jumped to adulthood: divorce papers, annulment papers, best wishes on the rest of your life, sincerely, your ex, cats I have known and lived with, break-up letters with Felix (multiple endeavors), getting back together cards (ditto), cards that came with long-forgotten flowers.

There were Christmas stockings for a former pet bird, a neckerchief for a long-ago dog, notes from both stepchildren, their college applications, AA sobriety chips (various denominations), datebooks without a whole lot of appointments from the mid-1980s, congratulations, your salary is now $18,500, household budgets ("fixed costs: rent = $355, psychiatrist = $150"), failed articles written and never published, our wedding ceremony, anniversary cards, goodbye cards leaving the East Coast, welcome to San Diego mug and matching ashtray, letters from the East Coast written long after you'd think I'd have been forgotten and saved long beyond when I *was*, resumes, travel diaries from my parents' trips, an Episcopalian Church's weekly flyer for Trinity Sunday, 1992—all the memories this unsentimental sort had apparently been unable to toss.

The Trinity Sunday flyer brought its own flood of memories. I was church-hopping in 1992, post–Catholic conversion but freshly disillusioned and newly returned to the seeking business. I'd been brought up Episcopalian, so it made sense to check back with them. St. Peter's in Del Mar was a gorgeous cedar-wooded church above the Pacific with a lively, informed priest.

"I don't know if I'm a Catholic or Episcopalian anymore," I complained to Father Corey.

"Episcopalian," he said promptly. "We're a very welcoming church. You were baptized and confirmed Episcopalian. Welcome back."

"Thank you. Then what was I when I *thought* I was Catholic?"

"Lapsed Episcopalian," he shot back. I had to love his quickness, and I returned to try out the church service, like a taste tester of spiritual flavorings and bouquets. It was too far from where I lived, and I didn't want it to be the church I went to, but the cedar wood buildings were gorgeous, and as I walked inside the church itself, I hoped for a kind word, a sign, anything.

A "high" Episcopal church with stained-glass windows, an ornately wrought gold altar, crucifix and Stations of the Cross, it was surprisingly full at 8:00 A.M. For an uncertain, unhappy Catholic—or lapsed Episcopalian—it was a welcoming place to be.

It was Trinity Sunday, which meant nothing to me except that we were finally past the Sundays of Easter. Father Corey seemed to think otherwise. He marched into his little pulpit and said, "Okay, I'm going to explain the mystery of the Trinity and try not to fall into too many heresies."

It was the kind of church where half the congregation began making notes on the back of their bulletins while he spoke. At the end, Father Corey said, "So I hope I've taken the mystery out of the Trinity for you today."

"Not bad," the gentleman in front of me muttered to his wife. "And I only picked up two heresies in the whole talk."

I was smitten. I saved my bulletin scribbled full of cryptic notes, maybe hoping that someday they'd unveil their own mysteries. The bulletin was filed next to the dream notes I made in the middle of the night when I'd been given the meaning of all human existence. I woke up and said, "I've got to get this down on paper!" and scribbled as fast as I could. It was a good thing I did, because by the morning I'd forgotten everything. But my notes, scribbled in the dark on a two-inch square of paper, a complete blackness of scribble, were incomprehensible then—and now.

I tossed the dream notes and the Trinity Sunday bulletin in the throw-away pile.

Now it's Trinity Sunday again, and I'm the lector for some pretty cryptic readings on the subject. My lector workbook begins: "The concept of God as three persons (Father, Son, and Holy Spirit) in one is impossible to grasp, and yet the Trinitarian notion of God is absolutely central to most (although not all) Christian believers. . . ."[1]

Well, if *that* doesn't have ordinary believers between a rock and a hard place, as my father would say, to pick our way between multiple heresies as well-intentioned people try to explain the unexplainable and trip into the land mines of church doctrine.

Add to the landmines my own cranky complaint—undoubtedly heretical—that at least two of the three "persons" are given masculine identities (Father, Son)—even though we're *told* that God is beyond gender. Well, if that's true, could we have changed the labeling practices by now? And what's up with Spirit, which *did* get a new handle?

If the separate identities aren't impossible enough, we Christians get to know them as *one*. A writer in the Anglican Church tradition gently joins my lector handbook's philosophy when she writes, "Trinity Sunday became a whole new way for our religious forebears to fight with the mysteries they feared. . . . The concept of monotheistic Trinity is one of the most difficult of the mysteries celebrated in the season."[2]

But wrestle with it we must, as Christians, even risking heresy in our understandings. In the old Anglican liturgical schedule I knew growing up, half the church year was counted from Trinity Sunday. Long after memories of Easter glory and Pentecostal fervor, well into the dog days of August, you would attend church on the Twentieth Sunday After Trinity. Labor Day would come and go, the kids were back in school, the leaves were falling from the trees, and the nights were long and dark and cold, and it was *still* Trinity, the Twenty-ninth Sunday After . . . the Thirty-third Sunday After . . . all the way to Advent, which bumps into Thanksgiving in house-decorating time. It seemed like you could never let go of Trinity.

Now the Catholic Church, and many Protestant Churches as well, refer to that great chunk of the church year as *Ordinary Time*. Technically, it's ordinary only in contrast to the extraordinary times of Advent, Christmas, Epiphany, Lent, Passion, Easter, and Pentecost. But I agree with the writer who declares flatly that such a name "is stark in its simplicity, for, as we all know, there is no such thing."[3]

There's nothing ordinary about Trinity, and its very richness and complexity can create some difficult reading. Take, for example, the deathbed pronouncement of St. Theophilus of Corte, who uttered, among his final words, "a profession of faith in the Trinity": "One God alone, one in three persons, one spirit, one eternity."[4]

Which proves that I will never appear in a *Who's Who of Likely Saints*. Granted extreme grace and a relief from crankiness, my deathbed words might echo the Hail Mary that I have said so often in this life (*pray for us sinners now and in the hour of our death*), or, more likely, "Is it hot in here or is it me?"

Sorry, St. Theophilus of Crete. Your sermons may have moved obstinate sinners to conversion, but your profession on the Trinity isn't terribly helpful, you know?

Then there's Blessed Elizabeth of the Trinity, who lived at the end of the eighteenth century, dying of Addison's disease at twenty-six. She lived a Trinitarian spirituality, which piqued my curiosity. What

THE WHOLE • 139

does Trinitarian spirituality *look* like? Her brief biography says that the Blessed Trinity dwelt in her soul, inspiring her to "live a life of praise and homage to God dwelling in her." Her vocation would be a "praise of glory," she decided, praising God dwelling within her, offering a ceaseless Sanctus.[5]

This has got to be one of the happiest vocations I've ever come across; it reminds me of dear Father Stanislaus at our abbey, shouting to us to "praise everywhere and always," praise without ceasing, impelling me to invent that praise rosary of psalm bits to send to him before he died.

Before her death, it seems that Blessed Elizabeth received an extraordinary grace. "The Blessed Trinity was made manifest to her within her soul."[6] What on earth does the Blessed Trinity look like when it becomes real in your soul? The answer I get back is: You'll have to see for yourself.

When I look harder, trying to see for myself, the manifestation is written out as Blessed Elizabeth's famous Prayer to the Trinity. The same rich complexity pours out: "O my Three, my All, my Beatitude, infinite Solitude, Immensity in which I lose myself, I surrender myself to You as Your prey. . . ."[7] It is a beautiful prayer. It is quite possibly Trinity manifested in a soul. But it isn't my manifesto, and it still doesn't help me intelligently proclaim the Word on Trinity Sunday.

It's Memorial Day, the first long weekend that bookends summer. It's Trinity Sunday. In the pulpit, I read from Paul's second letter to the Corinthians: "The grace of the Lord Jesus Christ and the love of God and the fellowship of the holy Spirit . . ."[8] My cheat notes say that Paul is giving us Trinity's calling cards: grace comes through Jesus as God's favor. Love comes from God in Jesus. Fellowship is the unifying force of the Spirit that makes us one in community.[9]

Can it be that the Spirit is the glue that holds the whole mystery of the Trinity together? Is that what I'm hearing and reading today? The congregation looks up at me with bland, unsuspecting faces. I suspect I am not alone in my Triune difficulties.

## Step 7: Littleness

The idea of littleness as anything other than lack of bigness never entered my spiritual vocabulary until I met Sister Pat, a Franciscan nun who offered spiritual counseling on a sliding fee scale.

Until then, littleness was a derogatory term of non-endearment, a way of keeping me in my place. I once told Felix that I was five feet tall. He denied it flatly. I insisted, heatedly—as if being *all* of five feet tall was a big deal.

He threw a hundred-dollar bill on the kitchen table. "Hundred dollars says you aren't five feet tall."

My eyes got pretty big; I'm used to carrying denominations that spit out of bank teller machines. Two thoughts went through my head: (1) This man is getting too much pocket money, and (2) It's mine!

I got the tape measure, we marked the wall, we agreed to the marking, and I stood at the wall. He marked off 4'11 ¼". We did it again. I watched him mark. We did a best out of three as he marked where I told him my head reached. Then he put his hundred-dollar bill back into his wallet.

At work the next day, my office mates were disgusted. "Carol, for $100, I could have stretched a quarter inch!" my administrative assistant said.

"Hey, for a hundred dollars, I got from 4'10" to 4'11 ¼"!" Littleness is my destiny. My father towered over the rest of his family at 5'3". We came from the smallest state imaginable—Rhode Island. Forty miles or so gets you tip to tip, but our geographic sense is smaller. I grew up my whole life in Pawtucket, but I'd never been *near* the Benedictine monastery in Portsmouth, didn't even know it existed until I found a list of U.S. Benedictine monasteries on the library wall of the abbey. And why would I? Portsmouth, thirty-three miles from Pawtucket, might as well have been on Mars.

You get on the United flight from Chicago to Providence, and you smile at *all* the passengers, just to be safe. The odds are the guy sitting next to you went to school with your sister's boyfriend. Or else he married your ex-husband's cousin. Littleness is endemic when you come from an environment like that.

So I bristled when, after a few months of spiritual counseling, Sister Pat said, "I'd like you to consider littleness." I was pretty sure she was making fun of me. I didn't think she was trying to help me grow.

In the Old Testament, God tells his chosen people, through his faithful servant Moses, "It was not because you are the largest of all nations that the LORD set his heart on you and chose you, for you are really the smallest of all nations."[10] I'm a small person from the smallest of states, so I get that. Understanding that God loves us in our little state helps me appreciate Benedict's insistence on littleness as a step to humility. Benedict says the monk must *be convinced in his heart that he is inferior to all and of less value.*[11]

A belief system like that won't fill my calendar with radio and television talk show dates. Could I even bear to listen—that great first word of the Rule of St. Benedict—to someone else say, *I'm the lowest of the low, the least among anybody* without rushing her off to a psychiatrist and giving her a subscription to the Oprah magazine, while keeping an eye on the sharp knives in the kitchen drawer?

But forget about my inclinations—the ladder of humility goes against my footsteps with every rung. What would holier, more learned people say? How would people less tuned in to the dubious wisdom of popular culture look at Benedict's call to littleness?

Sister Joan Chittister, a Benedictine nun who sees the holy through feminist eyes, has no problem with this embrace of littleness. "Aware of our own meager virtues, conscious of our own massive failures, despite our great efforts, all our fine desires," she notes, "we have in this degree of humility, this acceptance of ourselves, the chance to understand the failures of others." And then she nails it: "We have here the opportunity to be kind."[12]

Now there's the knockout punch: I am not kind. I am impatient with inferiority and imperfection in others. This is one place where a step up a ladder of humility makes perfect sense. This step offers me the chance to move up to the level of everyone I think inferior and imperfect—and to know their failings as my own.

But littleness needs others, while its opposite—grandiosity—feeds itself in isolation. I'm king of the world when I'm alone—a fact I find miserably hard to deal with. "Have I told you lately how ironic to end up a Benedictine in community values," I said to Abbot Antony last month, "when my heart was set on becoming a hermit?"

"But you would have learned selfishness alone," he said. "And you wouldn't even know it without others to teach you what you had learned!"

Score: Abbot one. Carol cranky.

St. Francis de Sales wrote a how-to book like Benedict's Rule, but more detailed, called *Introduction to the Devout Life*, that discusses humility as an asset to the devout life. "The virtue of humility consists in knowing and freely admitting our lowliness," Francis writes, "to love and delight in it."[13]

Littleness in itself isn't the virtue. Admitting it, owning it, and being cheerful in it is. We've all seen the smaller dog roll over on its back defenseless before the larger dog and emerge from the encounter intact for admitting its littleness. But delighting in it takes work. I've managed it a few times and realized how good it feels not to have to play the starring role in my little head drama *all* the time.

Jesus had something to say about this, too. He tells a parable about a wedding feast to a roomful of his era's leading men, all of them edging for the best in the house. Don't sit in the best seat, he warns. Someone greater than you may show up, and you'll be embarrassed when you have to move down. Choose the lowest spot; your host might come along and move you forward.

Jesus finishes the parable with the words: "For everyone who exalts himself will be humbled, but the one who humbles himself will be exalted."[14]

This happens all the time at concerts. When the lights go down, the bold move forward to the best empty seats—only to be forced back when the latecomers arrive. I saw it in reverse when Felix and I were visiting a distinguished businessman in Korea. We were nobodies to him, yet when we got into his car to be driven to our destination, our translator, the businessman's relative, gave us the seats of honor in the back of the limousine while he sat in the front, next to the chauffeur. It wasn't necessarily about embracing littleness, but about hospitality. As our host, he took the lowest seat to give honor to us.

Father Casey hits the nail on the head: Humility, he says, "leads us to find contentment in the ordinary, obscure, and laborious occupations that constitute our daily existence."[15] Littleness, in other words, is all about us, *is* us, if only we stop wrestling the world for bigness. It uncovers who we really are, and who we see in each other, if only we drop the masks and the striving. Ironically, it allows us to move from the way we are to the way we can be, as one commentator puts it.[16] Less *of* us becomes more *like* us.

Littleness, like any other step of humility, vanishes as soon as you announce it. Consider this story. On the Jewish high holy day of Yom Kippur, a day of fasting and repentance, a rabbi, in his zeal for humility, jumped up during a silent moment of reflection and shouted, "Lord I am nothing! I am no one!"

Inspired, the synagogue president did the same, standing up and shouting, "Lord, I am nothing! I am no one!"

Witnessing all this, the synagogue's caretaker rose and blurted out, "Lord, I am nothing! I am no one!"

At that, the president turned to the rabbi in amazement and sniffed, "*Now* look at who's saying he's no one."[17]

Who indeed do we think we are, anyway? I look at this step and ask myself, "How **BIG** can *little* get?" The answer that humility must take is "not very." Otherwise, little becomes something else. In the topsy-turvy world of spiritual growth, "the last will be first, and the first will be last."[18] Sit at the lowest place so you may be called to the place of honor.

It's a concept that the great writers of religious tradition—who seemed utterly unaware of their greatness!—are totally in step with. Thomas à Kempis, in *The Imitation of Christ*, suggests, "If you want to learn an art worth knowing, you must set out to be unknown and to count for nothing."[19]

For a change, this is something that gets easier as I get older. The culture I ruled when the world was mine for the taking in my twenties and thirties notices me less as my requirement for bifocals increases. In ten years, I think, the world won't notice me at all. Benedict is only giving me a head start and putting a positive spin on what the culture will do to me anyway. "Embrace littleness," as Sister Pat said.

The *Imitation* warns about the pitfalls of not embracing littleness. For "want of prudence," à Kempis suggests, some people bring about their own personal downfall. "They wanted to do more than they were able, *taking no account of their own littleness*, but obeying the urges of their heart rather than what reason judged to be right" (italics mine).[20]

This contradicts every little kernel of wisdom I've ever gleaned from every talk show I've ever watched and every self-help book I've ever read. But it makes me think of a job I *had* to have. I'd been toiling away at secretarial positions for years at a large research university, anxious to make my mark, eager to become a true professional, which I defined as having the kind of job where you could take work home with you. As a secretary, I could never take work home with me. This seemed to be a weakness in my career life. I might work hard or well or creatively, but I only supported the efforts of others. I wanted my own work, but I was a generalist without a specialization.

"Become specialized," a friend advised me. She had successfully made the transition herself, and I wanted her input. "Your problem is that you're good in lots of areas. Pick an area and become great. See where the jobs are that you want."

I decided that I wanted a job in finance. Research funding was part of what I did well, so I honed in on it and went after jobs in that field. I was acting right out of the career and personal growth checklists you find in women's magazines.

There was an opening for an assistant fiscal officer and I just *had* to get it. "Why?" asked Felix. "You don't even *like* math." Which was true, as my school grades, *summer* school grades, and long-suffering father, the CPA who got stuck doing homework with me, would all have attested.

"It isn't math. It's money," I said. "*Big* difference. Put dollar signs in front of numbers and see how I do."

It was also a promotion—more money, better benefits, more prestige. In research institutions, the administrators are as big as the research contracts they manage. If I got this job, I'd become a big dog indeed. I wanted to be **BIG**.

I got the job. My work ethic and determination were matches for the nearly pathologically driven center that I applied to, which micromanaged macro-sized federal research projects. My new boss appreciated brains and attitude and a little experience over lots of experience and the wrong attitude. "You graduated from college *cum laude*," he pointed out to me. "That means you're smart. You can learn things. You've got a can-do attitude. That means you *want* to learn things. Welcome aboard." He introduced me to my office mate, my support staff—a team of six people to support the assistant fiscal officers—and my computer. He promised me a computer station and modem for working at home and predicted I'd be doing a lot of that.

To me, it sounded like heaven on earth. There was only one problem: I'd obeyed the urges of my heart and the demands of the marketplace, but I'd disregarded the littleness I brought to the game along with my *cum laude* diploma and my can-do attitude.

It was the math. Dollar sign or no dollar sign, I couldn't manipulate the numbers. Even with computer spreadsheets, I still had to create the calculation formulas. At least I could bring work home. I did that a *lot*.

And when I couldn't, I'd make sure my office mate was out of the office and the support staff fully occupied, and I'd call my stepson when he got home from school. I wasn't checking in to make sure he'd arrived home safe and sound. I was a desperate professional careerist. "Okay, if I know what 80% of somebody's salary is, how do I find 100% of it?"

He'd go into his tutor routine. "See, you have to solve for $x$, where $x$ equals 80%, and y equals 100%. So, $y$ equals . . ." I wrote little math cheat cards and hid them in the locked part of my desk. It was 1986, and I was handling over $40 million of research dollars spread across twenty separate accounts, in the days when $40 million wasn't chump change—BIG dog! How **BIG** can *little* get?—and nobody could ever find out I couldn't solve for $x$.

I knew littleness and stared it in the face every day in those monstrous spreadsheets and micromanaged $100 purchase orders. I became painfully familiar with every aspect of it, although I sure wasn't embracing it. I was hiding it in a locked drawer in my desk with my cheat notes. I was terrified of being found out. I was making my career at this institution—I'd been there nearly ten years and Personnel wasn't going to let me transfer out of this job for at *least* two years. And transfer to *what?* In specializing, I'd narrowed my options. The only thing I'd be eligible for would be bigger and better fiscal management jobs—if I didn't get fired for incompetence first.

My salvation came from a totally unexpected quarter. Felix took a business trip to San Diego in February and looked up a colleague who'd moved there. They played golf together. When he called me, he sounded as happy and excited as I'd ever heard him.

"It's 80 degrees here, and I've been offered a job. Let's talk."

It had been snowing, and the hour commute to work was clocking closer to 90 minutes. And because it was fiscal mid-year review time, I was working at home, too— I'd already worked 80 hours for the week when he called. It was Thursday.

"Okay. We'll talk."

When I gave notice, my boss was crestfallen. "You adjusted to the environment so quickly, and you worked harder than anybody. Why, my biggest battle was the size of your dial-up charges from home! Double the others! What will you *do* in laid-back southern California? Surf?"

As I cleaned up spreadsheets and prepared to make the cross-country move, he said, "There's a big research company in San Diego that hired our former director. They're always hiring fiscal officers and contract managers. I'd be glad to put in a word for you. They'd *love* your work ethic."

"Thank you. That's so kind of you." And maybe he did put a word in for me. I never checked in with that company. I became a Kelly Girl, a temporary office worker, hired to plug in the holes in a vacation schedule or to perform a task the real help didn't want to do, while I looked for jobs I *did* want.

"Quite a come-down for you, I know," Felix would say sympathetically, trying not to prance too gleefully at being madly in love with San Diego.

It was littleness for sure, at least in the career sense. And I embraced it.

## Trinity

Trinity bugs me. Maybe it will always lie beyond my understanding. The doctrine makes my eyes bug and my head spin no matter how earnestly I attempt to understand. Even some of the clearest attempts at understanding seem muddy, like the explanation in a book designed to clarify Catholic life:

> [T]here is one God, and there are three persons in the one God or Trinity. The three divine persons do not share the one divinity among themselves, but each of them is God whole and entire. Yet each divine person is really distinct from one another. Hence we say that God has one divine nature and three divine persons.[21]

Maybe it belongs forever in that big bag that the abbot simply refers to as divine mystery where for some, like a heavenly Santa Claus, God hands out the understanding as a sort of grace present.

But how can faith grow within such mystery? For most of us, without some understanding, our faith will grow alongside and separate from such mysteries, or we'll develop a cafeteria-style pick-n-choose spiritual life.

Several years ago, I pored slowly over the letters of St. Paul as daily *lectio divina*, or sacred reading. In Galatians, Paul, after speaking of the unhappy results of living by the flesh in the secular world, writes, in contrast, about the fruits of the spirit. "If we live in the Spirit," Paul says, "let us also follow the Spirit."[22] And I, who had never heard of any saints like Blessed Elizabeth of the Trinity, jotted in my prayer journal as response, "It is as though the Trinity works with an indwelling Son, and a traveling companion Spirit, all on a journey to join together with the Father."

Maybe I was getting closer to an understanding. But all the father and son language—how could that dwell in me, a woman? An editorial in *Magnificat*, a monthly collection of daily prayers, Mass readings, meditations, and saints' stories, helped.

The editor, Peter John Cameron, suggests that the remarkable thing is that we usually come to the Trinity backwards. That is, "we start with an experience of the Holy Spirit that unites us to the Son who reveals to us the Father." Some people's first acquaintance with the Trinity is the touch on the shoulder that allows the embrace of Jesus and opens them to the Father. Pentecostal Protestants are well acquainted with such discoveries; Catholics probably less so.

In many ways, Father Cameron suggests, this order of embracing Trinity "mirrors the Blessed Virgin Mary's own intimacy with the Blessed Trinity in the Annunciation."[23] Aha, now *Mary* knew indwelling! The Spirit within, the origins without, the Word made flesh and dwelt among us. Who better to know the indwelling Trinity than a woman? God is now fully gathered up from the law and prophets, and spilled out fully into creation.

Christ's Incarnation began when Mary was overshadowed by the Holy Spirit. With Christ's death and victory over death came the great wind, the great fire, the great comforter that begins our own incarnation from the Spirit to Christ, to Christ's origins, like a triangle perfect within a circle, and the circle is all of us.

Trinity is wholeness, like the unbroken circle of the old hymn. We talk about inclusion in the secular world, particularly in academia, as if we really mean that including everybody will make us somehow better. But when the discussion turns to diminishing resources and raising standards, inclusion gets squished a little to one side. But *real* inclusion—why Christ came to save all of us, even the ones who only come to church once a year—matters because, in the Trinity, inclusion makes us whole.

Imagine wholeness. The very word seems to reveal our splinteredness, our fractures, our separateness, our selective blindness. Behold wholeness, Trinity, the round circle of inclusiveness encompassing the totality of God, including everything, even me—*all* of me.

I've seen Trinity's face.

I'd been in AA less than two years, and Felix and I were planning a trip to Hawaii. My sponsor was doubtful of the wisdom of a trip like that so early in sobriety, but I had meeting lists for Oahu and Maui. I even boldly called the contact in Oahu and told him it would be my second anniversary of sobriety when I was there, and would they have a cake for me, please? They did, and I celebrated along with sailors coming in on leave, some beach people trying to get it together, office workers from the high-rise skyscrapers of Honolulu, and tourists in matching aloha wear.

Going on to Maui, the only meeting I could fit into the schedule was one called Serenity Stop. It was held on the beach, and somebody brought donuts, someone else had the hot water and instant coffee, and a third brought "Easy Does It" and "One Day At A Time" signs.

We sat in a circle on the beach to talk. I was the only tourist this time, and a little uncomfortable with that status until one guy began to speak. His words were direct and fast and full of edges, not like the blurry softness of serenity the others had. He never took off his sunglasses. As he talked—"and this Higher power—I call him Jesus Christ, and he lives in my heart now that I stopped filling it up with booze . . ."—you could see all of us reflected back, right out of his eyes. It didn't matter then if you were a tourist or a local, a recovering alcoholic or somebody sniffing around for coffee and a donut. We were all just there, a circle of hope and courage and brokenness and betterness, coming out of his eyes, all of us.

That's what Trinity's face looks like.

In graduate school, they taught me to look at what *was*—in the history book, the legal argument, the art on the wall—and see what was *not*, the stories unsung, the strands of thought not chosen, the definition that limited visibility, the hole in the donut that would make it whole.

Trinity is the donut, whole, the allness and awfulness of God who creates and sings songs, who suffers and breaks, who speaks through stringed instruments.

Blessed Elizabeth of the Trinity talked of the indwelling Trinity. It's like God within, only labeling the parts, a circle with sides.

The sides are made up from Trinity's revelations—Father, Son, Holy Spirit, no matter how masculine and exclusive the names seem—and the circle is *us*, God's creations. That means there's no single indwelling—who am *I*, alone, to incorporate all of Trinity? The inclusion and wholeness comes with all of us together, male, female, children, in all our pretty colors. Wholeness within, wholeness without.

# Interlude
## *Safe Place*

"What time do you get up in the morning?" the old abbot asks as we make small talk in his beloved little oblate library in the quiet of the late afternoon before Vespers. He has just confessed to needing to stay in bed until 4:30 A.M. nowadays since his heart surgery, an hour later than he had in the old days.

"During the summer, four-thirty," I say mournfully, a most reluctant, unwilling morning person, who thinks four-thirty in the morning is practically still night.

"And when do you retire for the night?"

"I'm not much after a ten-hour workday," I answer. "I'm not up past nine-thirty. I come home, eat dinner, pray the Evening Office, and that's it." I'm too embarrassed to admit that after the Office, I try to practice the ukulele most nights. The ukulele seems to be a funny instrument to everybody else—thank you, Tiny Tim—but to me, it's almost about the sacred.

In a meditation I was reading, the author talked about the safe places we can create to store the truths we learned about life. It may be a journal, she says, or somewhere to go alone and think, "or maybe it's a particular piece of music that will release its memories each time you hear it played."[1]

Each night when I play my ukulele, I warm up for ten or fifteen minutes playing basic chord progressions in various keys. They are my safe place, these musical keys, and warming up is my entry into safe places I have known. The key of C is Kohala, where the Monday morning group played ukulele until Auntie got tired, which was long after I did. There, an older man from Ohio with a tenor uke showed me the C chord. Auntie showed me the F, and the guy who practiced every night in front of his TV set showed me the little triangle my fingers had to form to make a G7. And then we were off: "You are my sunshine, my only sunshine. . . ."

The key of G is the Kealani's Uke Pickers, where George showed me the crazy G chord. We meet on winter Saturdays in Encinitas, when the surfers aren't around to fill up the place, and we play until we freeze. We even got a gig once, and tee shirts in honor of the gig.

The key of D is Waimea, the place the old ones call Kamuela, where Auntie taught me to crowd my fingers together to make a "ladies D"—I bought L'uke the Uke in Waimea the next day, and declared that the first song I would write for uke would be called "Rush Hour in Kamuela," where the rainbows, which are everywhere, practically lay on the ground gridlocked.

The key of F is Hilo, where a lady who only knew that one chord tried to sell me a high-priced uke. I never liked spending much time in Hilo. It rains every day, so much I can feel the webs growing between my toes. But now that I'm home where it never rains, I can watch daybreak over Hilo Bay via web cam, and each day it rains in Hilo, a mystical experience of lushness to set off and contrast with the coastal desert where I live.

And then there's A, the bright open sound of Ka'u, the flat, open yellow place in the southlands of the Big Island of Hawaii. There isn't much there that isn't yellow—except the beaches of black, or white, or extraordinary green sand, all hidden away in the open-stringed key of Ka'u.

This is what it's like when I practice the ukulele at night. These are my safe places, released every time I play. Playing music in this safe place has become my delight. Benedictines take delight in the balance of work, prayer, and recreation. I was on the short end of the recreation part of the triangle until making music entered my life. Now my life is lit up with delight.

Delight is such a lovely, unexpected thing. You can either laugh or clap your hands in it. When I took a master uke class, Jumpin' Jim took such delight in the close harmonies of the four-stringed uke. It was "like a barbershop quartet," he declared. I had been delighting in the open strings of Ka'u, but since he shared his delight in closeness, I have delighted in closeness, too. It makes you want to clap in delight. But your hands are busy, so you laugh God's laugh. Trinity manifests in us, as Blessed Elizabeth of the Trinity discovered in her vocation. I would like to make my vocation that of the one who laughs God's laugh of delight. Somebody has to do it, so why not me?

This safe place is a funny place. "It's playing the instrument *together*," Jumpin' Jim emphasized, "the twenty-five of us in this room, or a hundred of us, or a million of us, all tuned a little differently, all of us at wildly different levels, and the music we're making blends together until we only hear ourselves in others. And we think, "Wow, I'm good. I could get pretty good at this. And together, we are good. Together we get there.""

What if the Psalmists included women? I know better than to think that David wrote all the psalms in the Bible. Why don't I admit women may have penned the poems or broken out into songs of joy or rage or storytelling? We have done so in all times and places, with—or usually without—power. If the Psalmist is sometimes a woman, I don't have to worry about my inclusion in Trinity's wholeness: "Together we get there," as Jumpin' Jim says.

Heck, I sit in the sunroom and fall in love with music nearly every night. This heart rejoices, this soul is glad, and even this body rests in the safe places of the music, sung for the Lord.

"How do you seek unison with God?" asks the student.

"The harder you seek, the more distance between you and God," answers the teacher.

"Well then, how do you bridge the distance?" asks the student.

"Know that it isn't there," says the teacher.

"Am I one then with God?" asks the student.

"Not one. Not two," the teacher says.

"Well then, how can this be?"

"The sun and its light. The ocean and the wave, the singer and the song. Not one. Not two."[2]

Allowing a woman psalmist into the edges of the Psalter softens the songs with love. The lady psalmist finds and chooses great loves, and her song is the prayer of the Trinity—the singer and the song. Not one. Not two. *Maybe three.*

That delightful noise—"Shout joyfully to the LORD, all you lands"[3]—that's coming from my instrument and my arthritic fingers, going out and back to heaven, available whenever I take up my ukulele and hug it to my heart, hearing my instrument in others.

It is the delight of wholeness, of Trinity made whole in us.

# —8—
# The Gathering

## St. Benedict, Feast

For a while, Felix and I tasted a little of what the many military families based in San Diego feed upon: apartness. The military take their overseas assignments, and the big boats sail off without much hurrah, and disappear for months at a time. For years, the *San Diego Union-Tribune* would publish a two-page world map every six months or so, and then list map coordinates several times a week so you could follow the carriers' journeys.

Felix followed the fleet vicariously. He would tack up the map in the garage when the new one came out, and then the little colored pins would appear, tracking the routes of the *Stennis*, the *Constellation*, or other carriers. I'd look up from folding laundry a few weeks later, and see carefully drawn, dotted lines showing the paths where the pins had been.

"Why?" I asked. "Why do you care where they are?" We weren't military, had never been military, and didn't know any military. So why was Felix "standing the watch," as the *Union-Trib* called it?

"They're part of the community we live in," he said. "I'm just keeping an eye out for the neighborhood." And so he did until the neighborhood became a threatened place, and military families asked the paper not to publish ship coordinates anymore. Felix marked the last ship coordinates, then pasted a military locator map for Afghanistan on the wall and left it up in the garage. Part of his neighborhood went off-line—untracked, but unforgotten.

I suppose he related to the military families as a concerned neighbor might. While the ships left San Diego without much notice, they always returned to fanfare—TV cameras, waving flags, smiling sailors, and excited spouses. The return was always the front-page headline, the lead story on the six o'clock news. "He's been gone six months," a happy young woman, maybe just out of her teens, would tell the cameraman. "Our son was born two weeks after he shipped out, and this is the first time he'll see the baby." And some of the sailors would cry, too, at the heartbreaking sudden rush of homesickness you get when home is finally, safely, in your view: It's just what I remembered, but everything is a little different. It feels right. It feels very strange.

When we lived in New England and he worked for a German-owned company, Felix traveled to Europe often. Once we relocated to San Diego, though, most of his trips were domestic—until his company was bought by a Korean-based group, and the decision was made to move all manufacturing to Korea. Felix headed up manufacturing.

After a two-week introductory trip, Felix began commuting between Carlsbad, California, and Inchon, South Korea—a one-way commute of more than 6,000 miles and sixteen hours of fly time.

Unlike the military families who spend long periods of time apart and then a shorter "long" period of time together, we bounced between apartness and togetherness. He would be in Korea for six weeks, home for two, Korea another five weeks, home for three. He called Korea "the other woman in my life." At some point, I stopped laughing at the joke.

After one particularly long stint, I met him at the airport as usual, but I was a little quieter than on most homecomings. Somewhere in the drive home, Felix said, "What's wrong?"

"I didn't recognize you at first when you got off the plane," I said. It felt so terrible—a familiar face coming through the gate, a familiar stranger not quite in focus. It only took a few seconds to recognize him, and to rush forward to greet him, but those few seconds had a scary, guilty aftertaste: I am not recognizing my own husband. What's wrong with me?

"I always have a little trouble, too," he said quickly, as if relieved to finally unburden a guilty secret of his own. "You're always shorter and blonder than my memory thinks you should be."

Memory is such a liar. It holds the beloved face tightly like a photograph, unwavering and loyal, unchanging, like a perfect flame of constant love. But love isn't constant. It's a shifting reality between two constantly changing people, as the military families always learn again at re-entry. We change, we age, we move along the continuum of time, however imperceptible that movement seems. And then a beloved aunt you haven't seen in twenty years says, "My, how you've grown!" You realize she's pasting your picture of now on top of the one on her dresser that's been there unchanged for a couple of decades, and she's in shock.

With close relationships, lived in daily contact, even an absence of six weeks is long enough for the mind photos and the reality shots to separate. There is that momentary shock before recognition sets in.

It happens with groups, especially the tightly knit ones that speak in a coded shorthand. I was visiting Rhode Island some fifteen years after my move to California, and ran into somebody I'd known since junior high school. "Isn't that something about the mayor?" he asked. To him, it was like I'd been gone since yesterday. To me it was, "Huh?" I was still embedded as a small part of his cultural framework, whereas neither he—nor much of Rhode Island—was any part of mine.

Jesus had only been dead three days when Easter came and the stone was rolled away from the tomb. He returned to face family and friends who couldn't recognize the *now* because they were still filled with the horrible memory photographs of *then*.

That sort of unfamiliarity with the familiar happened to me with AA. After years of being nowhere near a meeting or the language of AA recovery, I was working on my master's thesis on the rhetoric of the self-help movement and went to several meetings to refresh my memory. The strange 1930s boosterish language of AA's Big Book hit me full force with near incomprehensibility—as it must have when I first entered the program. "We thought we could find an easier, softer way. But we could not. With all the earnestness at our command, we beg you to be fearless and thorough from the very start."[1] I could have quoted it from memory at some points in my history, and referenced it in my daily experience, but my absence, and the changes in me that my absence embraced, led me to say, "Huh?"

During six months of heavy travel, I missed many of the monthly oblate meetings Abbot Antony hosts, and I didn't even have the time to write him or stop by for Mass and lunch. I could manage church *somewhere* once a week, but that was about it. Even the daily office became too burdensome to lug around with me, so I stopped praying it. I took a month's vacation and then plunged back onto airplanes and into rental cars.

But missing the monthly oblate meetings wasn't plunging me into peril—not in the way that stopping AA meetings can be perilous to the newly sober.

When I stopped going to AA meetings, I was not told I'd fall off the wagon or start drinking again—at least not by the social worker who had supervised my entry into AA. His only caution to me was, "Don't isolate yourself." It was the isolation that would lead to problems, he felt, not necessarily a lack of meetings.

I took that wisdom into my Benedictine oblation. It wasn't about the oblate meetings or even praying the Office that would make or break my oblation. It would be isolation. The old abbot had made it pretty clear that my spiritual journey would be made in community with others.

I found a new community when my life became too busy for my old one. I found a pick-up Saturday ukulele group to join after the one disastrous experience when I returned from Auntie's beginner class. They said in Auntie's class that you learned in a group, not through videos or solitary practice. Jumpin' Jim added encouragement with his emphasis on "all of us together."

Isolation is a dangerous thing for all-or-nothing types like me, and the uke club kept me from finding the edges where I might slip and fall. While I couldn't find a Sunday a month for the oblate group or an hour a day for the Office, I *could* find many Saturday afternoons near one of the best surfing spots in California to join my fellow uke pickers and play some tunes until we all got tired. The Office was too bulky to fit in my luggage, but the ukulele case managed to become carry-on.

A group is a group, I decided. A gathering is just that. And whether they are joined together specifically for love of Christ, or in their common effort to apply the Rule of St. Benedict to everyday lives, or to figure out how to sit in the sun together and sing and strum in joy, we are a collective body of people, and you can learn many lessons you just can't as a soloist.

The more time I devoted to the ukulele group, the more I discovered that everything I knew about living the Rule of St. Benedict was coming from playing ukulele in the band.

Well, maybe not *everything*. I would like to think that Abbot Antony taught me a few things, too. But the fundamental theme that underlies the Rule is community. The Rule is a set of regulations for "a school for the Lord's service"[2]—the old fashioned, place-bound, time-honored school like we grew up with, the one with the rows of desks, complete with the class clown, the brain in front, the tease in the back. For Benedict, the school is the monastery. For me, it's the ukulele group where we all learn together, rubbing off our rougher edges, shoulder to shoulder, strum by strum.

I saw the Rule lived out in the ukulele culture when I showed up at Auntie's, the mainland tourist in Crazy Shirt gear and upscale sandals, here today, gone tomorrow. As the regulars shuffled their chairs to include mine and tuned my borrowed plastic ukulele to match their pitch, I thought, "Is *this* what Benedict meant?" His instruction manual of the school for the Lord's service says, *Once a guest has been announced, the superior and the brothers are to meet, with all the courtesy of love.*[3] I have met wonderful guides like Ron, the social worker, or Abbot Antony, the monk, along my journey, but this was the first time an entire gathering had embraced me, the stranger in their midst. I fell in love at that moment—in love with the wholeness I was suddenly engulfed in. I fell in love with the knowledge that I was part of something. It happened again at the uke pick-up gathering in Encinitas. They pulled up a seat and handed me the music and said, "Welcome. Next song, key of B-flat." I played what notes I could manage, and stayed in the circle.

Everything I learned seemed to come alive in ukulele school. *On arising for the Work of God*, says Benedict, *they will quietly encourage each other, for the sleepy like to make excuses.*[4] That's for sure. As the newest, and absolutely worst, ukulele player in the group, I watched carefully, asked a few key questions of those around me ("You're putting your fingers how???"), and accepted their encouragement. "Sounds good!" they'd beam, and I'd laugh because I'd only played two chords over and over, and "air uke" for the rest.

And then the glorious irony happened, as it does in AA and other groups, and you learn what you can't learn any other way except this way, together. Somebody arrived with a new uke and a nervous smile, playing *much* worse than even me, and I found myself encouraging strums and strings that I barely knew a week ago myself. I still had sore finger pads, but suddenly I was the coach and teacher—but not the only one. Just the one sitting closest to the newest. I couldn't get bored and sleepy and wander off. I was too damned busy worrying about her encouragement as well as my own, and thinking, "Is this *right* out of old Benedict, or what?"

My uke groups provide a community even when I'm traveling far from home. The Rule of St. Benedict talks about travel, and I've paid special attention to see what I can learn. If you can't be where you're supposed to be, says Benedict—and clearly you are *supposed* to be in your designated place of prayer at the designated hours with your designated community—then at least perform your work of prayer where it finds you.[5]

So when I take off on my travels, I bring a list of uke players and groups from the Uke Yak website. There are two registered players in Rhode Island, and fifty-four players and eight groups in California— what more do I need when I travel? In my old life as an AA member, I had to find a meeting wherever I found myself. As a Catholic of stubborn, if not orthodox persuasion, I use www.masstimes.org to help me find a Catholic church when I'm on the road. And now I've got Uke Yak. I can find community wherever I am.

My uke groups also give me the kind of discipline that the Rule fosters: *let us stand to sing the psalms in such a way that our minds are in harmony with our voices*,[6] says Benedict. So I've added daily discipline and practice to the sheer joy of playing my uke: ten minutes of chord transitions, twenty minutes of reviewing old favorites, twenty minutes of new work, five minutes of speed or dexterity work. It looks a lot like my gym routine, but I've realized it's a way of getting mind and fingers in harmony with my voice.

Finally, my playing was bringing alive for me Benedict's famous good zeal, the grand finale he uses at the end of the Rule, when he writes: *let them prefer nothing whatsoever to Christ, and may he bring us all together*.[7] In my newfound devotion, to which I preferred nothing else, I was being drawn into a larger circle. For a former soloist and overactive lobbyist, I sure was learning a lot playing a non-solo instrument.

By now, though, I'd missed two more oblate meetings, and the old abbot was sending *me* little catch-up notes. But the abbey seemed far away from my travels. The picture of myself now no longer fit with the photograph then, taken at the abbey. In that picture, Abbot Antony and I stood facing the camera. I squinted directly into the sun, so relieved to finally get a picture taken with my beloved abbot, while he, delicately, looked away from the camera to the book he had just loaned me. In retrospect, my oblation had always been about my spiritual guide, the old abbot, not about the oratory of oblates that I was pledged to.

There was a new photograph sitting on my desk, a new me, taken with Auntie and surrounded by her group in Hawaii. A ukulele is not a solo instrument, and I knew that in my bones and in my ears when I heard how good I sounded in the circle where everybody else was making music so much better than me.

One day, I mentioned to a coworker about the uke group on my calendar, and she said, wistfully, "How nice to be a part of a little group like that." Is this a metaphor of spiritual life? I wondered. If it doesn't come with a bumper sticker that says, "Christian values here," would I even recognize it as such? Or had I finally come to live the Rule through the unorthodoxy of a ukulele group?

## Step 8: Following a Spiritual Guide

Humility doesn't have to be complicated: The eighth step of humility is only one sentence long—*that a monk does only what is endorsed by the common rule of the monastery and the example set by his superiors.*[8] Follow your leader, in other words. How complicated can this be?

Well, we can complicate it. Guru-following is a very Eastern tradition, and I am a Westerner. For Christians, the ultimate spiritual guide is supposed to be Jesus, the Good Shepherd, which, unfortunately for my touchy ego, makes me a sheep. Sheep only follow their own shepherd's voice, and that's where the following part gets tricky— there are a lot of bad imitations running around. My lector workbook commentary for Good Shepherd Sunday says, "When we know the true shepherd's voice through informed faith, we will not follow false shepherds or mistake the allure of self-centered fantasies."[9] But how am I supposed to know what informed faith is, let alone recognize the true shepherds?

When I was an impressionable teenager, I was fascinated when the Beatles flew off to India to study meditation under a guru. It was my first experience of gurus and of watching famous people submit to a teacher. But it was an Eastern concept. I first heard the term *spiritual director* when I attended a Franciscan retreat that offered spiritual direction. I signed up every day. It was like therapy without Freud. It was what I thought therapy *would* be like—and had never been. It had questions, but answers, too; beginnings, but also endings. But outside those retreats, you paid for spiritual direction, just like therapy, only with spiritual direction, your insurance wouldn't co-pay. Or you trotted yourself off to confession, which the priests are hasty to announce is *not* therapy at all.

The monks at my abbey will serve as spiritual advisors if you ask, but that assumes you know to ask, have some idea of what it is you're asking (therapy versus spiritual direction versus confession), and are prepared to follow through. That's asking a lot of the ordinary, screwed-up, spiritually thirsty human being.

According to the monks of New Skete, the student had an obligation "to make his own way to a teacher, an indication of the genuineness of his desire and an appropriate act of humility. Distance is never an issue."[10] Crisply put—but do you look in the phone book? I know very, very few people on the spiritual journey who have the luxury of a guide. No wonder we all keep getting lost. The few I know who have a guide are clergymen or women who maintain ties with a former teacher, the way young scientists do with their advisors.

And what do you look for in a spiritual director, anyway? Some sources spell out knowledge of God, knowledge of people, and some knowledge of communication between God and people.[11] Other traditions have a simpler, Zen approach: when the student is ready, the teacher appears.

Perhaps it happens that way, and your readiness is confirmed by the arrival of the teacher. But you still have to be pretty careful about listening for the *good* shepherd's voice. It seems to me that Catholic priests are too few—and too burdened by their duties and the size of their flocks—to enter into advisement with individual members. Other Christian clergy have the worship committees, stewardship goals, capital campaigns, and Bible studies to suck the time and talent from their calendars. That leaves professionals in psychological fields, making for relationships that are more business-like, with issues of finances and confidentiality.

So who listens? Who guides? In AA, it was your sponsor, who was nearly always the same sex, always sober for at least two years, and always somebody with "good sobriety," who liked who she was. Come to think of it, those would have been perfect guidelines for our Catholic sponsors, too.

Joanie was my AA sponsor because she'd been around the longest and seemed to know the stuff, but I hated slogan answers to questions, and the implication that if I followed her way, I'd get exactly her results. In Catholicism, I asked my next-door neighbor to be my sponsor because I didn't have a clue who else to ask. We both stumbled along cluelessly through the conversion classes. He was as ill-prepared to guide as I was to accept guidance.

Looking back, I don't think I'd seek an advisor with certain knowledge or even willingness to serve, or even demand a letter of recommendation. I think I'd look for someone who has what I want and I'd ask how to get it—the same way the young woman in my university saw my job, decided she wanted it, and asked, "How do I get there?"

In AA, everybody, once they'd sobered up and were wild with not drinking, wanted serenity. But those who'd been at it for a while knew how tough it was. "My serenity is like a duck," the old ones would say—rather smugly, "floating across the water so calmly, paddling like hell underneath." To get to that smooth, calm place, you had to stay within the group's guidelines. To become like them, to obtain what they had, you had to imitate them. It's like art students copying the masters' works.

I didn't realize Abbot Antony was my spiritual advisor. I never asked him to be—wouldn't *dream* of asking him—and I didn't think I needed or wanted one. And then one day, my oblate buddy Hildegard, talking to her friend about spiritual advisors, turned to me and said, "And the abbot is Carol's spiritual advisor, isn't he, Carol?"

"The old abbot? I don't think so. Why do you say that?"

"Well, you meet with him all the time, and write to him, and he writes to you and gives you things to read that sometimes you read."

Well, I guess he *is* my spiritual advisor. My faith has been placed not as much in God—humbling as that is to admit—as in the little abbot who has tried to serve him faithfully all these seven decades he has been a monk. I've tried to do whatever the little abbot has given me to do—the Rule, the daily office, sacred reading, really icky reading, whatever—as if it were given to me by God because the little abbot is my earthly substitute. Imitating Christ is too overwhelming. Imitating his little abbot, Christ's humble servant, seems like an easier way to start.

For Benedict himself, the monk's attitude to his abbot was the "paramount expression of humility."[12] That means there's hope, even for me, in the climb to humility. I may be an aging baby boomer, anti-authoritarian and a spiritual do-it-myself kit, but when it comes to the old abbot, I've got nothing but undying reverence and devotion. When I see how readily I would obey whatever he asked, no matter what, then I understand what the Buddhists say about guru devotion: it's a tremendously effective way of surrendering the sense of self.[13] Fortunately for me, as for others in traditions of guru devotion, the little abbot tolerates the stubbornness and ignorance I bring, "adjusting," as a Buddhist nun says of her master, "by developing several alternative suggestions in advance before assigning me any major task."[14]

When he saw my sullen resistance to the idea of praying the whole Office, Abbot Antony showed me how to use the abbreviated one first, then lured me into the large, full Office, by promising me it had poetry in it. It did. He won. I won. He led me to daily lectio five minutes a day and the Rule a little bit daily, like vitamins, or weight repetitions at the gym. He led me slowly. *And the sheep learned his voice and followed* . . .

Following a spiritual guide is an extraordinary experience. Like many of the steps of humility, spiritual direction goes against the American grain. It strips me of my self-sufficiency and grates as a discipline, correcting, molding, and perfecting me in ways I might not necessarily choose. It's about humility.

Perhaps most importantly, following a spiritual guide is all about finding my way to Christ. Benedict promises me the exaltation of heaven if I climb the steps of humility in this life.[15] It's not humility for humility's sake. It's humility for the sake of Christ.

And it surprised me how much I wanted direction to get me there. I spent five years and a great deal of money I didn't really have on weekly therapy, just trying to decide if I wanted to be happy. Forget the *how* of happy—was it even worth it? I was suspicious. I was twenty-seven years old and full of existential angst. What was in it for me? I was pretty sure happiness was a concept sold by the media to get me to buy stuff. I was pretty screwed up.

The recovering alkie types wanted serenity, and saw it in the faces of the long-sober. I definitely didn't want serenity. It sounded like dead with your eyes open to me. When my social worker decided to bring to his alcohol recovery group a stress reduction expert to help us on the way to serenity, I literally left the room. I liked having what I called nervous energy. (Other people tended to call it something quite different.) I didn't *want* no stinkin' serenity.

And so it went. St. Paul writes in a letter to his little flock, "You have followed my teaching, way of life. . . ."[16] "Not me," I could have answered before I met the old abbot. Up until then, I had never found the teacher or the thing I wanted enough to become a follower. I never had a mentor. For me and people like me, there were self-reliance and self-help groups, and if they didn't work, there were professional counselors or for-profit secular gurus selling lifestyles and all the paraphernalia that went with it.

"I'm surprised you never really went into New Age spirituality," a co-worker told me once.

"I know," I said. "I look the type. I just couldn't afford it." My favorite bookstore in a funky part of Encinitas was called Phoenix Phyre. They had New Age books, beads, oils, and incantations for sale. There was the obligatory resident cat, a collection box for "kitty's surgical procedure," and private rooms for psychic counseling. It just seemed a little *too* self-consciously Californian—and they didn't take credit cards. So I never got into having a psychic advisor. And in the more mainstream world, the priests and ministers were too busy for individual sheep and usually didn't seem to possess anything I wanted for myself anyway. Even St. Paul noted that his followers were responding to both teachings *and* way of life. What I wanted couldn't just be taught. It had to be lived, and I had to *see* it being lived. And somehow—maybe this is where the grace of God comes in—I had to recognize what was there for the asking.

And then Abbot Antony stumped into my life, and I don't know if the student was ready or not, or if even the teacher was ready. All I know is that he answered the door and invited me in. And I looked at him and *through* him, and saw Christ and wanted Christ, and fell hopelessly in love with Christ, and would do anything to be near Christ, always, forever.

Abbot Antony became my Paul, my spiritual guide. I try whatever he suggests, and sometimes his suggestions actually stick. Other times, it grieves me that I am such a poor oblate—that my reading is not the sort that edifies, that my perseverance needs maintenance, that my attitude flirts with rebellion, that my attendance at oblate meetings is so spotty, that part of the community of oblates is nearly nonexistent. It's my failure, not the abbot's, when I make time for a pick-up ukulele group but not an oblate meeting, when I'm attracted to saints more than to their Savior and to rosary beads more than to the solemnity of sung psalms. It's my fault when I'm drawn to cheerful small indulgences rather than to quiet self-denial, to happy talk instead of reflection.

It's my failure because I've been given an example of the holy life and how to live it. My teacher is patient, but he will not be here forever. And even when his teachings (and my homework) lag, the little abbot's example is still before me. "I will help you as much as I can while I am here," he said right before our oblation vows. "And when I am no longer here, I will help as much as I can."

There are days when every belief that is central to Christianity or part of the glorious burden of Roman Catholicism is ludicrous to consider, too heavy or slippery for me to assume. On those days, I believe because Abbot Antony believes, and because I believe in *him* and his faith, if not in me and mine.

Is that enough to get me to where I want to go? It has to be. I can't will a feeling or make a belief. I can only act in accord with it and follow my old abbot.

I'm a follower of Christ—that's the big picture, the big C of Christianity. In a more personal way, I am a follower of Paul, the little tent-maker, the convert like me, the man of great heart and message, so great that he brings me into *his* heart, which is Christ.

And—even more personal, more immediate—I'm a follower of Abbot Antony, who shuffles along to the New Jerusalem on surgically mended hips and knee and a heart complete with replacement valves. Before he gets to his New Jerusalem, he introduces me to St. Benedict as a teacher and Blessed Joanna Mary as a fellow Benedictine traveler, who even has the same last name as mine— perhaps a relative! All of these become my guides, too, in the daily journey. They are my teachers.

It's different in other cultures. They understand. An old Peace Corps volunteer was retiring as a higher education lobbyist, and one of my breakfast meetings was paying tribute to his service.

"Let me tell you what matters," Jim said as he clutched yet another glass-etched tribute award. His eyes got shiny. "Let me tell you why it matters what we do." He was teaching English in a remote village in Thailand, and once a year, he brought his best students to the capital to compete in the foreign language competition, "where, remember, English is just *one* of the foreign languages."

It was nearly always the first time, and sometimes it was the last time, that these kids would leave their native villages. That competition represented the world to those kids, and the place that not only they, but their entire forgotten village had in the larger world. They worked hard to be chosen.

His best student one year was an exceedingly shy, humble girl, overwhelmed by the bigness and importance of the capital, by the number of important people rushing about, by the bright lights and indoor plumbing. She was speechless from the moment she arrived, and her Peace Corps teacher worried about the girl's presence of mind as she sat, eyes cast down, before the judges as they tested her command of English.

"You have a teacher you admire and respect, who tells you the truth," said one judge at the end of the questioning, gesturing towards the Peace Corps worker. "The next day, another teacher, whom you also admire and respect, tells you the opposite and says that *it* is the truth. Who would you then believe?"

Without even lifting her eyes, the shy country girl in the big city replied, "Well, I should try my best to believe them both."

## St. Benedict, Feast

"God does not simply wait for us," writes the abbot in his latest monthly letter to his oblate-flock before summer break. "He is preparing a place for us and besides, has left superabundant aid to prepare ourselves as well. Our Benedictine vocation should constantly alert us to the using of these aids. Let us develop that spirit of wonder and amazement at God's concern for us. He desires no profit from our good behavior, yet He is immensely pleased with our efforts and will reward us as long as we die trying!"

Dang it, if that isn't enough incentive—Abbot Antony copies God as much as anyone can, and he is *thrilled* at every bit of effort his flock makes. At the end of his letter, he invites us to join the monks for lunch on the Feast of St. Benedict on July 11.

Okay. I'm coming. I got the message.

It's been months since I've been up the hill. The oblates who have managed to attend this midweek, midday celebration—some of them driving in from as far as Nevada to join us—look reassuringly familiar, but the language of celebration is jarring to my ears. *The man of God, Benedict, left behind the glory of the world, for the Spirit of God was in him.*

Didn't we just sing the exact same thing in the dregs of Lent when we actually celebrated Benedict's arrival into Heaven? This day commemorates his birth—but why must we gather again, this oratory of oblates who have dropped their work in the fields and offices of their daily world to join in this hymn of honor? I can't think that Benedict would be pleased at rating "twofer" feasts. It's not humble.

I'm not exactly pleased myself. My months-long absence from the oblates has created a distance that rubs me wrong even as I return to the little body. It doesn't *have* to be about community, and certainly not *this* one. There are ukulele pick-up groups you can learn from. Why do I have to be here anyway?

"You'd love the Camaldose Benedictine oblates," Ed told me over the Christmas retreat. Ed was visiting the abbey to meet with his spiritual advisor who is a monk here. "It's a lot quieter than here. You eat, pray, and reflect alone in your own private hermitage and come together to pray the Office."

I looked them up on the web when I got home. They have a monastery just six hours away along the most gorgeous part of the Californian coastline. The monks practice *deep: deep* silence, *deep* solitude, *deep* interior prayer of quiet, work, and shared life.

I agreed with Ed. This was my kind of life—although, of course, it really *isn't*, in either temperament or lifestyle. The Camaldolese oblates face the challenge of setting up their own structure of life in silence and solitude.[17] When I told Felix about them, he looked at me like I'd just hatched the most *outlandish* harebrained egg and said, "How does being a hermit fit with a married lobbyist? What am I missing?"

Oh, phooey. Can't anybody have any fun around here? Apparently not. I want to do something else. I want to *be* somebody else. "You want the selfishness of being alone," said Abbot Antony, a bit sharply. Rebuffed, I got sulky, and stayed away from my monastery even more.

But the abbot's disapproval stung. He was a gift, plain and simple, who appeared, like an angel, when I needed him.

And I had no place else to go by the time he appeared in my life. There was no room at the inn, no place to hide, and he was not only my saving angel, but the end of the road. My old abbot angel appeared, so close to the doors of heaven, so transparently holy that you could practically see right through him to heaven itself.

Okay. Maybe I'll do something more solitary or exotic after he dies. And, heck, as one of the old desert ammas said, "It's better to live in a crowd and desire a solitary life than to live a solitary life, but all the time be longing for company."[18]

Maybe she's right. Like most kids who had brothers or sisters, I would have preferred to be an only child if only I'd gotten a vote. In the psalms, God says, "You are my son."[19] Who wouldn't want to be God's child? The bad part of course is trying to live up to such a parent's expectations and never getting to be an only child. But on the other hand, as Abbot Antony reminds me, only children, like half-time hermits, don't get to learn the lessons of playing with others. God wouldn't want us to be selfish in our spiritual toy box: share and share alike.

What a radical moment *that* would be at Eucharist—this broken Body, this saving Bread, given up for you—*all* of you. There was only one body dying on a cross, but in the breaking of the bread, there are many bodies given up, enough for all, like loaves and fishes, multiplied endlessly.

In front of the stark altar, the monks have placed a two-foot high statue with trumpet sections of white lilies. I'd never pick Benedict out of a police line-up. Like most of the male saints, he's white-skinned, bearded, and vaguely Eastern, only recognizable by his accessories. Benedict holds open his Rule, and somehow you just *know* it's not the Ten Commandments. In front of the statue is a relic in its white containment, lit by a blue-stained glass votive candle. Like the candle denoting the Presence of the Blessed Sacrament, this candle says, "Listen!" as authoritatively as the Rule's opening command.

This Benedict, this holy man—we oblates are pledged to follow his Rule to the best our stations in life permit. When I complain that this is too vague, the monks will murmur, "moderation," until I want to throw my shoes at them and yell, "when do we get to the good stuff, huh?"

Alas, after a year of try-before-you-buy (officially called the novitiate year) and some final vows before the abbot, after the annual renewals of those vows—after all that, I'm not sure there *is* any good stuff.

There is only each other. Today the monks stand together, as they live and work together, and pray for Benedict—"You made St. Benedict an outstanding guide to teach how to live in Your service."[20]

We oblates, though, don't live and work together. Some of us have come great distances today to gather together near a relic, in the spirit of our guide and teacher. We're like bits of the flame, flickering off the main source of light, shimmering off the old block of the Holy Spirit—coming together, praying with each other, and rekindling ourselves into one flame.

Abba Lot, one of the desert fathers, asked Abba Joseph, "Abba, as far as I can, I say my little office. I fast a little, I pray and meditate. I live in peace and, as far as I can, I purify my thought. What else can I do?" The old man stood up and stretched his hands towards heaven. His fingers became like ten lamps of fire, and he said to Abba Lot, "If you will, you can become all flame."[21]

So *this* is what all-flame looks like, I think in the lunchtime roar of the Retreat Center cafeteria—probably not at *all* like the Camoldese, who pick up their food at a central dispensary and then return to the solitude of those solo hermitages. They obviously have reserve and dignity and solemnity in their prayer life. We are like a noisy bunch of piddling puppies, all *over* the old abbot, the food, and the abbey today. We celebrated the holy man, Benedict, on his happy passing to God in March, but today we celebrate his entry to the world and the community that would become the hallmark of his spirituality. His passing is a reminder of Easter, but here, today, it feels like Christmas, the miracle of entering into humanity. They both matter. I need them both.

I force myself between two noisy oblates, one a classmate of my novitiate year. I'm not an only child of God *at all*: "Pass the salt and pepper, Gregory?"

I need them all to complete Trinity's circle.

# —9—
# The Dream

## Transfiguration

There are the dreams you dream when you're deeply asleep—the ones painted with the richest of colors, swirling with absurd connotations, well-meant, and usually misunderstood. "What could it have *meant?*" we ask each other. A few of my more psychologically playful friends consult dream dictionaries, looking up a dream, symbol by symbol, to come up with a meaning. Usually it comes out like a literal word-for-word translation from a foreign dictionary. *I, me, we go, car, sex, forever*—missing in its literalness the essence of what they were attempting to capture.

Felix has these deep dreams. When he recounts them, you hear the poetry of a wonderful unconscious mind—maybe the language of a soul.

"The bishop drove up to my house," he'll say at breakfast. "He was wearing robes of red and gold, and his high hat nearly reached the sky."

"I found broken rosary beads under the porch and they were so beautiful, even broken, that I felt like I had to fix them," he announces another morning.

Again, another dream: "I was floating along on a junk in the South China Sea when the Devil found me and tried to strangle me. He was completely dressed in white, but I knew he was the Devil."

All these poems of deep-sleep language, coming from a nonbeliever, give me pause. I am in awe of their vivid textures and characters, even as he's saying, "So what does it mean?"

169

I try. I never owned a dream dictionary, never took a psychology class, never kept a dream diary. But there's something about a dream, even in its jumbled timeframe and nonsense settings, that seems like communication in a language deeper than mine. If you listen as deeply and openly as possible, sometimes you hear what the dream is trying to say.

"Okay, 'dressed all in white' would be a Western notion of goodness and salvation, like a white knight coming to the rescue. But in your case, Western notions of goodness and salvation are turning against you."

"Yeah. I like that." When I'm listening well, Felix can hear the dream, too, with my ears and heart. Of course, there are other times when my little mental flag doesn't go up saying, "Listen! now!," or when he's so busy talking about a dream that he's burning my English muffin, or when I'm mentally rehearsing for a presentation I'm making at nine o'clock and my listening antenna isn't fully extended. "Well, maybe the car represents teenage mobility, and you'd like to have those years over again," I say, sounding like those dream dictionary translators: *I, me, we go, car, sex, forever*.

And Felix, who is listening harder than me, scowls, pokes the petrified English muffin out of the toaster, and says, "I don't like that meaning. Try again." If he were a biblical character, like Jacob dreaming of wrestling angels, or the Pharaoh getting dream analysis from Joseph, he'd be a very tough customer indeed.

And then there are the twilight dreams, when you're not sure if you're awake or asleep because the veil between conscious and unconscious—mind and soul perhaps—is thinner. It's an afternoon nap, or early morning before the alarm goes off, and you're in a gray twilight world that looks a lot like this one, and things are happening. Or are they?

My father was a great afternoon napper, and once as he was sleeping upright in his favorite chair, my grandfather walked into the room and began talking to him. My father struggled with his annoyance because he *liked* my grandfather and wanted to hear what he had to say, but was really enjoying his nap. He decided to forgo the nap because, after all, my grandfather had been dead for a while now, and the opportunities for visits were growing further and further apart.

*That* thought woke him up. He could almost still see where my grandfather had been sitting, and my grandfather's distinctively raspy speaking voice was still an echo in the room. Daddy almost cried because his waking up had disbursed the twilight world. He stayed in his chair a long time until he was sure he was really awake.

I live on a golf course, and my bedroom faces east. It really doesn't matter if I announce ahead of time that I'm sleeping in tomorrow and firing the alarm clock. I'll also have to convince the grounds crew and capture the rising sun. Sadly neither man nor nature will stop their course just because the sleepy princess wants an extra hour on a weekend morning. So I spend some time in the twilight of pre-dawn, backstage rehearsal for another perfect day in San Diego paradise.

Twilight dreams: I lose my wallet, and I'm frantic to find it. It has my money, of course, but knowing me, very little of that. It has my credit card—do I know how to stop charges on it?—and most important, it has my driver's license. How will I ever replace it? My whole identity is in that wallet, dammit, and I need to find it!

Somehow, because it's twilight and not deep sleep, I can take hold of my panic and say, "It will be fine when you're awake." I drift away from that dream and into another. Now I've just lost or misplaced the three new outfits I've been so anxious to claim. Father! Son! Holy Spirit!

"So, what do you think it means?" Felix says solemnly at breakfast in his best Dr. Freud voice, obviously entertaining himself at my dream-world expense.

"My identity is such a fragile, escapable thing," I say mournfully.

"I don't like that one," he says promptly. "Try again."

"Hey, buster. This is *my* dream, and *my* meaning," I snarl back—and stomp off to pray the Office of Readings for the Feast of the Transfiguration.

Now *this* is a story that needs some meaning enhancers. According to one version, it's eight days after Jesus breaks the news to his disciples: he's going to Jerusalem, where he'll suffer at the hands of the religious authorities, die, and return from the dead. This isn't exactly what the disciples signed up for. But when Peter jumps in to protest, Jesus hears Satan in those words, and tells Peter to "bug off" (my translation).

Now, eight days later, according to another version, Jesus takes Peter and two others on a mountain day-trip. As Jesus prays and the rest of his trekkers fall into a deep sleep, Jesus is suddenly transfigured. His face becomes dazzling as the sun and his clothes as radiant as light, and, if that's not enough, Moses and Elijah—representing the law and the prophets—appear for a chat. The disciples awaken, perhaps, or enter the twilight realm where they witness what's happening.

It's enough to send you scurrying to the footnotes, or skimming to find something that makes sense. Even poor Peter could have used a footnote or two—and he's one of the eyewitnesses. "It is good that we are here," he cries—a good, supportive response. But then, he gets a little odd, too. "Let us make three tents, one for you, one for Moses, and one for Elijah"[1] It's one of those moments, between sleeping and waking, and Luke's Gospel adds the obvious parenthetical remark: *he did not really know what he was saying*. Poor Peter didn't have a clue what to think.

And neither do we. Maybe it's because, just as Jesus' warning of trouble in Jerusalem turned political expectations upside down, his Transfiguration upends our spiritual expectations We expect spiritual realities to manifest in non-physical ways, but transfiguration, by definition, changes things from the outside. That sounds more like expectations for losing twenty pounds on the latest diet, not the latest from the spiritual world. Says one writer, "What is revealed [in the Transfiguration] here is not only the glory of pure, angelic spirit, but of the spirit through the body, glory of the spiritualized body of man."[2]

How interesting, I think, as I pray the Office for the Feast of the Transfiguration, to replay those twilight dreams of mine, about loss of identity and loss of appearance. And how interesting that Jesus is transfigured, not to the whole gathering of disciples, or to the thousands he fed on a few loaves of bread and a couple of fish just a short time ago. He is revealed for what he truly is among just a few of his closest disciples. And while they may not have understood, the three friends probably shared Peter's heartfelt remark: "It is good that we are here."

This Gospel story reminds me of going on a retreat, leaving behind the familiar landscape of home and family, jobs and troubles, to go away to a hilltop or a desert, and remove the stoppers between you and God, between who you appear to be and who you really are.

I've gone on many retreats—thematic ones, silent ones, self-directed ones, other-directed ones. I've spent money to have properly trained retreat leaders teach me to embrace midlife, and I've spent entire retreats knee-deep in glue, crayons, and paper. I've been directed and I've been left alone. I've been undeniably in the presence of God—and absolutely, miserably alone in a retreat house full of guests.

One of the principal attractions for me of lay monasticism was its offer to retreat together. That was listed on a brochure for the Secular Franciscans that I picked during a retreat at a mission. The Secular Franciscans "meet together, pray together, and go on retreats together," said the brochure. I thought that sounded like heaven—to be with other people like me (whatever that meant on any particular day). My world is a heavily populated one; the overwhelmingly full churches I attend are faceless, anonymous places. "For where two or three are gathered together in my name, there am I in the midst of them," Jesus promised.[3] But I'd never recognize him among the sea of faces, and I have to get there an hour early just to find a seat. Outside of church, my world is filled to overflowing with work and activities. It is also noisy, restless, and busy.

But my prayer life is nearly always solitary. As a kid in a church-going family, even our church activities separated our family into choir, altar guild, and money counter. As an adult, I went to the megachurches alone. The idea of a pray-together retreat-together community really grabbed me.

As a Benedictine oblate, I've settled into a three-retreat-a-year routine. The holy days of Passion are a spiritual journey we tumble through at the abbey, anybody who signs up a year in advance. At the end of the calendar year, I spend a few days totally alone in my room at the abbey with my prayer journals and art projects. But in the summer, an oratory of oblates come together to pray, listen, eat, walk, and generally encourage one another in our way of life together. It feels like Transfiguration as we retreat up the hill to find ourselves in God and, instead, we find that God is in ourselves, where God has been, all along, abiding the haste and noise of our ordinary life, waiting for a bit of silence and the witness of others like us to return us to the extraordinary of our divine lives.

My mother has always said that as we age, we become ourselves "only more so." If she's right, I'll move even more deeply into those labels like Catholic, artist, or Benedictine that I strive so hard to collect and become.

When we retreat as oblates together, we become ourselves through the witness and prayers of one another. That's what the Transfiguration is, say the Monks of New Skete—"not some pious story about going up a mountain and having light shine on everything," but about "gaining an insight into who Jesus really is."[4]

It might have been about who Jesus really was, but you have to wonder if we'd have ever caught a glimpse if the apostles hadn't managed to wake up in time. Maybe they'd have heard the end of the conversation Jesus had with Moses and Elijah, the way my grandfather's twilight words faded off so gently as my dad awoke. They were just ordinary men, after all, fishermen yanked from their nets into a call they couldn't comprehend during Jesus' life, men who seemed asleep when all the important stuff was going on—these men were who the Transfiguration was for. Jesus already knew. Jesus couldn't witness his own Transfiguration. That was for ordinary witnesses to know and understand when they could.

There's a story of a young man who traveled all over the world, and, arriving at a particular monastery, asked to speak to the abbot. After the two men spoke awhile, the abbot said, "So what have you learned in your travels?"

As if he'd been waiting to be asked for a long time, the young man burst out, "Abbot, I've learned that the whole world is asleep!"

At this, the abbot laughed and said, "You may stay as long as you like."[5]

There's a lot to be learned up the hill with a few fellow trekkers, if we can only stay awake.

## Step 9: Practicing Silence

"What do I know about silence?" I asked Felix as I studied this step. Before he could answer, I continued, "Nobody can believe I've ever been on silent retreats for five days at a time. Everybody thinks I'm such a chatterbox that I'll *explode* if I shut up for fifteen minutes. I know that isn't true, but nobody else does. And how many words do I get to describe silence anyway?"

There was a moment of careful silence while I took a breath and my slower-speaking spouse determined whether or not I was actually done. Then, speaking with more care and deliberation than usual, he said, "Well, you know a lot about silence. You practice it when you're praying and when you're writing in those little notebooks, and *of course*, when you're taking those long walks of yours on Pluto."

Benedict devotes an entire short chapter of the Rule to silence as "restraint of speech." As a restraint or discipline, it's probably a very good part of the Rule. But it's not necessarily a stepping stone to humility. There have been times when I've filled the quiet with scornful, solitary judgment. Such restraint of speech follows the letter of the Rule on silence, but it has no community, and probably no God in it either.

Within the steps of humility, practicing silence involves others. It involves listening. I began to learn about humble silence at AA meetings. Behind closed doors, with only alcoholics present, we would go around the room and share our experiences. It seemed there was *always* a "share hog" going over the same old problems again and again. I'd zone out, unable to *bear* the sound of Henry droning on. Since these weren't professionally moderated therapy groups, I'd wait for the chair to shut him off, or the old-timers, or the newcomers, or *anybody*. But poor Henry would run the clock out until nobody had time to say anything more than, "I'm sober. It's great."

I was. It wasn't. I wanted my turn. I wanted my issues. I *really* wanted Henry to find another group. Eventually he left AA altogether because we weren't responsive enough for him. He clearly needed to be heard, but it was less clear why I needed to listen. I wanted a wall of words of my own, to block out anyone who annoyed me. Unfortunately in those days, that was everyone. I could restrict speech, but I couldn't practice silence.

One of the old ones of the desert said,

> Every man who delights in a multitude of words, even though he says admirable things, is empty within. If you love truth, be a lover of silence. Silence like the sunlight will illuminate you in God and will deliver you from the phantoms of ignorance.[6]

This lovely "silence like the sunlight" bears no resemblance to the glowering, glaring silence of my self-absorbed anger. Poor Henry needed listeners practicing silence. He got restraint from speech instead, and left when he knew he was not being heard.

What makes talkers of us in the first place, suggests the author of *The Imitation of Christ*, is the escape our words provide: "We want an escape from the tedious whirligig of our thoughts," à Kempis writes.[7] Anyone who hasn't had the dubious pleasure of sitting in a university's academic senate meeting need only turn on C-SPAN when Congress is in session, or catch a school board meeting on a public access channel, to figure out that there's way more yakking than thinking, lots more talkers than listeners, and hardly any humble silence. What we really need instead, the old text continues, is "more watchfulness, more prayer."

Watchfulness, mindfulness, and attention beyond our own self's borders are the things that get us to this practice of silence. At AA it was all about me—my sharing, my suffering, my discoveries—and Henry was usually in *my* way. But it was at an AA meeting where I caught the tail of the bigger silence, the one, ironically, that leads to humility.

AA recovery, like Benedictine spirituality, was founded as a communal movement. AA wasn't born when Bill W. stopped drinking, but when he realized he was about to start drinking again. In desperation, he called a non-alcoholic friend and asked if she knew another drunk he could talk to. Henrietta introduced Bill W. to her favorite hopeless case, Dr. Bob. AA dates its founding from the day the two men met in the friend's home: one dying to drink and the other dying from it. On June 10, 1935, one man listened in the silence of the truly humbled and humiliated, as the other man spoke from his knowledge of that place. Fifty years later, a celebration was held in Montreal to commemorate that event. As close to the first actual moment of Dr. Bob and Bill W.'s meeting as could be found, each AA group all over the world was asked to hold a minute of silence in tribute on the East Coast at 9:00 P.M. on Monday, June 10, 1985.

Exactly at 9:00 P.M., thirty minutes west of Boston, in a tiny town with nearly as many sheep as voting adults, Norm banged his coffee cup on the table and announced: "Fifty years ago, Bill W. was introduced to Dr. Bob, and AA began. Let's join the meeting in Montreal and alcoholics all over the world in a moment of silence." He set an egg timer on the table, and it began to tick off 60 seconds.

It was the longest, loveliest 60 seconds of my life. In my mind's eye I could see, like the live TV satellite feeds that flash over the world on New Year's Eve, all the groups sitting in smoky church basements and schools and hospital cafeterias. I could imagine everybody silently waiting, thinking about how they came to be there, knowing the ugly broken lives before and the battles still ahead. But for now, for one minute, we were all together.

As the egg timer ticked, I could see the face of Henry, who long ago left us in a huff; I could see John, so ashamed that he couldn't read the AA steps with us that he went out, got arrested for drunk driving and hanged himself in his jail cell. I could picture the ones who couldn't stay, or wouldn't, or got a better offer, or came in a few more times. I imagined the ones holding hands and probably crying in Montreal, the ones stumbling in from the street, drunk. I thought of the old ones sober nearly as long as AA, who couldn't remember what it was like before, but knew the gratitude of what it was like now, and tasted it every day, with every tick of an egg timer on a beat-up old table in a dusty church rec room on a buggy June night in a one-stop-sign town outside of Boston.

In the silence, we were all crowded into that living room in Dayton, Ohio fifty years ago, listening as Dr. Bob was listening, incredulous with hope over the stumbling words that a barely sober man spoke, desperate to stay sober, desperate for that silence.

And just that once, a bunch of has-been drunks practiced silence. I had to take off my glasses to wipe my eyes when the timer went off. For the first time in my secular, sober life, I was part of something bigger than myself, and I could feel it with every wide-open pore of my sniffy-faced being.

"Would anybody like to share before we close the meeting?" asked Norm.

Silence.

"Then we'll say the Lord's Prayer and leave it at that," he said. But it was the first time we standoffish, mind-your-space New Englanders spontaneously reached out, held hands, and began anew: "Our Father, who art in heaven. . . ."

The poet Ezra Pound grew increasingly silent in his last years. Toward the end of his life, he admitted to his French publisher, "I did not enter into silence, silence captured me."[8] Like the one at that special AA meeting, this was a silence that captured me and gave me a grateful surrender into those who had gone before and the lessons for me of those who had fallen away.

There are many, many times when I cannot approach God. In the practice of silence—even if it's only in prayer, writing in a notebook, or walking around Pluto's perimeter, as Felix calls it—God has the opportunity to enter me. This is a silence filled with mindful watch-fulness that sets a banquet of humility.

At my church, Deacon Henry, from Singapore, told us in one of his homilies the story of the silken drum. A mighty warlord, realizing he was nearing the end of his days, urged his only daughter to marry and carry on the dynasty. "The green of the plum tree has come and gone, and it is the time of the blossoms," he told her. "And yet you do not blossom. Will I die without seeing you married, without knowing my grandchildren?"

"No," his daughter said. "I will fashion a drum of silk, stretched over a bamboo frame. The man who hears the music when my fingers strike the drum, that man I will marry."

"Foolishness!" the aging warlord said in frustration. "A silk drum will not make any sound. I shall die without heirs."

But his daughter had her way, and so the silk drum was fashioned as she wished. Many young men came to listen as she played, but none heard any sound. The months and seasons passed. The plum tree blossoms withered and fell to the ground. And then a handsome young man, finely dressed, came and paid his respects to the aged ruler.

"I have traveled from beyond the mountains that you can see, over the seas before the mountains, to take your daughter's hand in marriage," said the stranger, looking directly at the silent daughter who sat nearby with her silken drum.

"She will only marry the one who can hear the music of her silken drum," sighed the old man. "Don't tell me you heard the sound all the way from your distant kingdom!"

"You are correct," said the suitor. "No sound of the drum reached my ears."

"Then be on your way, like all the others before you," the old man said. "Why do you linger here?"

"Because, my lord," the stranger said, "I hear its silence."

And the young woman smiled and put away her silken drum.

## Transfiguration

Transfiguration is a quiet feast, barely a blip in the long liturgical stretch of Ordinary Time that is really the beginning of our life in Trinity. Transfiguration, unlike, say, Ascension or Pentecost, isn't pushed to the nearest Sunday and celebrated communally. And unlike other feast days—the Assumption of Mary, the Immaculate Conception—it's not a holy day of obligation. The Transfiguration— that brief glimpse of godly glory a few apostles nearly accidentally witnessed in their twilight sleep—is an ordinary day feast. If you attend daily Mass on August 6, you get those strange and wonderful readings. If you pray the daily office, you're brought along up Mt. Tabor with Peter, James, and John, to witness anew: "It is good that we are here." Otherwise you are one of the many who still sleeps. Transfiguration is a summer sleeper.

"The Transfiguration is the summer lightning of the coming resurrection," writes Romano Guardini.[9] We get this visual of the Resurrection first during Lent, when it makes for good storytelling, setting up the luminosity of victory alongside the drums of doom, as Jesus presses forward toward Jerusalem, teaching his followers.

But now we're hearing the story again, in the wastelands of Ordinary Time, far beyond the Resurrection and the pain that preceded it. We need to remember it again, just as we are ready to forget.

Summer lightning comes unexpectedly when the atmospheric conditions demand relief. Growing up on the East Coast, I'd be playing on the beach one minute with the world at my feet and sand up my suit, and there would be a low rumble or two, and the elders would grow wary. A few more rumbles would sound a little closer, the sky would darken, and we'd hear: "Would you please pack up your pail and rubber rafts and I said we're leaving early!"

Oh, *why?*

Flush in the middle of life at its grandest—the sudden *crack*, and lightning forked into the ocean, and we would make the mad scramble back into the safety of the car. I forgot about lightning. You always did. Sun, moon, rain, snow, fog, you knew them; they were calendar constants. Lightning was the surprise package in August, the *crack* that caught you napping.

Southern California lives in the playtime of August without the wake-up call of lightning. It thunders over the mountains and sometimes you can hear it, but you never get the pull-up-short and run-for-cover experience. I've lived here nearly fifteen years, and experienced summer lightning just once—my first summer in San Diego.

I'd just returned from a visit back East, where our house was still up for sale. Felix stayed east for business, and I came back alone. It was a quiet, sniffy return trip. My temporary job was miserable in every aspect, and to make matters worse, Felix and I were living in a converted motel room while we waited for our house to be sold. All the familiar comforts of home were in storage, and all that was familiar and wonderful was behind me in New England.

At two o'clock in the morning, I was jolted awake by thunderclaps that sounded like they were right outside my window. I looked out—our cabana was just two blocks from the ocean, and lightning forked madly in all directions before belly flopping into the ocean and splattering into thin sheets of white coating on the water.

The storm raged all night, was still at it when I got up at six. It looked outside like I felt inside. "Go get 'em," I thought. There was no need to turn on the lights inside because the lightning was still that constant and bright. According to my radio, much of San Diego was minus electricity—a funny idea when you saw how much of the stuff was running around loose outside my window. I showered, nervously—is this something I want to be doing in an electrical storm?—and went into the kitchen to make breakfast. The radio man was imploring people to stop rushing to the beaches to watch the lightning hit the water. "Dummies," I thought, willing to root for lightning over a San Diegan at that moment. Go get 'em.

I popped an egg in the electric frying pan just as the power blew. The traffic lights outside went dark while inside the cabanas there was a moment of stunned silence.

Bank of America's alarm began screaming. Dottie, the little girl in the next cabana, followed suit. Two cars in the parking lot began their unearthly hoots and whistles of outrage.

Everybody at work was bleary-eyed from staying up to watch the storm—a once-every-fifteen-years phenomenon, according to the *Los Angeles Times*. Welcome back, Carol. What exactly did you need a reminder of? In the average thunderstorm, lightning hits Earth about 100 times. This storm managed over 1,800.

". . . the summer lightning of the coming resurrection . . ."

What is it we need to remember that plops the Transfiguration, like a quiet, unnoticed rumble of thunder into the breathless ordinary of August? One biblical meditation suggests, a "celebration of the memory of the Jesus wrapped in glory."[10] There are all kinds of memories, all kinds of ways of seeing the same memory.

The Feast of the Transfiguration is actually placed in August to correspond to a Jewish feast of another transfiguration, layering memory onto memory like a collage. In Exodus, Moses stayed on the mountain with God, writing down God's commandments. When he came down from Sinai, "he did not know that the skin of his face had become radiant while he conversed with the LORD."[11] How could he? He was facing God, not a mirror. It was the witness of others that drew attention to his transfiguration.

Maybe, on second thought, he was looking into a mirror, as Jesus also may have been—but the mirror image was God in them, their extra-ordinariness looking back, not their ordinary faces of Ordinary Time.

To know God in ourselves transfigures us. Every life, no matter how ordinary, can hold moments of God-in-us awareness—moments of deep distress, of dying, of sublime joy, of momentary silence—when God's presence takes over and takes our breath away. In the stillness of death, the silence of adoration, the sight of the fat, full moon struggling to rise over the mountains, the moment of thrill and the lostness of creation, we know God better than we know ourselves. Suddenly, the moon crests the horizon, the earth holds its breath in wonder, and it all stops.

Then the breath rushes in, and ordinary life goes on.

But we had that moment when God was looking back at us, and we were transfigured, trying on our wardrobe of heaven.

If we don't know what we looked like facing God, then maybe we should ask, "So what does God look like?" For really, transfiguration just pokes a finger between a twilight land of dreams that looks like this one, giving us a glimpse of that other land before the ordinary closes in again like a veil. After all, if eternity is forever, it's also now. As Guardini puts it, "This eternal life does not wait till after death to begin. It already exists . . . whether given by grace, or seized by faith."[12]

In AA, we always said, "God, *as I understand Him*," to emphasize that we had come to terms with our need for God and were meeting God now in a new way. It was a Make-a-God kit (some assembly required). But it was still God, still a chip off the old block, as my father would say, only you chipped off whatever face you could look at—a piece of nature, a historical Jesus, the Virgin Mary. And you took it, looked into its face and proclaimed God. And sometimes God looked back in infinite fondness at your feeble efforts to be better. So pleasing those efforts were!

The Transfiguration rolls around, another arbitrary August 6, unnoticed, except for a few who are chosen to symbolically climb Mt. Tabor with their beloved friend and teacher. "Wait for me!" I practically yell. My legs are little; I started way back from the others. "I want to go, too. I'm with Him."

There is an ancient sermon by Anastasius of Sinai appropriated for today's Office of readings. I take it as my ticket to climb Mt. Tabor:

> Therefore, since each of us possesses God in his heart and is being transformed into his divine image, we also should cry out with joy: It is good for us to be here—here where all things shine with divine radiance, where there is joy and gladness and exultation.[13]

Me too! I want to remember!

It's been a lousy week at work, maybe a lousy couple of weeks—huge workloads, collapsing budgets, and front-page headlines full of bad news about us. There is no God anywhere in any face, and I don't blame God. I'd bail, too, if I had the option. At the very least, I should close my office door to all the jangly nerves and noise, bear down, get some work done.

Instead I tell everybody I'm leaving for an early lunch with friends. Well, sometimes they are. I drive away from all the commotion and head up the hill to the abbey. It's the Feast of the Transfiguration. It's summer's lightning. I'm coming too, dammit.

The regulars shuffle in, but that's it. How perfect. This isn't Pentecost's mob scene, or even Benedict's community. It's the little Feast for Christ and his buddies. But the bells of the abbey clang exuberantly. *They* know a feast when they see one, and their joy knows no bounds.

Father Aloysius of the amazing, mellifluous, resonant voice presides. "It's the bicentennial!" he crows, leaning forward at the pulpit for emphasis.

Now stop it. I was *there* for the bicentennial. It was 1976, and I went to the Bristol, Rhode Island, Fourth of July parade decked out in full, sweltering colonial costume. But Father Aloysius explains. Monks make their vows on various feast days, and three monks here made their vows on the Feast of the Transfiguration. Father Aloysius is celebrating sixty years of vows today, Father Cornelius sixty-eight

years of his vows , and my own beloved Abbot Antony, seventy-two—
two hundred years between them.

Abbot Antony, eyes closed and hands clasped together, seems to
be in the happiest prayer I've ever witnessed. It is a memory, this
feast. Two years ago, Abbot Antony stood there alone with his
cracked old voice and renewed the vows he had made seventy years
earlier, and his face shone so brightly and he appeared so beautiful, I
could scarcely look at him. And while he stood there facing God,
with God's face reflected back at him, Nancy, my oblate friend, and I
cried because we were witnessing what heaven looks like for one brief
instant, and that's all you need to see to want it forever.

The feast is a memory, of Jesus' glory, of God's face, of promises
fulfilled beyond the wildest imaginations. As Abbot Antony stands
there with his eyes closed and hands clasped together, it could be the
light reflecting off the Pacific Ocean below, or it could be the light
from heaven above, but his face is becoming beautiful again. For no
reason at all, I glance away and see Nancy out of the corner of my
eye. She's crying a little, and so am I.

*Lord, how good it is for us to be here.*

# $-10-$
# The Call

## St. Matthew, Apostle, Feast

They think highly enough of you at work to send you to your professional society's annual meeting, like a 4H Club's show goat. Or they think well of your potential to let you go off to network and learn from others in your field. Or maybe you invited yourself—stuck the meeting into your annual budget, fit it into your goals and objectives, so you could get away for a few days to spend some time with people like you. Just once a year, you plead, it's good to spend time with others of your kind, to learn a few new tricks and maybe to commiserate.

And so you go, however you finagled the trip this year, to the annual meeting of People Who Do What You Do For A Living. There will be workshops that freshen or add to your skills, new people to meet, old ones to catch up with. You promise to return refreshed and rejuvenated though this is hardly a glamour trip: San Diego to Washington, D.C.—in February, no less.

You arrive after a long, cross-country flight through difficult winter stopovers like Denver or Chicago. It's Friday night and the capital empties for the weekend. You're a little time lagged and a lot cold and cranky. You're a member of the governing board of your association—quite an honor, you know—and that means a full day of board meetings and an evening get-together before the association meeting begins on Sunday and goes through the day. And then the society's annual meeting starts immediately after that.

It is good scheduling, actually, packing so much in to your five-day stay. There's only one problem you can see as you review the schedule in the hotel lobby one last time: there is no opportunity to get to church.

You're sure to be the only one who worries about this sort of thing. *Real* professionals are right now unpacking and getting prepared to join other People Like Themselves. You, and you alone, are not being professional. You're trying to adhere to a few simple rules you added to Benedict's Rule when you became a Benedictine. You get to church at least once a week, no matter where you are or how awkward it is.

It's pretty awkward now, you see, looking at that blasted schedule again. Board meeting Saturday, 8:00 A.M.–4:00 P.M. Association meetings Sunday beginning at 8:00 and concluding an hour before the annual national society meeting starts Sunday evening, running straight through Wednesday.

And this is your first year on the board, a great honor that you would like to acquit with some style and ability. Your employer paid for your attendance, endured your time away with the understanding that they benefit somehow.

And dammit, you're the only professional in the universe who seems to think church-going matters, although you're starting to wonder—again—*why* it matters, and why can't you be like everybody else just *once?*

But it is no use. A rule is a rule, and nobody made you sign on, but you did, so you walk up to the concierge and mutter, "Do you have a list of churches nearby?"

Of course, she chirps loud enough for the entire lobby to hear: "No list. What kind of church do you need?" She might have well have substituted *psychiatrist* for church the way a few people—undoubtedly newcomers to the profession who will be meeting you at Saturday's dinner, looking to you for guidance—look over at you now with glances of pity. "Obviously some hick from a small town. Needs that church-crutch, the poor thing."

"Catholic," you mutter, feeling anything but Christian in your murderous embarrassment over being made conspicuous and needy and churchy.

"Oh, goodness. You don't know the *cathedral* is just four blocks away? St. Matthews Cathedral!"

You look suitably ignorant in your frozen-faced conspicuousness. She draws you a map. She declares they serve Mass at least three times a day, like breakfast, lunch, and dinner, and adds, "Why, if you leave now, you'll make the 5:30 P.M. service just fine."

You've been Catholic less than ten years. You know about daily Mass in the morning, but you never heard of one at 5:30 P.M. on a Friday. As you hurry off, hand-drawn map in hand, she says to the bell captain, "It's only the Catholics who ask about churches. I wonder why that is." You escape before the bell captain tells everybody why.

You find the Cathedral of St. Matthew the Apostle easily. It's a short walk, brisk and hurried in the raw February chill. The Cathedral is large and imposing on the outside, dim and candle-lit inside—the way churches looked before you moved to sun-drenched San Diego, where "light and airy" are the first words of every real estate agent's creed.

As you take a seat near the front, you see a marker in the aisle in front of the altar. You stretch your neck to read in the gloom on an early winter:

Here rested the remains of
President Kennedy
At the requiem mass November 25, 1963
Before their removal to Arlington
Where they lie in expectation
Of a heavenly resurrection.

Oh my. The little flyer you grabbed on your way in says this cathedral honors the patron saint of civil servants. Though you're not a civil servant but a lobbyist—you've never been able to uncover a patron saint for lobbyists—you work for a state university, and you interact with civil servants every day. They are your people.

You look around in the gloom just as a priest, altar attendant, and lector come quietly out to the altar without fanfare. "In the name of the Father, Son, and Holy Spirit," begins the priest, and you all make the sign of the cross hurriedly, from wherever in your mind and thoughts and lives these words find you.

The words of the Mass find *all* of you—and it's not just you, needy, churchy little you after all. In the gloom of a Friday evening, when you'd think the civil servants who fill this city would be racing out to the suburbs to start the weekend, when this is already the third Mass of the day for the Cathedral, when it's 40 degrees and sleeting outside and only a little warmer inside this drafty old cathedral, there are thirty to forty of you, people just like you, huddled together in the front rows, around the place a fallen president rested before awaiting the expectation of heavenly Resurrection.

And you all cross yourselves and take your hope and strength in the presence of each other, this night, in the broken bread shared at the table of the Lord, in the knowledge that you are never a solo act in the work of the Lord, under the eyes and patronage of St. Matthew, Apostle.

The Cathedral of St. Matthew the Apostle introduced me to St. Matthew himself, whose feast day is celebrated in the quiet of Ordinary Time, in late September. The kids are back to school and political campaigns are picking up momentum as November election ballots fill with candidates and issues demanding our interest, our money, our votes. Civil servants—well-named because as servants they serve no matter how they feel about the candidates or issues—wonder how it will all change what they do. Lobbyists like me—we get busy educating people on these issues and their effects.

And in the middle of everything, nearly unnoticed, comes September 21, St. Matthew's feast day. So little is actually known about the saint we call Matthew. Even the name we know him by is an Aramaic version of an old Jewish tribe he was named for in Jesus' time: Levi, Son of Alphaeus, "Gift of God," now "Matthew." We don't know anything about his life or death beyond his call to follow Jesus. Old traditions claim he died a martyr, but even those details are disputed—some stories claim he was stabbed, others that he was beheaded or burned, still others suggest he was eaten by cannibals. His bones are reported to be in Salerno, or maybe in Rome. We're not even sure if he actually wrote the Gospel attributed to his name.

What is not disputed is his profession: tax-collector. Nobody loves tax collectors today, when everything is calculated by formula, collected on schedule, and maintained by civil servants. In the first century, though, Roman tax collectors were despised. Signing on for the job would have made Matthew, a Jew, a traitor to his own people—

people who he would have bullied, harassed, and extorted for his own personal and professional interests. Even if he'd been an ethical tax collector, his fellow Jews would have hated him for doing business with non-Jews and handling their money.

When you go to a chamber of commerce event and pass out your business cards, people find out you're a lobbyist and treat you like a leper. It would have been the same for Matthew.

Lobbying isn't illegal, and neither is tax collecting. Nor was it two thousand years ago when Jesus "went walking and saw a man—Levi the son of Alphaeus at his tax collector's post—and said to him, *"Follow me."*[1] And the man got up and left his life, both lucrative and despised, and followed Jesus and became the patron saint of account-ants, bankers, bookkeepers, custom officers, financial officers, guards, money managers, security forces, security guards, stockbro-kers, and tax collectors. In short, he is still very busy with career groups that we still have mixed emotions about.

Whether or not he actually penned the Gospel that bears his name, it has the temperament of the numbers man: five loaves, two fishes, and five talents, an indirect tax and a poll tax, drachmas—the meat on the bones of the good news. But the numbers man, proba-bly well-to-do, left it all for two words: *Follow me.* He became one with the story that appears in his Gospel of the lilies and the birds who never did a day's calculation, but were cared for anyway.

There's just something about Matthew that the working, calculat-ing stiff has got to identify with and admire.

Felix and I returned to the East Coast to witness the marriage of his daughter and then to revisit and play along Cape Cod, where we'd celebrated our honeymoon, summer vacations, and just about every three-day weekend we could find before we made the westward trek. We spent much of the vacation driving between the seaside villages of Truro and Chatham, without much to see.

We stopped at a large shop whose name caught our eye: Lilies of the Field. As it turned out, it didn't stock lilies, but it did catch Felix's attention. "That's a Bible thing, isn't it!" he exclaimed. Having never been knowingly near a Bible, he still just knew. "I want it," he said.

Home two weeks later, I looked up Matthew for him and found the passage about the lilies. Matthew isn't the patron of engineers like Felix, but they share some of the same fondness for numbers. Here are the words of the man called Matthew, who left everything to follow Jesus:

Consider the lilies of the field, how they grow; they toil not, neither do they spin: and yet I say unto you, That even Solomon in all his glory was not arrayed like one of these. Wherefore, if God so clothe the grass of the field, which today is, and tomorrow is cast into the oven, shall he not much more clothe you, O ye, of little faith?[2]

Felix took the card that I wrote the verses on and propped it against his computer in a way that constantly called to be straightened out or moved. It seemed to enchant him. It seemed to allow him more reasons to play golf in the middle of the week. Finally I asked him, "What gives with the lilies of the field? Why did you want it?"

"I've been considering the lilies," he said. "I've decided I like roses better."

Matthew would be okay with that, I think. Roses exact their price in time, energy, and talent in return for the higher dividends they pay in beauty. Matthew had respect for prices paid, talents used, and returns on investments.

## Step 10: Soberness

The article in the *San Diego Union-Tribune* talked about emotions, and how some movie scenes almost carry a crying towel guarantee. "It's happened to most of us at least once," the article begins. "There in the dark in front of forty-foot images on a screen, tears well up and we begin to cry. Why?" There are reflex tears from dust and onions, the article explains, and emotional ones from current and remembered feelings, even those projected on a screen. The why of emotional tears is still a mystery, but scientists think it may be instinctual, like smiling or frowning. Tears tell us how people feel.[3]

When I hung around the Franciscans and did my retreats there, Sister Mary Lou always spoke with great approval about the gift of tears. I liked her spin on it, because when it comes to tears, I've got the gift that keeps on giving—it seems like every day is Christmas.

But I've also got the gift of giddiness—seemingly uncontrollable guffaws, giggles, quips, and a larger-than-life inability to take—or be taken—seriously. I'm also pretty gifted in sullen silences and rancorous rages. When it comes to emotions, I've got full sail and no anchor.

That makes for trouble for this step of humility, where Benedict talks in favor of soberness and against ready laughter. "What a drip," I thought when I first read this. "Doesn't he get the joke?" Apparently not, for this step is a single sentence long, a model of brevity and soberness.

When I first stopped drinking, the word *sober* was in my vocabulary, if not in my heart all the time. What a prune-faced word it was, too, not the opposite of drunk, but the opposite of fun. Who wanted it?

I walked around using the phrase "alcohol-free" for months because it sounded liberating. It didn't catch on. Everybody in AA was sitting in smoke-filled rooms, grimly talking about their gratitude for sobriety. It still sounded icky, but I talked the talk so they'd leave me alone.

In my heart, dammit, I was *free!* And then Jack the Barber showed up at my Sunday morning "Sobriety Forever" meeting. He was a well-known institution in the western suburbs of Boston. Once a down-and-out street drunk, he was tougher than nails sober. He ran a barbershop in downtown Hudson, picked up the drunks off the street at night, let them sleep and live—probably illegally—above the barbershop until they stopped shaking long enough to bathe. He'd cut their hair, tell them to get a job—*any* job—and spend whatever time they weren't working in an AA meeting, any meeting. Twice a week, he'd load up his bunch of guys in a van and drag them to an open meeting as a commitment. That was the word we used in AA for groups who visited your group and did the speaking. Being the AA bookie who filled the schedule of commitments was never fun, because speaker groups could be pretty unreliable in their various stages of recovery. But not Jack the Barber and his boys. They showed up clean and barbered where they said they would, and Jack made them all talk, even the ones just a week sober. There was some unwritten rule in AA groups that said you had to be sober ninety days before you could go out and speak at commitments. I never found where the rule was, but everybody knew it. Jack ignored it.

It wasn't the dainty rehab *my* insurance plan covered, and they sure weren't my kind of drunks. Jack's boys sitting up front, some of them still shaking, talking through anxious puffs of cigarettes were poster boys for how bad you *could* get if you didn't shape up and stay shaped. They'd look at Jack, and he'd look at them, the whole time they talked, and they never told funny stories of setting the cat on fire or going to work with their clothes on backwards like the rest of us did when *we* talked.

And when the last one finished, Jack the Barber would take the floor. He never talked about where he'd been, although rumor had it he'd been a rough drunk. Heck, you'd just *seen* his story in the boys he dragged in to the meetings. He filled his van with his story, twice a week, filled the room over the barbershop with it every night. He'd get up there—a fierce little man you could barely see over the podium, and he'd thank us for inviting his boys and listening to them. "It's a simple program," he'd finish. "I tell the boys to keep it simple. And when they get distracted and it ain't so simple anymore, I got a little prayer I say over and over: Let not my thoughts disturb my peace of mind. Let not my thoughts disturb my peace of mind. Let not my thoughts disturb my peace of mind. You, too. God bless."

Wham! End of commitment. And we'd stagger to our feet for the Lord's Prayer, and we'd chant, "Keep coming back! It works!" and you'd see the shakier boys with Jack the Barber, their lips moving, "Let not my thoughts disturb . . ."

Even Benedict couldn't do it better than Jack the Barber. There's a difference between getting the joke and being the joke that Jack's boys understood quickly. Soberness was too important and too fragile to pre-empt with frivolity. One Benedictine writer suggests that the problem with frivolity comes from being an outsider, and therefore poking fun "at the conventions and pretensions of the group on whose margins they lived, to point out when the emperor had no clothes."[4]

It seems silly to think of us laughing and joking away in AA, storytelling as outsiders, while the down-and-outers were the inside job, all respect, decorum, and soberness. But in the upside-down-world of the outcasts from normal life, there's something to this step of humility, this kind of soberness—something maybe Jesus with his ragtag friends of tax collectors and women might understand.

Most of us were pretty genial drunks in our time. Ladies who looked like your Sunday school teacher—and maybe *were* your Sunday school teacher—stood up and said, "My kitchen table was my bar-room." There's no denying the degradation of the fall from middle-class grace. "Higher bottom drunks," we called ourselves. "We didn't hit bottom; the bottom came up and hit us," as it said in the AA Big Book.[5] With that careful distinction in place, we could accept the label of recovering alcoholic, at least while we were in an AA meeting.

The stories we told were told funny. We got the joke, dressed it up, and presented it to others for a laugh. The well-dressed high bottom articulate woman, seven years sober, talking a story that flowed from the pits of Hell to the joys of sobriety at the West Acton group is the one I still best remember. "I loved being in rehab, playing the lead in Sylvia Plath's novel *The Bell Jar*, when I wasn't busy playing cards with the other patients all day," she said. "They called that 'settling for less.'"

And all of us high-bottoms laughed like hyenas, got the joke and the literary allusion, and we fed our illusions of being different than Jack the Barber's boys. We weren't *real* drunks.

Jack the Barber's boys were the inside job. They didn't need fancy words; the words would only disturb their peace of mind. A lot of them came from the places in society where they didn't have much to lose—and they lost it all anyway in the freefall of booze. You heard the voices of brain-damaged drunks, and you saw the faces of the liver-destroyed ones, and true humility would have understood the difference a little money and a little luck gave to separate you from them. Their barroom was a grate on a city street, where, if luck was with them, they wouldn't die from fumes or burns, or get rolled or beaten up or drink lighter fluid by accident.

Their stories were different, too. They never laughed or came out with any good lines. "I just got out of the state facility," a young man with terror fresh in his eyes blurted out at one group. "They said I had a wet brain, and I'd never be any good. There was an old guy there who had what I had. He had wet brain, too, they said. And this morning, just as I was getting ready to leave—well, the old guy fell down the stairs. I ran over, and I held his head in my lap and there was some blood coming out of his mouth, and I'm screaming, "he needs help!" and nobody stops what they're doing, and the old man looked at me once, and then he's dead. Like that. Right there in my lap, and they don't care cuz it's just another old drunk with a wet brain." His eyes were full of terror and tears, and he could barely say what he had to say. "I came straight out of there to Jack's and he said, come to a meeting, and I did, because I don't want to die like that, and it's me who needs help now, not the old man anymore."

And he stumbled off the stage, with Jack and his boys applauding heartily, the rest of us tepidly following suit because maybe we've had our problems, but we still have our manners.

Soberness is about emotional stability. Jack's boys had it in such intensity because its alternate would leave them for dead.

Much as I disliked being sober, and as much as I disliked the soberness connotations in early AA, the lessons it teaches about humility are invaluable. This kind of soberness is less about balancing emotions like a careful tightrope, and more about the peace of mind you find when you've met your match—alcohol, ego, political mechanisms on the job, whatever—and acknowledged your loss. In humility's game under St. Benedict's rules, you just won.

The whole point of these steps, as Benedict eventually says, is *love*. Soberness—mindfulness—is one important way to get there, while giddiness, or mindlessness, is not. "So that we may no longer be infants," says St. Paul, writing to the people of Ephesus, "tossed by waves and swept along by every wind of teaching arising from human trickery, from their cunning in the interests of deceitful scheming. Rather, living the truth in love, we should grow in every way into him who is the head, Christ."[6]

"Let not my thoughts disturb . . ."

This step is about mindfulness. We don't learn soberness alone, as Jack's boys knew. They drank alone and faced the world alone, but once they were rounded up by their hard-assed savior, they learned soberness together. They were no longer the joke—maybe that's why they no longer *got* the joke.

Perhaps it's easier to see this soberness through the lens of its opposite, what St. Bernard of Clairvaux calls *giddiness*. In a lovely act of humility, Bernard took the ladder metaphor and the steps ascending to humility, and went *down* them to show our steps of pride. "The proud always seek what is pleasant and try to avoid what is troublesome," he tells us across the centuries, cutting to the bone as he dissects our difficulties with this aspect of humility. "You are scurrilous, overcheerful in appearance, swaggering in bearing, always ready for a joke; any little thing quickly gets a laugh."[7] Both soberness and its opposite—giddiness—are the ways we respond in community, ways that either set us apart in humility or together in the blind cheerfulness of denial and good will.

We can approach soberness by being mindful of ourselves and others, by paying attention, by listening deeply. "Keep your head where your feet are," as the old ones at AA say. And maybe they should have added: Watch where everybody else's feet are, too.

I was the group secretary of the Sunday morning group, which I *thought* meant you kept the records, signed the court-ordered attendee slips, and remembered anniversaries for the person in charge of the cakes. But it also meant that if the commitment speaker didn't show up, you had to pull together a meeting on the fly yourself—a pick-up meeting, it was called.

One morning, just a week shy of one year sober, I was the secretary and the commitment didn't show up. I'd had a feeling they wouldn't, so I started the pick-up early. Asking people to speak at the last minute does *not* make you popular, and I felt so drained that I wanted to sit in the back with my needlepoint and let AA come to me. But I could only get speakers if I chaired the meeting.

I didn't have time to pray or think about what I would say; I didn't have a moment to murmur Jack the Barber's mantra. I felt like I'd said everything I could—and a lot more besides—in the Friday commitment *I'd* been on, where I did forty-five minutes of my story that sounded a lot more hilarious in the telling than it ever was in the live act. John V., an old-timer who was my first speaker on the pick-up meeting, must have felt the same way as I did. He got up, said a few sentences, and then sat down.

I had an hour Sunday meeting to fill: a half hour of speakers, a raffle break, and another half hour of speakers. At this rate, I'd run out of speakers before the half-way mark.

Then Beverly got up, looking shaky and emotional. Five minutes into her story, a guy in the corner went into a seizure and collapsed on the floor, banging his head on the radiator as he went down. Half the group rushed over to him. I thought Bev should stop speaking and wait for the confusion to die down. But she clung to the podium, to the shreds of composure she still had, and to the soberness she had so painfully acquired, and she kept talking to the half that stayed in their seats, kept the meeting going. The show was going to go on this morning, and Bev was going to keep it on track.

God certainly gave me Bernie, my next speaker, and also the guy who knew Bernie, suggesting that I ask him to speak last as the meeting's anchor. Bernie was an excellent speaker; twelve years sober, with enough emotional stability and vocal power to pull the rest of us back into focus—a necessity, as he spoke against the noise of the EMTs, whose patient was now conscious, still drunk, belligerent, and very loud. And even when the EMTs had gotten the man outside, Bernie kept it going inside, for the drunks who presumably *wanted* help. He kept us seated and listening by his very stability, right until the end of the meeting. Then he said, "My sponsor told me if you want to be noticed, stand up. If you want to be heard, speak up. If you want to be appreciated, shut up. Thanks."

My own thank-you's to close the meeting were more heartfelt than usual. I was sticky with nervous perspiration, disoriented, angry at the EMTs for not getting the guy out, angry at the drunk for the attention *he'd* sucked dry from the meeting. But for a shaky drunk and an old-timer in emotional stability, the show went on, as it must for all of us climbing this ladder to love.

## St. Matthew, Apostle, Feast

"Why are you going to the monastery in the middle of a Saturday, and we have a party to go to tonight?" asks Felix.

"It's the Feast of St. Matthew today," I say. "Can't miss it."

"Oh. Right. Of *course*." There are some places in relationships where one of you says to yourself, "You know, I just don't want to go there." For Felix, the "can't miss" of celebrating St. Matthew's feast day is clearly on that list.

For St. Matthew, it was different. We'll never know for sure what propelled him from his place of doing business at the come-hither of Jesus, to leave his life behind and follow him. Maybe it was the first welcome sign the tax collector had seen from his own people. I can relate to that, to the refreshing warmth of an unexpected welcome. After decades where I wandered in a spiritual desert, Abbot Antony rolled out the welcome mat at his abbey, and I made a mad dash for the open door before he could change his mind. I could ask questions later. The important thing was to say yes and get inside.

Bird of paradise and tricolor moreae grace the front of the altar, orange and purple colors splashed against a red votive and a place-setting of colored glass and wood for St. Matthew. Oh, that I had my own occupational patron! In a way, I'm here today out of respect for my father. Matthew is his saint.

The monks march in for Mass, and the priest-monks wear the red of St. Matthew's possible martyrdom. The opening prayer opens a memory of a tax collector.

God of mercy,
You chose a tax collector, St. Matthew,
To share the dignity of the apostles.
By his example and prayers,
Help us to follow Christ
And remain faithful in your service. . . .[8]

"My goodness," I think, "if you would call, and then dine with, a tax-collector, well then maybe also the lobbyist, the lawyer, the used car salesman and who else? Does your call encompass anyone who will listen?"

"Will you stay for lunch?" Abbot Antony asks after Mass. It's not part of my plan for today, and I hate disruptions to my plans. But the call requires an answer. Matthew left his counting tables and his outcast life when he answered. Even sinners and outcasts get to say yes and enter in.

"I'd love to stay for lunch. Thank you for asking."

On the campus where I work is a nearly life-size and very lifelike statue of Cesar Chavez, facing north, as the migrant field workers have, with the words underneath, "Si, se pueda," "It can be done."

Brought up in a devout home in an agricultural area devoid of churches, Mr. Chavez learned the faith through his mother, who was devoted to the saints and their relics. "My mother was very religious," he recalled years later, "without being fanatic, and she believed in saints as advocates, as lobbyists, to pray to God for her."[9]

It's nice, putting lobbyists with the saints for a change, instead of with the publicans and the sinners. That puts us alongside St. Matthew, a tax-collector whose presence at Jesus' table scandalized the neighborhood—and who is now patron of civil servants, the soul of hard-working anonymous respectability.

My father, a convert from the Catholic to the Episcopal Church, didn't place much faith with relics and saints, but surely St. Matthew would have found him anyway. An accountant and, later, a tax collector, he thought tax collectors got pretty bad press in the Bible, and tended to take the slander against them personally.

Sometimes, thinking of St. Matthew, I slip into my dad's story. His religion was low-key, practical, humble. He did his church's bookkeeping and the rector's taxes free of charge. Although he was just starting out in private accounting practice, and could have used the income, he gave free tax advice to any parishioner, especially the widows, who asked.

His favorite Bible story was the one about the five talents, detailed by the mathematically precise Matthew. One biblical footnote[10] suggests that five talents equaled $26,400—which seemed like a pretty big gift to me when I was a child. In the parable, one man got five talents, one got two, and one got a single talent. The first and second men doubled their talents through investment and hard work, but the third buried his to keep it safe. In the end, the first two men were rewarded, while the third, who hadn't used his gifts wisely, was banished.[11] My father loved that story. He fully expected a final accounting some day, and he was determined to make it a good one.

What his determination looked like to an outsider, a non-relative, I learned the night that Felix and I went out for a big evening on the town. When we got home, Felix counted his cash. "I had $50 in my pocket when we left, and I *still* have $50 in my pocket!" he crowed. "Does that make me an Al Papineau?" Before I could say anything, he looked at his stash again, and said, regretfully, "Nah, if I was an Al Papineau, I'd have gone out with $50 and come home with $75."

Al Papineau was the city tax collector, the family man, the stalwart churchman. He was one for St. Matthew's books. A high school dropout who worked in the same dusty textile mill as his aunt and uncle, he married at nineteen, became a father at twenty, and still managed to complete college, get his CPA license, and become a municipal tax expert by the age of forty-five. He didn't love money for power or goodies. He loved it because it meant numbers, and numbers were what he loved.

Numbers made him a father of a different sort. When my sister and I wanted to earn money with extra chores, he taught us how to submit sealed bids for the project of shoveling snow. Our New Year's Day tradition wasn't watching parades or football games; it was stuffing envelopes for Dad for a five-dollar fee (it was a much better deal than the snow-shoveling gig).

Mindfulness about numbers wasn't grim to him. It was fun, and he tried to share the fun with me. When he decided to earn his spending money through the weekly double deck pinochle games he played with the guys, he asked if I wanted to stake him.

"What's that?" I asked.

"You split half the winnings with me. You share half the losses."

I signed on. It was fun when he came home with $65 but the next week, when he came home with a loss of over $200, I felt sick. That was twenty weeks' of allowance for me. He announced the stake was off, and absolved the debt. To this day, I can't bear to bet as much as a lottery ticket.

He didn't agree with the ways I chose to spend money as an adult. "Extravagant Sam," was his nickname for me—while Felix was calling me El Cheapo. For Dad, money wasn't for spending—it was for giving away, and for multiplying, like talents, or loaves and fishes.

Felix and I were living together, unwilling to legalize the arrangement. If the morality of that bothered my dad, he never let on. What he *did* say, finally, in his best I've-given-this-some-thought-and-run-the-numbers voice, was, "You know, you're filing two individual tax returns. You could save a bundle if you could file joint."

Felix and I got married before the end of the fiscal year. At the wedding reception, my father remarked, "We should have taken up a collection. There was a good crowd at the church. You could have the reception all paid for by now."

After I moved to California, my calls to him on his birthday were always the same.

"So are you doing anything special for your birthday?" I'd ask.

"Well, I'm at the kitchen table, calculating my net worth, and your mother's making me banana bread."

"Banana bread? Gee, Dad, that's so . . . humble. . . ."

"But I *like* banana bread!"

Yes, he did. And he *was* humble. He didn't have to work it step by step. He adored calculating his net worth each year. It was the yearly test, measuring his progress in multiplying his talents.

His progress in technology was less remarkable. "I want to get a new computer for home, but your mother won't let me," he informed me by phone. "Of course, with my luck, I'd find out when I got it home that it had a black-and-white monitor or something." He laughed at his bad technology luck, and then began coughing again.

My mother would have let him have anything he wanted at that moment. He was dying of lung cancer, suddenly, rapidly, just sixty-five years old. The numbers had turned against him.

It was the last time I heard his voice.

A funny thing happened at his funeral—if you knew Al Papineau, it was screamingly funny. There was a good crowd at the church for a Wednesday morning—he would have liked that. And I got up and did one of the readings without crying—he would have liked that, too. And then *the usher came down the aisle and took up the collection,* just like that, just like any regular morning service, even moving around the casket to make sure he didn't miss anybody.

And *that* would have gotten him laughing until he began coughing.

People scrambled to get to their wallets to plunk money into the plate, stunned and surprised. Later, the usher said he wasn't thinking so much as acting out of usher habit. We put the money collected into the church's capital campaign fund. There was nothing my dad loved more after family, cats, and banana bread than a capital campaign to redo the heating system in an old church.

It was so Al Papineau, so St. Matthew. Meet the world empty-handed; come to God with $250 from the collection plate.

*"Follow me,"* Jesus said.

And they both left their counting tables, and followed.

# −11−
# The Church

## Dedication of the Abbey Church, Solemnity

Once a year, whether I need it or not, Open Studios comes around in the autumn, like the reminder of a new school year.

As a kid growing up in New England, my new school year began like clockwork the Wednesday after Labor Day. Whether the temperature was sixty degrees or (more likely) eighty degrees, we sweltered in our new wool skirts and sweaters. The start of the new school year had nothing to do with the weather.

No, it was the internal thing, the prompting to begin again, that filled the new school outfits as well as any perspiring body could: This year will be different. This year I'll study harder and get better grades. This year I'll try out for the play and not pretend it doesn't matter. This year I'll make a new friend. This year I won't eat lunch alone. This year will be different.

Whether it was different or not scarcely mattered as much as the fervent desire of those new school year resolutions to become our best selves, however we defined that.

And even when our school days were long over, the start of a new academic year could still fill us with nostalgia: I could have applied myself more. I should have been the soloist at the concert. I would have done it differently, if I'd known then what I know now. The steady, heartfelt yearbook of new school resolutions became the dull bore of New Year's Resolutions that had no hope of fulfillment: Lose ten pounds. Exercise daily. Learn computer. Somehow the noble hopes of new school years, which always involved a community, became solo quests for self-perfection. It was all about me.

Here in San Diego, the land of year round schooling, I have Open Studios to pin my aspirations and dreams of betterment and bravery on. It's a series of weekends in early fall designed to let the public into the privacy of the artist's working studio.

Before I went to my first one, I subscribed to the notion that art required suffering, gloom, and copious amounts of alcohol to flourish, and none of that seemed possible in fair-weathered, beach-volleyballed, sun-drenched San Diego. The joke of Open Studio would be finding the five working artists that I figured a place like San Diego would be able to support.

After a full weekend of art, artists, and studios, I stood humbly corrected. The sheer number of people who managed to make art in this high-rent market dazzled me. The kindness of those artists who opened their work, their methods, their drafts, their notebooks, and their studios to the strangers with nothing more than a purchased program to admit two overwhelmed me. I was experiencing a hospitality that Benedict himself would know and approve. *Great care and concern are to be shown in receiving poor people and pilgrims, he writes in his Rule, because in them more particularly Christ is received.*[1]

A few of the visitors to Open Studios may be patrons looking to buy or commission art, but most of us, I think, are the poor, the pilgrims, the wanna-be's, come to adore, like the Magi, come to respect the artists' bravery or seek their inspiration. Felix sculpts, I make collage diaries. They are the poor entrees we bring, like gifts, when we visit Open Studios.

Some of the artists are the exceptionally brave and seasoned ones, whose studios are also part of their homes. For them, Open Studio is opening everything: heart, hearth, notebooks, and life's work to the stranger who clutches that purchased program. Others, usually younger, newer in the journey, rent lofts downtown in old barnlike, abandoned warehouses beneath the flight path of planes landing at Lindbergh Field. There's community there in the old warehouses, and some of them, newer to the journey, need that community.

"No heat in the winter, no air conditioning in the summer, no hot running water anytime," Candy told us as we visited her loft this year. "But we can get as messy as we need to in our work, and it's still presentable enough to bring people here. Did you stop by to see Pru?"

Pru does oil painting, abstract landscapes, which sounds funny until you realize that all landscape is abstract until you choose to make order of it. She believes in being responsible, Pru tells us. That means, despite being a full-time artist—which doesn't even translate to a part-time salary—she buys health insurance and car insurance. She doesn't want the cost of any of her mishaps to be borne by anyone else. "I take risks all the time," she says, but by that she means in living off her art as well as through it. "I market myself heavily, and there's constant rejection in that. But then I closet myself in and produce a new body of work. It's all in the balance."

She is speaking from a place of self-knowledge and self-confidence and in her artist's path. She is speaking in a place no bigger than half the size of my bedroom with a window that looks out on a flat roof and some cawing crows. A few large canvases are posted on one white wall, and dozens of smaller ones are stacked against each other along the other. There are empty Maxwell House coffee cans filled with brushes, and greasy turpentine oil paint rainbows. I can stand in the middle of the room and nearly reach everything without taking a step. This is her world, her hospitality, her hidden heart, exposed today for Open Studios.

It was the first time Pru had been a part of Open House. "Fran asked me to," she explains. "She wanted there to be a group of us displaying together, to make it worth your while to stop here. Please make sure you see Fran."

This little community of make-do, make art has its elder—Fran, older than the others, is respected and obeyed, like a secular abbess. The younger artists even cough up the $30 entrance fee—a lot of money for them—to put themselves and their art into the catalogue and expose it all to strangers. Fran makes art books but also works in melted oil and wax on canvas, a medium where she can't predict the colors she'll finally get.

"Aren't you worried about losing control of your work?" I ask her, since I think life itself is the messy draft, and art is where the sense-making begins.

"Oh, no," says Fran. "This is the only way. Otherwise everything gets tight and restricted by the controls you impose." Her studio, her heart and hearth, is large, white, and orderly. Her window carries your eye all the way to the bay, and the strong sunlight turns everything to white light until you get to the graceful blue ribbon of the Coronado

Bay Bridge. There are inspirational poems and refrigerator magnets hung on the corkboards, and the books she uses to make her art books in the built-in bookcases. The place is big, spacious and light-filled—but it, too, is also crammed with life—her life, her art, her heart.

By the end of the Open Studio, I'm slack-jawed like a tourist to Europe visiting six cathedrals in one day. I'm drunk on images and on creative juice flow and on the freedoms and risks these women know. Who needs alcohol, the depressant, when there is art, the intoxicant?

"You would love it," says Felix as we leave our last Open Studio for this year, "having a place like that where you could escape and create, and go deep."

"Oh, but I do," I want to say. And it isn't escape at all, but more like a honing in, an opening of heart. And once, why, they even held an open studio of sorts at the abbey, that place that holds my heart and maybe my art as prayer.

After four years of hanging around the edges of the abbey as a retreatant, an oblate, a student, a penitent, and most certainly a pest, I watched in amazement the day they opened up the cloister itself and let me in. It was nothing personal: they let everybody in during the weekend's open house.

"Why are they doing this?" I asked sweet-faced Pat, a fellow oblate, even as I anxiously pawed the ground, first in line for the first escorted tour of the enclosure.

"Why, to say thank you, of course!" she answered. It was evident to her, the why. The program that Brother Mark handed me began with the heading, "Your Generous Heart Made It Possible." But I didn't know. I thought the cloister had always been there. I didn't know my donations were going into a building fund, or that I was a benefactor. I didn't feel any different, even knowing now that I had a generous heart. But if they were going to open their heart, I would be first in line.

I already knew the public space that we visited first, of course: the porter's office, the Retreat Chapel, the cafeteria, the retreat rooms. I knew the library where we held monthly oblate meetings, and the abbey church where Mass and all the public Offices were prayed. I really knew the prayer walk well, as an engine-racing sort of oblate on retreats. And I knew the oblate library, right near the oblate master's office, where we oblates found books to read, videos to watch, and a place to work. The oblate library was *my* open studio.

Beyond the oblate library was the infirmary; visitors from outside could come to visit the sick without disturbing the monks. "You are either staying here after a hospital stay, or staying here on your way to the cemetery," Brother Stephen, the infirmarian announced cheerfully. They are, all of them, so cheerful and nearly envious of those who have died. I forgot that in the tour: I know the cemetery, too, and know three of the ten names on crosses there.

And then we slid inside the cloister, and its world opened up like an artist's heart. The monks' cells (a vacant one was available to tour) were spartan, but had private little garden areas for meditation, and some of the older monks had ocean views beyond. The novitiate monk cells were in a separate block—no ocean. We walked through a classroom where the twelve steps of humility were posted about, like a child's A-B-Cs, and the refractory, the chapter house, the recreation area, all linked by winding pathways and desert plantings. Regimented and stark, it felt like a kindly jail you chose to enter, complete with ocean views.

The ladies in my group loved it all, possibly because it was all so tidy, and these monks were quiet as well as tidy, unlike some of the husbands being dragged through the Open House. But this hard, stripped-down life seemed almost as difficult a way to find God as our own messy, secular ones.

I left the tour as refreshed and as desirous as after Open Studios. These open hearts lure my own closed one out to live the life God has in mind for me. It reminds me of what Father Martin de Porres said in a homily just a few weeks ago. "The church is a city," he said, "a place to live."

The abbey may be my artist studio, where I go to study in the oblate library, pray in the chapel, or walk along the prayer walk. But it is not the city where I live, the way it literally is for the monks who inhabit the cells and dine in the refractory. I've heard other oblates say, "This abbey is my church." But it really isn't.

*Monastery, abbey*—I use the words interchangeably, but they are not quite the same. A monastery is a place of residence occupied by a community living in seclusion under religious vows. An abbey is a monastery under the supervision of an abbot. For me, the abbey is the place where my community—my fellow oblates—meet once a month and retreat once a year, and run into each other at odd times in between.

But we don't live there, and so the abbey church never feels like a parish church to me. No lay people lead the songs or the prayers, or read the Word. There are no announcements about church picnics, Bible studies, or fundraisers. The abbey is the "oratory" in Benedict's sense of the word—simply a place of prayer.[2] The Monks of New Skete find it a messy search for God in the tidiness of the monastery. When you enter, they say, instead of finding the God of your expectations, what you gradually discover are your selves as you really are.[3]

Parish churches are messy, noisy places, with too many non-prayerful activities going on—too many conversations between the pews, too many crying babies, too many restless children, too many bored teenagers, and too many check-the-box-went-to-church adults. In southern California, there are just too many of us, period, and if you get to church on time or a little late, you may end up standing in the foyer for the entire Mass, hoping the Word catches you by osmosis, since you can no longer hear it.

So much for control, as the artist Fran would have said. Who wants it anyway? Some churches are places of discovery, places where you live more fully than others. You go shopping for a church, and one has striking preaching, one a glorious choir, and one (I am thinking of my church now) has the best art you've ever seen in a modern church. You respond because you love a word given that you can chew on for a week, or you love the music that makes your heart sing, or you love the art that feasts your eyes and gladdens your heart. And you pick a church because it's what you're looking for. You have found God in the manner you had hoped.

But what makes you stay, what makes you live there is what sneaks up on you and envelops you, the mirror that claims you as you really are. And that, inevitably, is the person sitting next to you, coughing behind you, fidgeting in front of you, singing horribly out of key across the aisle. That's what a church as city is all about—the people alongside you, mirroring the person that you are.

## Step 11: Brevity

This is one of the easiest steps of humility to understand. When Benedict's monks *do* speak—silence has already been placed before them—they speak briefly, reasonably, and quietly. They are men of few words.

I came to the concept of brevity as a virtue, if not a step of humility, when I decided in my twenties to become a writer, and began reading books to teach me how. I read them all—big, fat, wordy tomes, with lengthy, self-congratulatory examples from the author's other works. And then I picked up Strunk & White's *Elements of Style* because it was supposed to be a fundamental text on the subject.

It was a skinny little paperback, and didn't cost much, so I didn't respect it as much as the big tomes that cost more. But then I hit a little story in the introduction that E. B. White tells about his teacher, William Strunk:

> When he delivered his oration on brevity to the class, he leaned forward over his desk, grasped his coat lapels in his hands, and in a husky, conspiratorial voice said, "Rule Seventeen: Omit needless words! Omit needless words! Omit needless words!"[4]

I was stunned by this stern edict, and gave up the idea of becoming a writer for a career where words would hold more value—lobbying and speechwriting, for example. But every speechwriter, too, subscribes to the maxim: Be brief. Be gone.

"How many words does it take to explain brevity?" I tease Abbot Antony. His eyes grow bright with amusement, and he spreads two fingers a quarter inch apart—and says nothing.

Well, I know brevity of the unhumble kind. It isn't words or their lack that create a humble heart, but their purpose in being uttered. It was Labor Day weekend. I wasn't scheduled to be the Sunday 8:00 A.M. lector at church, but Helen forgot she'd be out of town. She called on Thursday to see if we could swap days.

It wasn't a big deal to swap, so I did. I had only two days for preparation instead of a whole week. And, as first reader, I get the Old Testament to read. Sirach? I need more than two days! Sirach isn't part of the Protestant Church's canon, so there's no cozy familiarity in the reading:

> [C]onduct your affairs with humility,
> > and you will be loved more than a giver of gifts.
> Humble yourself the more, the greater you are,
> > and you will find favor with God.[5]

Oh, this is *so* not funny. I peek at the Gospel reading—the homily theme—and I notice that it finishes with Jesus saying, "For everyone who exalts himself will be humbled, but the one who humbles himself will be exalted."[6]

"Have you ever heard of St. Benedict's twelve steps of humility?" asks the gentle, retired Father Bill while we're preparing for the Sunday 8:00 A.M. Mass. Looks like I've become substitute reader on Humility Sunday—though they'd never label it that way in the bulletin the way they do with Good Shepherd Sunday. *Everybody* would be out of town for Humility Sunday.

"Yeah, some," I say, because you can't brag about expertise on humility. "By the way, I have a 9:21 tee time at the Lake San Marcos Country Club. I'm not supposed to be the reader today. I just thought you'd want to know that."

Father Bill's eyes get a little wider. "I was going to start my homily by saying 'I'm humble and proud of it.' What do you think?"

"I think we have to finish by 8:45 A.M. if I want to make my tee time."

He rushed the opening of his homily. Nobody laughed at his humility joke—three seconds saved right there. I read to my natural East Coast speed, and my East Coast accent came back as a result, rendering the wise words of the son of Eleazar, Sirach unintelligible to the early-morning faithful. I "accidentally" got up and read all the announcements while the collection was still rattling through the pews. Father Bill barely got to the back of the church to shake hands, and I was in my car squealing out of the parking lot at 8:44 A.M. Brief it was. Humble it was not.

"Humble persons won't make braying jackasses out of themselves," writes one monk,[7] while another more sympathetically notes that "the eleventh step of humility is to be expected only at the eleventh hour." You can't force it on newcomers, he suggests; it's "the normal outcome of a lifetime in search of wisdom."[8]

I can't speak of outcomes yet, either briefly or at length, because, as the needlepoint sampler says, "God isn't done making me yet." But I remember the *beginning* of my lifetime's search for wisdom as if it were yesterday. And if St. Bernard can show us the steps of humility through illustration of their opposite vices, perhaps I can illustrate brevity through its opposite vice as well.

I'd signed myself up for weekly psychotherapy sessions, where, in the days before pharmaceutical cures, you talked—a lot—about feelings and fantasies. It was the poles-apart opposite of brevity.

It was four years of once-a-week verbal intensity. I think I signed on because my employer had wonderful benefits and I hated to see any of them, including the once-a-week, twenty-dollars-a-visit psychotherapy sessions go to waste. It meant I did all the talking and got all the one-on-one attention I could want for fifty minutes a week. I felt like a kid in a candy store.

I was also a weepy, confused woman in that candy store, which might have been my underlying reason for seeking out the only help I saw being offered at the time. I quickly fixed my adoration onto Dr. B., and wrote many poems and short stories out of a relationship that develops from an imagination without nourishment. Unlike conversations with God or with your next-door office mate, therapeutic conversation is all one-way.

I spent a year being weepy and confused. Did I want to be happy? What constitutes happy? And what's in it for me anyway? ("I remember that discussion," groans Felix. "Are you sure it only lasted a year?")

"If you could be anything, anywhere in the world, what would you be?" Dr. B. would ask.

"A flawlessly beautiful, emotionless woman on her deathbed, surrounded by weeping, emoting lovers," I'd answer. Then I'd cry because it sounded so beautiful and so impossible to attain.

"Now *there's* a happy ending I somehow missed," he would say. "Okay, if you had a million dollars, how would your life change?"

"It wouldn't. I'd still be miserable and try to stay afloat each day." Then I'd cry because there was no hope, and I was always going to be miserable.

"How would you characterize your attitude toward life?"

"Life is what other people do. I'm into being an escape artist. Let me drink it away, write it away, read it away, sleep it away—anything to get out of it." And then I'd cry some more because escape sounded so nice, and here were a few options I'd never really pursued seriously.

("It was a very long year, if it was really only a year," sighs Felix. "But what could anybody do? You had all the answers, and let me tell you now what I didn't tell you then—they were really lousy answers.")

About once a month, I would decide to terminate therapy because I wasn't getting any better, but my reasons never sounded convincing. I usually cried when I tried to figure out why.

THE CHURCH • 209

Maybe the talking helped. Maybe the diary I began helped. Maybe I just got older and outgrew my nihilistic angst. (Maybe God was there, even then, looking out for you, offers Abbot Antony, decades later.) For the next two years, I talked about Dr. B., about his other patients, about his life off stage (*my* stage, of course). I suppose it was a way of trying to locate myself in a larger world that didn't revolve around me all the time. It wasn't *much* larger, but there was a little wiggle room. I was still confused and weepy a lot of the time.

Once, as I walked through the reception area after an appointment with Dr. B., probably looking like a sister to the snotty, soggy tissue I clutched, I saw what I thought must be Dr. B.'s Other Woman: not his wife but a *real* Other Woman—his next appointment. She was my age, dressed similarly in Depressed Denim, a tissue all ready in hand. I imagined Dr. B. with an endless cycle of weepy, confused women. It sounded like a dreadful waste of his Harvard Medical School diploma and his rugged good looks.

"Do you have a 4:00 P.M. patient?" I asked the following week. You never got a real answer from a psychiatrist, just blinkie blinks and silence. I got blinkie blinks and silence. "Come *on*. Don't say, 'Why is this important to know?' or stupid shrink stuff. I'll tell you why I asked if you'll just answer. I promise."

Blinkie, blink, and then with reluctance, he admitted to a 4:00 P.M. patient.

"Is it a woman?" I had to give more assurances that I would *tell all* if he just *cooperated*.

His 4:00 P.M. patient was a guy, he said. I cracked up laughing, while he said, "Now you have to tell all. You *promised*, and *I* cooperated."

I told him about the Other Woman in the reception area, how I'd spent a week in a competitive, jealous fury, alternating with high praise—now rendered null and void, you understand—for his workload of treating an endless stream of weepy, confused women patients.

"You're right," he said. "If all I saw were weepy, confused women, that high praise would be justified."

That was the first time I laughed in therapy. I never wanted to terminate again. I was having a good time.

In the fourth year, it began to seem like the outside stuff was crowding my fifty-minute spots and the little room we met in. There were long discussions about mortgages, as Felix and I tried to secure a house together, marriage issues, issues with friends, work issues, even hobbies that came to play in those fifty minutes. Sometimes I had to bring a list so I wouldn't forget anything. Sometimes, I forgot to cry. And then the oddest thing began to happen: I was done before the fifty minutes were up. There was nothing more to report. I was reporting, not emoting.

It sure wasn't the way it used to be, and I'd say, like a report card at the end, "Well, this wasn't a good session, was it?"

"*I* thought it was," he would answer. "You covered your topics in a logical, orderly way. You articulated the things that weren't right, and assessed what could or couldn't be done about them."

And then one session, I said, without thinking, "I think we should terminate therapy."

"Really? What makes you think that?"

And I hadn't thought about it, not for a long time, but I said, "If I add up what I'm spending in co-payments to see you, I could really use that money for living room furniture for the house."

"Sounds good. Shall we make the end of the month the final session?"

"*That's all there is to it?*" I'd spent months, maybe *years*, discussing therapeutic termination, and suddenly it was as quick as a sneeze. Oh, Traitor Mouth, what have I gone and done?

"Sure," he said. "A couple of weeks to wrap up and . . ."—a sudden, surprisingly mischievous smile—"time to pick up another 3:00 P.M. weepy, confused woman."

"I *have* gotten better these four years, haven't I?"

"Can't you tell for yourself?"

"Yes, but I want official verification."

He gave me the passing grade benediction. "You've gotten much better."

I might have cried for such a momentous moment, were I not so busy preening my feathers and smirking.

So many, many words, boatloads of them, capsizing on themselves for all their weighty grief and woe. ("It was a *very* long time," Felix sighs one last sigh.) And it finally came to a halt because one day I looked up and the existential angst was gone, and I really could use the money for new furniture.

In AA, they say you have to walk the walk, not just talk the talk. That's how they measure your recovery: not in the pretty words, but in the not-drinking. And not only the not-drinking—we all knew the trembling-fingered, white-lipped dry drunk, and knew where that person was heading. They measured your recovery on *where* the not-drinking was coming from.

For Benedict, brevity isn't just the briefness of words, but where those few words come from—the good walk with Christ, along the road to the New Jerusalem. I think it's like the companionable quiet of the old couple, still deeply in love, still caring and courteous, long beyond the limitations of words.

Brevity is the occupant between the words and the silence. It engages us in their tug of war. It's an "eleventh-hour step" that can't be mastered before words or silence are mastered.

> An arrogant monk in a crisis of faith went to his abbot saying, "Give me a word."
> The abbot responded, "No."
> Shocked, the monk demanded, "And why not?"
> "No is not good enough?" asked the abbot.
> And the monk left, and repented of his arrogance.[9]

# Anniversary of the Dedication of the Abbey Church, Solemnity

> How lovely your dwelling,
>     O LORD of hosts!
> My soul yearns and pines
>     for the courts of the LORD. . . .
> Happy are those who dwell in your house!
>     They never cease to praise you[10]

As a choir member, and later as a soloist, I've sung these words of Psalm 84 in every kind of arrangement, from hackneyed to holy. It's a psalm served best in song, the kind of song the birds enter each sunrise from the old magnolia tree in my tiny backyard.

Any Benedictine will tell you, within the first fifteen minutes of your chat, that the first word of the Rule of St. Benedict is "Listen." If you never progressed past that point in the study of the Rule (and the truth is that most of us only dabble along in spurts), you could spend a long and productive spiritual inquiry right there with the first word—*listen.*

What they don't focus on is the first word of the *psalms*, that massive body representing the full range of humanity and its relationship to God, the stuff the monks sing even more than they read the Rule. The first word that opens us up to the God of sung psalms is *happy*. Psalm One is the preface to the whole Book of Psalms, and "Happy are those who do not follow/ the counsel of the wicked,/ Nor go the way of sinners."[11]

If, as one writer suggests, God is one of us and is with us as we try to get home,[12] then Psalm 84 sings of home—God's dwelling place and the happy ones who dwell there. Whether that means a particular church, a sense of interior, or even a tree in a tiny back yard, the psalm sings of the deepest comfort—home, with God.

The holy ones rest in God nearly as perfectly as the starlings and sparrows outside nest securely in my overgrown magnolia tree. St. Catherine of Sienna knew and accepted her religious call long before her parents could know or accept it. They sought to dissuade her of her place with God by denying her the time and the privacy for prayer. St. Frances de Sales writes, "Our Lord inspired her to make her soul a shrine to which she could retire with him in spirit in the midst of her exterior occupations."[13]

Such a spiritual, virtual oratory is difficult for some of the less saintly of us to manage. That's why it's good that we build and inhabit our churches. They are the external shrines to which our souls can return and know we are with God.

It's the solemnity of such a place that we celebrate today, the anniversary of the dedication of the abbey church. In the ranking of liturgical days, this is right up there, Level I, along with the solemnities of the most holy days of the Church, like Easter or Christmas, Epiphany and Pentecost, above all the feasts, memorials, and ordinaries that fill so much of the liturgical calendar. The anniversary of the dedication of the abbey church, solemnity, shines out like the highest beacon of light against the ordinary, rocky shores nearing the close of this long stretch of Ordinary Time.

It is an odd celebration, this solemnity of a church on a Monday morning at the end of Ordinary Time. The bells at the abbey ring with the unbridled joy of Easter, but the Monday Mass crowd—on an extraordinarily dismal day for October—is a bit more subdued. There can't be thirty of us huddled in the abbey church, and none of us look like we're about to burst into a chorus of Happy Anniversary.

None of us look like the first word of the first psalm. The only reason I even know it's a special day is because it's listed on the calendar
that the monastery mails out to its oblates and benefactors each year.
Otherwise, it would just be Ordinary Monday for me, too.

Will the bells never stop? What if you gave a solemnity and
nobody came? But even if just two or three are gathered together in
his name, the Spirit of God is here, too. I used to think of those
words of Jesus and look around the church—particularly the cold,
uninviting ones—to see if I could see God standing among us. Even
the Spirit must enjoy these places we build, like nests for birds that
fly about, where we can gather ourselves up and know that God is
among us. We sing during communion, "As the sparrow finds a
home/ and the swallow a nest to settle her young,/ My home is by
your altars,/ LORD of hosts, my king and my God!"[14] Here we come,
like little Capistrano swallows, to celebrate the building of this nest
some fifteen years ago.

Less noticed, never marked on any calendar, is the knowledge that
such great moments of celebrating the sacredness of God's dwelling
places on earth can also be undone. It's not that God ever leaves us,
internally or externally, but that we—for whatever reason—must
leave this place and find another. I have no intention of ever removing the old magnolia in my backyard, but if earthquake, fire, or pesti-
lence renders it unusable or uninhabitable, the birds will find
themselves another sanctuary.

As a young college music student living in Rhode Island and
singing at local congregations, I witnessed the deconsecration of a
church. I was a sometime-soloist at St. Paul's Episcopal Church,
which meant I also covered summer service at its mission church,
Trinity. Singers notice things that impact the sound and frequently
the choice of song. Trinity's congregation, at least in summer's single
Sunday service, numbered maybe a dozen people, whereas St. Paul's
numbered hundreds. Singers tended to notice things like that. It
indicates how long the singing gig might last.

That was an accurate assessment measure for Trinity. I drove there
one hot summer Sunday morning, wishing I could be doing anything
but singing "Morning has broken" for ten people and ten dollars. I
wasn't a member of Trinity, and only a nominal member of St. Paul's.
For me it was just a singing gig—and a poorly paid, poorly attended
one at that. I left the politics of church management to other people.

"Morning has broken, like the first morning, Blackbird has spoken, like the first bird . . ."

I sang, and the collection plate quickly rustled through the small, somber-faced group of mostly older folks. I felt like I was singing at a funeral, the air was so heavy and dead, and I blamed it on the typical New England heat and humidity summer combination. The borrowed summer rector got up to read the announcements as my last note was clearing the hot, heavy air.

"As you know, the deconsecration service is next Sunday," he began. He was speaking to the same few people I had just been singing to. His voice was kindly; but the faces in front of him seemed frozen with grief. I *was* at a funeral: these people were losing their sanctuary.

Like much that is old and wonderful in New England, this tiny chapel had formed as a parish in 1843, and the chapel itself was consecrated ten years later on what was probably an equally hot and equally un–air conditioned summer morning of 1853. Now, nearly 125 years later, it was too small for self-sufficiency; its members would fold into St. Paul's or scatter to other Episcopalian churches.

It made sense to fold it up, at least from the numbers point of view, but you saw those frozen old faces and almost heard the prayer unanswered: "I wanted to be buried from this church. My parents were buried from here. My grandmother was buried from here. We got married here. This has always been our church." Instead, this tiny congregation would perform last rites on their little church.

I returned the following week, mostly out of curiosity. The frozen faces were back, thawed now with tears. Here was the place where they worshipped God, found God, sang and played, studied and celebrated the transitions of life. The little church was filled this time, not just with those who loved Trinity, but also those who loved the ones who loved Trinity. "If it was full like this every Sunday, we wouldn't be closing," said one tart-faced elderly woman in the front row. Nobody shushed her.

Deconsecration is the funeral for a place of God, the way the Solemnity of the Abbey's founding is the anniversary of a wedding vow between God's place and God's people. I had never understood church as anything but a building you go to until I saw the faces of the people who attended that day. *They* were the church; it was their collective funeral, too.

"All things are new in Your grace, Lord God, and old things pass away," began the summer fill-in rector, in a voice as gentle as a summer breeze.

"Help us to hold on to memories enriched with time and meaning," we responded. With each response, there were fewer and fewer voices, as the congregants choked on memories or tears. By the time we got to rector and congregation together—"There is a time to mourn and a time to dance. . . . Deconsecrate this site from its religious purpose begun in 1853 . . ."—it was mostly the voices of the rector and me left. We were the temporary ones, the ones without the memories. We represented the new face of this old congregation.

They disbursed, as they knew they must, a tiny diaspora in Pawtucket, Rhode Island, moving onward to be buried from strange churches, scattering their collective memory as the body of the church called Trinity. St. Paul's accepted some of Trinity's treasures, the way we distribute the special items of the deceased to the living as a form of living, distributed memory. St. Paul's Church named its chapel for Trinity's honor, as we name our children for the memory of our beloved dead.

But the life of God's people in the Spirit of God continues, because St. Catherine had it right: God rests in us, and we in God.

Christ was the sanctuary made by God into humanity, not the sanctuary made by us into God. We get them mixed up. I certainly do. I tie the tags called Episcopal, Catholic, Franciscan, and Benedictine, as brightly as I can onto buildings associated with these tags. Then I go inside. I am enchanted by it all, sometimes welcomed, sometimes not. Then I realize that there are just *people* inside, dammit. And boring, frozen-faced people at that. Where's God? I thought this was God's address?

"For Christ did not enter into a sanctuary made by hands," says the author of the Letter to the Hebrews.[15] He was destroyed—at least temporarily—by human hands, but his sanctuary always surpassed our limits, even as we struggled even harder to contain him. This glorious Solemnity, ever so quietly celebrated, has its reasons, even within our human limits. These public oratories, or places of prayer, do matter to us spiritually.

I attend church weekly, no matter where my travels take me—and sometimes they take me to wonderful, unexpected sanctuaries of God. If I am not traveling, my parish church is St. Elizabeth Seton in

La Costa, which has the most wonderful little hidden day chapel, where you can experience the gift of a small worship community—like the one at Trinity so long ago.

I can worship at home, of course, and do. I pray the Divine Office sitting at my desk, where I have stationed a child's chair from the house's previous owner as a bit of an altar. On it is an embroidered cloth my mother made, a candle, a photo of the old abbot and me, a copy of the icon of Christ that also adorns the altar of my abbey, and a statue representing my patron saint, Blessed Joanna Mary, her hands full of shell necklaces from Hawaii, and a rosary my Auntie Blanche had in her hands when she was laid out at the funeral home in Rhode Island.

An interviewer once asked writer Flannery O'Connor how she finds inspiration. "If inspiration wants to find me," she responded, "it will find me at my desk." I try to find God in my everyday life, though I frequently forget what I'm seeking and get easily distracted and frustrated. God can find *me* in church, at least once a week, somewhere in the world. It's sort of like a prayer date.

You just can't get that knowledge of God as well anywhere else. This is where God lives for us. It is I who forget to leave a forwarding address. God's holy temples vary in spirit, and that variance never seems related to the grandness or plainness of the structure itself. I think it always comes down to (or rises up to) the people inside. In some places of worship, the people have found the spark that lights the Spirit, and it stays lit beyond their physical presence. Sometimes that's because of the priest or lay leadership, sometimes it emanates from the pews, like the little day chapel at St. Elizabeth Seton's. And I suppose sometimes it's the Spirit who chooses, who just likes the way a particular church looks, settles in to stay, and everybody responds accordingly.

The Catholic church near my mother's house, where I went to Mass hours after my father died, seems to possess its spirit through its priest, who pours out his love in song, as if one person could make a difference—and he does. St. Matthew's Cathedral in Washington D.C. seems sparked with the Spirit of the poor, who come inside for warmth, and by the good civil servants who come inside for the warmth of their patron, the tax collector. Sacred Heart Church, when I was back in Cambridge on a bitter cold Sunday morning, was dark and forbidding until you met the parishioners who loved their aged church, built in 1842, and who pressed into the cold stranger's ungloved, stiffened fingers a prayer card that I still have: "With God's help . . . all things are possible. With your help all things are made easier. Thank you and God bless you." The ten dollars I stuffed into the collection plate that morning was less a help to that parish than the presence of an ill-clad, shivering stranger from California, entering their dark church on a cold Sunday morning, giving the parish the opportunity to welcome a newcomer—which they did, as if I were Christ. A piece of my spirit stayed there with them.

There is less Spirit discernable to me in the churches of southern California. For one thing, they're newer, with fewer echoes of the spirits of our elders, baptized and married and buried here before us. The Franciscan missions have the old historical Spirit and the frenetic Spirit of their founders and reconstructors. This Benedictine abbey's church is new and modern and sterile to the eyes, but carries its charter all the way from Switzerland, and the chants are laced with the layers of Benedictines all the way back to before all the labels. And the Spirit rests along the Pacific below, and God swirls all about us like the swirling stained glass presentation of Spirit in reds and oranges that reflects all over the abbey church, mixing with the reflections of light and water.

At the abbey, it's the light that carries Spirit, and suddenly you know the psalms are not just sung, but lived. In the Office of Readings for the Solemnity of the anniversary of a church, we sing,

> The earth is the LORD's and all it holds,
>     the world and those who live there. . . .

> Who may go up the mountain of the LORD?
>     Who can stand in his holy place?[16]

*Me*, I hope, as I drive the hairpin turns to reach the abbey, to become a part of its glorious light. Pick me, God, for you have been in this spot all along—

—and this time, I know it.

# −12−
# The Saints

## All Saints, Solemnity

It's autumn in the southland. I can tell because it's time to close the skylights that have been open since May. The roses in my backyard are as tall and stringy as sunflowers as they seek out the passing sun. Felix's fig tree is in full harvest, and he has nightly battles with the raccoons, who know a good dessert tree when they see one. The pumpkin and kiddy ride booth is set up on its regular once-a-year station near Lake San Marcos. How fitting, since Halloween—the keynote autumnal event—rides into the potentially spooky and ghostly church feast of All Saints Day.

Late to the Catholic Church, I enjoy, collect, and amuse myself with the saints, probably more as if they were parts of a baseball card collection than part of the heavenly host. I don't say that out of disrespect but out of the joy of knowing a few of these virtual companions, like otherworldly friends from long ago.

I didn't know the saints when I was growing up, although the beautiful stained glass windows of St. Luke's depicted the basic ones, the apostles, in jeweled colors that glowed when the sun lit them. But they were just names, not acquaintances—St. Luke, St. John, St. Matthew, St. Bartholomew—as distant and unreal as the names of the dearly departed veterans of World War II listed on memorials. The saints were something to look at, like an illuminated manuscript, when the sermon grew long. They were not *someone*.

The someones to imagine and contemplate came to me from fairy tales. No wicked witch ever devoured innocent children the way I devoured Hansel and Gretel, Rumpelstiltskin, Cinderella, Lucky Hans, or—my favorite—Rapunzel. Lots of kids, I assume, have heard the old tales of good and evil, patience, pluck, and luck that stalked these pre–hobbit or Harry Potter characters. Generations of other kids know them through movie versions with catchy background songs and dazzling cinematography animation. Me, I just had my inflamed imagination: I was locked up in the high tower with nothing to do but sing—this didn't seem such a bad life to a ten-year-old chanteuse. Would I really want to go off with the mysterious prince, or stay with the life I knew? Was Lucky Hans really lucky to trade away everything he received until he was free of everything he owned? Or was he just dumb? Would I leave the glass slipper behind, and would a prince even know to look behind my scrubby appearance to see the princess within?

What would you do? Where would you go when the road turned? Who do you admire? When they make the movie, which part do you want? I struggled and entertained those questions. I colored their images in coloring books. I took the stories apart and made them into plays and tried the parts on for size. Sometimes, I was the helpless, hapless Gretel, beseeching God like a lost and found department. Sometimes I was the prince who braved all to rescue the distressed princess. Sometimes I was the narrator, moving the action forward like God.

I left the Grimm fairy tales behind in adolescence, and looked for myself instead in teen magazines, young adult magazines, and housekeeping magazines. Alas, I was nowhere to be found. The magazines were marketed to females or males, rarely both, while in the old fairy tales, I could emulate whatever virtue or tribulation I wanted, regardless of the gender of the person who possessed it. In the free market, unlike the world of Grimm's tales, I wasn't free. I was the new Cosmo Girl. When *Redbook*, *Ms.*, and *Seventeen* appeared in my mailbox on the same day, I realized—as did the mail carrier, no doubt—that there was a serious identity issue going on.

Then at the age of thirty-eight, I entered the Roman Catholic Church. I didn't join for the saints' honor roll—I can't imagine that many people would—but I knew I was entering a church that had all the stuff of a sacramental life. I entered the Church because I wanted a sacramental life, wanted to be drenched in sacramentals like the finest fragrances. When I was confirmed, I didn't realize that a community of saints slipped in with me. They didn't feel like ghosts and goblins, like the secular Halloween spin on the holy day that follows. They had names and stories, deeds and adventures, great martyrdoms and quiet resignations, these saints. They were a virtual community of friends I could choose to emulate or appeal to. Even better than my long-lost fairy friends, these saints were real-life action figures for my spiritual journey. We could take the train together to the New Jerusalem.

All Saints, this great solemnity that comes in the last, quickening days of the liturgical year, is like those stringy roses in my backyard, reaching upward for the last flecks of summer sun. We honor all of them, the great baseball card collection of them, the biggies with the biggest bang-for-the-buck name recognition (Mary, Mother of Jesus; the disciples; St. Paul; St. Francis of Assisi). We honor the lesser ones who had their time of popularity—St. Albert, St. Gertrude, and St. Mechtilde, to name a few who share November with All Saints. All Saints is a humble pie of goodness, in all times and everywhere. It's the day to sing praises on stringed instruments, with voices raised to all the saints. Brother Maurus at the abbey likes to say, "A saint is nothing more than a failed sinner." Today is their day.

The old desert fathers knew all about the saints. Abba Poeman recorded that Abba John said the saints "are like a group of trees, each bearing different fruit, but watered from the same source." Saints, differing in their practices and bearing different fruit, are watered and nurtured by the same Spirit.[1]

I like the reminder of the source of sainthood as much as I like the difference of fruits. Catholicism brings a narrower focus to the idea of saints, while Reformation Churches, like the Episcopalian or the Lutheran, paint saints with a broader brush stroke. In those traditions, saints are all believers in Christ, living or dead, made saints through their faith, rather than through bureaucratic processes.

Catholics alone believe in saintly intercession and prayer on our behalf. I like Catholicism's veneration of the saints because it puts names and faces, stories and deeds onto the lovers of Christ, and lets me pick or choose whose roles I want or need to emulate. "Show, don't tell," they teach you in writing class. Don't tell me she's saintly—show me. And this, the Catholic Church does amazingly well, in a diversity of stories and faces that any collector would envy.

There is something for everyone in the catalogue of saints, and I like that. A writer who loves the company of saints notes that they won't enter our lives unless we ask. "They wait for us," she says. "If we never get to know the saints, it's probably because we haven't taken the initiative to get to know them."[2] Catholicism, by its culture, calendar, and processes in saint-making, encourages the invitation. I learned about inviting the saints into my life long before I became a Catholic, from Ida, my personal saint matchmaker.

It hadn't been a pretty week, but at least I was safe in the infirmary, all eighty-eight pounds of me, trying to relax enough to begin eating, trying to rest from the strains of an alcohol-fueled breakdown, trying to stop spinning like a tornado in a life out of control. I had my cartons of cigarettes—you could smoke inside, even in an infirmary, in those days. I had my diary to keep me company and to chronicle my journey back from hell as faithfully as it had chronicled my descent. I had tons of visitors, since the infirmary was part of the campus where I worked. Friends and twelve step calls alike competed for my time with doctors, bosses, and my husband. The only thing I didn't have was my wedding band.

Somehow as the crises piled up and my weight crashed down, the ring Felix had put on my finger just six months earlier had slid off. I remembered putting it on in the morning, but not of taking it off. Trying to reconstruct from the whirlwind of that day, I could only assume—but couldn't remember—that I took the ring off to wash the dishes. I checked the kitchen and my clothes; tore the bedroom apart, then the bathroom, the kitchen, the clothes washer and dryer, and even the cat's litter box. Nothing.

Surely it was the loneliest night. I sat on the bed, crying my eyes out for the loss of my wedding ring and all that it meant, while Felix was far away on a business trip to Germany. When I was done crying, I went outside and sifted through two weeks of trash while the cold rain pelted me. It was no use.

"At least I never have to worry about losing my wedding band again," I told myself, trying to be philosophical. I went back inside and dried myself off, then poured my first drink after two months as a tight-lipped, teeter-tottering teetotaler, and tried to get riproaring drunk on apple jack. I hated apple jack, which was probably why it was the only thing in the house to drink. I failed to even get drunk, which left me in a miserable state. I tried to get drunk for five more days in a row and couldn't manage to even get a buzz. It

all culminated in the safety of an infirmary bed surrounded with cigarettes, a diary, and a steady stream of visitors.

Ida was the cleaning lady. She liked to talk, but the sick ones—
somehow neither she nor I put me in the category of sick—didn't
usually want to talk or listen. Ida didn't care if I was an anorexic, psy-
chiatric admission. She said the different people made her work more
interesting. She liked neatness. I was neat, she said.

As she cleaned the toilet, emptied the trash, and dealt with my
overflowing ashtray, I told her I was there to rest, that I'd gotten very
upset about losing my wedding band, and ended up here.

"You need to talk to St. Anthony," she said. "He finds things when
you ask."

Oh, how cute, I thought, and carefully wrote the conversation in
my diary, feeling very artistic for doing so.

The next day, Ida wanted to know if I'd found my ring. Regretfully,
I said, it was still lost.

"Did you ask St. Anthony?" Ida wanted to know. Damn, she was
*serious* about this.

"No," I admitted. She looked disappointed in me, so I explained
as well as I could. "I just don't know him, Ida. I can't start out by asking someone I don't know for favors."

Ida stopped wet mopping my bathroom floor to consider the
issue. "I see your point," she said. Then she brightened up. "Tell him
I sent you. St. Anthony knows me very well. Just tell him that Ida sent
you. Then tell me how it turned out—even if I'm not on shift that
day. Leave a note at housekeeping. Just a little note: 'Ida, St. Anthony
helped.' That way I can say thank you to him for you."

Oh, how cute. Ida left, and the lights in the hallway dimmed, and
the infirmary grew quiet. It was just me and my diary. Do I, or don't
I? I couldn't. I just couldn't. It was hokey, it was sentimental, it was
hypocritical of me—I didn't believe in that stuff.

But Ida did, and she was giving advice on the only thing that mattered to me at all that moment. All my other visitors were telling me
about AA meetings, higher powers, and gaining weight. I wanted
none of it. I wanted my wedding band back.

I couldn't do it. I couldn't pray at all, and never heard of praying
to a saint, and wasn't sure if Anthony was the one you saw being
thanked or petitioned in those weird ads under the Personal Notices
section in the paper, or if that was the Jude guy. I was a desperate
wreck. But I wasn't going to be a hypocrite. I hated hypocrites.

I would write him a poem. That's it. I could write a poem and call it "Poem to St. Anthony." Technically it wouldn't be a prayer. It would be a poem—a sideways prayer. Ida would be happy.

> The cleaning lady here
> says I should talk to you.
> She says you will listen.
> and so, St. Anthony, here I am.
> Ida sent me to talk to you,
> and she knows what it's about.
> It's about my wedding ring.
> Can you help me find it?
> It went the way of my sanity last week,
> and I'm beginning to recover that.
> The ring would be nice too . . .

The skies did not open over the infirmary, the heavens did not come down upon me, and I heard no heavenly hosts singing. I closed my diary, finished my cigarette, and went to sleep.

They released me the next morning with a prescription on a medical slip that I could have sold: Eat more. Stress less. Felix and I drove home quietly with a Big Book of AA on my lap to face the world anew.

I sacked out on the couch to check out my new book. Felix decided to help by removing the six weeks' worth of empty beer bottles taking up half the garage. Ten minutes later, he walked back in with red eyes, shaking hands—and my wedding ring.

"It fell out of an empty six-pack container," he said. "I don't know why I even picked up that one last when I was just grabbing them four at a time and throwing them into the trunk."

Unaccustomed as I was to small miracles, to prayers, to saints, even to luck by then, I knew it was going to be a different world from now on. I believe that St. Anthony listened—if not to me, through my self-conscious little attempts at poetry, then to Ida, who just *knew* what she knew, and lent me her faith.

I put the ring on a chain to wear for a while—I'd lost too much weight to keep it from slipping off my finger again. And then I went to the phone and called the infirmary. "Housekeeping? I need to leave a message for Ida. It's important. . . ." For I didn't know yet how to pray to St. Anthony, and I didn't know how to thank him either, but I had the feeling Ida wouldn't mind pitching in.

St. Anthony will always be special to me. We've got good history. Felix has lost his wedding band twice while traveling to exotic parts of the world, and St. Anthony got it back for him once, and once we had to learn to take better care of the things in life that matter, and it cost us the price of a new ring. I've become acquainted with other saints, too, sometimes because of their colorful names. There's St. Christina the Astonishing, of the twelfth century: she disliked the smell of humans, took rides on the arms of windmills, and prayed while curled in a ball.³ While I don't find much in this to emulate, I love that her wildness, and maybe her insanity, didn't keep her from finding God and holding God close. And her name is like a wondrous burst of a smile on a dreary November day.

Then there's St. Zita, among the ordinary of saints. Nobody will make a movie about a thirteenth-century Italian servant and nanny to a wool and silk-weaving merchant. No feminist Christians will rally around her acceptance of the kind of work that life dealt her. And yet I love her because she is the patron of a Franciscan nun I once stitched a bookmark for. The nun wrote back a thank you—the first one I'd received for my anonymous work, and it startled me. We didn't know each other. She was a name in a weekly church bulletin at a Franciscan mission for whom prayers and cards were sought. So I made her a bookmark and mailed it off with a little note.

A little note came back, like a dove, a messenger of good things. "From your handiwork and your handwriting, I know you are artistic and neat," wrote Sister Zita in a careful, spidery, aged hand. "It is a nice combination. I have such devotion to my patron namesake. Thank you for putting her name on the bookmark." Her devotion became a shared one with that careful note, and I had to go running off to look up Zita.

St. Adrian, on the other hand, was a problem. I found him in a book of saints, quite by accident, but he caught my eye because of my circumstances. I was at a crossroads. It wasn't a particularly bad set of choices to make, and I'd faced similar decisions in the past: stay comfortable, or move into the unknown. St. Adrian might be a guy, but he knew what I needed to know. Offered the position of Archbishop of Canterbury by the pope, he declined in favor of being the new archbishop's assistant. He chose the lesser path and became a saint.

Do I go, or do I stay? I appealed to St. Adrian on the wisdom of the lesser path, and decided that it was meant for me. I was in the process of becoming a Benedictine oblate at the time, and was ready to take Adrian as my patron for all his work on my career's behalf.

Then I got promoted anyway. It wasn't an easy adjustment—I was convinced the lesser position was the right one for me. So I unceremoniously crossed Adrian off my list of potential patrons to consider as my Benedictine namesake. When I found a website that gave instructions on how to fire a guardian angel, I decided Adrian qualified, and submitted his infraction: I got the promotion! I asked Adrian to help me to stay put! I was pretty indignant about the whole thing.

"Thank you," said the computer screen after I clicked the "Submit infraction" button. "Your complaints are important to us and will be answered in the order received. Express processing will be considered for hermits, altar servers, and selected saints-in-waiting."

I guess I didn't qualify for express processing, or there may have been a glut of heavenly complaints because I never got a return e-mail or a new patron, and I had to get past it and make the new job work.

There are also personal patron saints—the ones you're named for or whose name you take on in the profession of vows. I don't know any saints named Carol and I took as my confirmation name Blanche, after my sister-in-law. As a Benedictine oblate, I finally got to choose my patron. Adrian was certainly out, and by now, Paul was on my short list, although the old abbot would have feminized it to Paula. In the end, though, there was no choice at all, because the abbot was so excited at finding Blessed Joanna Mary Bonomo in the Benedictine martyrology. "You may have a saint as a relative!" he wrote me.

Hardly, since it's my husband's stepfather's last name. And Joanna Mary never made it to full sainthood, being only a Blessed, and therefore only suitable for private devotion. And I didn't feel devoted to her at all, mostly sulky at her obscurity. All around me, oblates wear badges with names like Benedicta, Scholastica (Benedict's saintly twin sister), Theresa (for the Little Flower of Lisieux), and various Catherines (Siena, Genoa)—and *I* get Joanna Mary Who?

Still, we've come to spiritual companionship together, Joanna Mary and I, joined in our obscurity and our attempts to become better than we are. And this summer, we began blending at the edges. For years, I've been cross-stitching baby quilts to give to the babies who crawl across my path or to my church's annual baby shower during its Respect Life celebration. So I've been searching for a place that makes custom labels to attach my quilts: "Made for you by

YOUR NAME HERE." I got a little pang in my heart when I finally found the needlework labels and ordered them. The pang came when the crispy-voiced order taker said, "Name on label? Please spell out."

"First word, B-l. Second word, J-O-A-N-N-A. Third word, M-A-R-Y." And once I said it, I felt like we were married, two spirits in one baby quilt.

The labels are quiet and lovely. I attach them to obscure back corners of each quilt I finish.

Besides the personal patrons, there are patron saints for countries—Our Lady of the Immaculate Conception for the United States—and for just about every occupation imaginable. St. Francis de Sales is the patron of journalists; even in translation, his 400-year-old writings delight and instruct. Firefighters, police, lawyers, even tax collectors have their patrons. Unfortunately, for all the searching I've done, I can't find a patron saint of lobbyists—which is really too bad, because it takes a lobbyist to make a saint.

The process of saint-making is arduous, both legally and medically, and requires supporters with patience and connections. After the candidate has been dead at least five years, a petition for cause may be submitted to Rome. Once the Vatican permits the cause to move forward, candidates receive the title "Servant of God," and their lives and writings, along with witnesses to their lives, are scrutinized. The candidate's corpse is exhumed, and proof of physical existence is made.

That part sounds silly or maybe morbid—back to ghosts and goblin time—but I remember when Rome decided years ago that some of those revered as saints, like Christopher, had probably been more legend than real. (Even after Christopher, patron of travelers, was demoted, my friend refused to remove his medal from her dashboard, but referred to the image as Mr. Christopher.)

The Vatican's Congregation for the Cause of Saints, if they approve of the results, confer the title of "Venerable" on the candidate. The earthly debate is now over, and heavenly work must begin: two posthumous, medically verifiable miracles. One gets the candidate bumped up to "Blessed," and faithful individuals may pray to this blessed person (like Joanna Mary) for intercession. The second confirmed miracle gets canonization, an official portrait, and a day of memorial. The standard for miracles is very high and medically exacting, but the public relations side of presenting a candidate and crusading the process requires a lobbyist's touch.

The saints you find in the compilations are heavy on members of religious orders, martyrs, and do-good royalty, not to mention a fair number of popes. This makes sense when you think of who would most likely have lobbyists to propel their cause forward in past centuries. But today the collection has grown to embrace the holy ones beyond the narrow halls of Caucasian religious: the church laity, the married ones, the parents, the poor, people whose lives give us mirrors of the saintly among all saints, so we can all turn to them for their example and their inspiration.

This big community in the communion of saints, somehow, leads me to see how much room there is in God for the person I am, and for the person I hope to become.

## Step 12: Constancy

"I think Benedict's steps to humility end in a whimper, not a bang," I told Abbot Antony not long ago.

"You want the whole orchestra for the finish?" he asked.

Damn, he's got that look of mischief again. Humility is still such a weird subject. And no, I don't suppose Benedict would finish this particular subject with bells and whistles and kettledrums. All he asked of us here in this last step—all!—is that we manifest our humility externally as well as internally, that it becomes who we are no matter where we are or what we're doing.

I think I'd prefer the bells and whistles. How the heck am I supposed to look humble? I don't suppose the answers will come from thinking about it. Abbot Antony tells me so often, "You can't give away what you don't possess." You aren't going to look like humble if you haven't become humble first. That's what the first eleven steps were about—becoming humble.

In twelve-step groups that offer the steps to recovery from various addictions and afflictions, it's called two-stepping and it's not the dance you want to dance. You saw it in AA. A person would stumble into a meeting however they could, and learn step one—admitting powerlessness over alcohol, that their life had become unmanageable. This is nearly an unreachable first step for an alcoholic, or for anyone who somewhere along the line found they'd turned the keys to the car over to a madman and they were locked in the back seat without a seatbelt. The people who never reached the meeting place were the ones who couldn't reach for this first step. The ones who managed to make it inside the meeting were usually the ones who had come to see powerless and unmanageable in the mirror every day. For them, it could be a relief, that first, hard step.

And then, in the twelve steps of AA, there are a bunch of steps in the middle that confirm your abject helplessness, cough up all the wreckage of the past, fix it, apologize for it, get a God, and get a life. Only then do AA's founders hit you with the glory step, number 12: "Having had a spiritual awakening as the result of these steps, we tried to carry this message to alcoholics, and to practice these principles in all our affairs."[4]

I remember lying on the couch reading my Big Book. It was a borrowed copy, and I couldn't make sarcastic notes in the margins, so I shared my sarcastic notes with Felix instead. He didn't seem to be getting the joke. It looked pretty serious from his point of view: twenty-four hours after he'd returned from an overseas business trip, I was in the infirmary for problems related to alcohol abuse. I weighed 88 pounds, and I couldn't sleep because my hip bones dug into the mattress. I wasn't eating because I didn't have the strength to break the seal of the refrigerator when I tried to open it, and I would come up off my feet tugging the handle. The two-car garage held one car and many, many cases of returnable beer bottles, all empty, all waiting to get returned.

No, he didn't get the joke at all.

At least my ridicule kept me from two-stepping. Once inside and powerless, you'd see a new AA member go rushing off to save everybody else. That was two-stepping. It rarely worked, and tended to be a slippery slope that sent all its dancers slipping over the abyss.

For Benedict, this is the culminating step, the capstone, bells and whistles not required for assembly. Of it, Benedictine writer Esther de Waal says, "It is vital that the inner landscape corresponds with the outer."[5]

I see so much that is disjointed about myself when I read that. I remember Norberto, a scientist from Brazil, working at MIT, announcing to the staff of my small research center, "I have come to know the secret of Carol!" Everybody stopped what they were doing and waited. Norberto continued, triumphantly, "She does not always know what she talks like she knows!"

Everybody, including me, went back to what we were doing. This was no secret.

Felix and his daughter and I were at the Pearl Harbor Memorial, and for some reason, I got separated from them. It was crowded, and they stood high on a knoll looking around to find me. When they did, the daughter asked the father, "Do you think she knows she's lost?"

"She sure doesn't walk like she's lost," answered Felix. I was stomping around with great assurance and direction, totally and completely lost.

Manifesting who we are can also find its mirror geographically. When Felix came to San Diego on a business trip, he said, "I felt like I belonged there. I felt like everything matched." And I look at the hard blue skies and the dashing blue Pacific, and the wilderness contained between them, and I think, yes, that's what he looks like inside, too. But what I say is, "I know. I had the same feeling once. Only it was in Cambridge, Massachusetts."

I found out that a woman I worked with—who encouraged me to apply to graduate school and lent me GRE study guides and kept repeating, "You can do this," until I began to whisper to myself, "I can do this"—was pregnant for the first time.

"Would you like me to make you a baby quilt or a sampler?" I asked. I had not seen a lot of these type of crafters in southern California, and it was probably because the sun's strong enough to strip the colors from your yarns, and everybody's outside all the time anyway.

"I'd *love* a baby quilt!" she said, and then hesitated. "You do that kind of stuff?"

"I do that kind of stuff, yes."

"I just don't think of you that way. You don't look the type."

"What type do I look?" This was a golden opportunity to see ourselves as others do, since she was supportive and highly articulate.

"Why, I see you sitting up late at night, drinking coffee, reading Virginia Woolf."

"Well, but I do that, too."

The difficulty in constancy for me is that we are constantly changing, growing, shifting, shedding. Our externals change, too, although sometimes to a different rhythm or theme. How many women have I seen in photographs, including myself, barely recognizable from picture to picture as we try on different looks, practice new personas, and ask the camera or the bathroom mirror, "Is this me? How about this one?"

And if we can't hold to constancy, how can we expect others to? We freeze-dry our friends and acquaintances into fragments of a person—organized, creative, tempestuous—and squeeze the entire person through that keyhole, regardless of fit.

The keyhole to humility is pretty small. Like Alice in Wonderland, I'm not going to fit through the keyhole if I'm constantly mixing-and-matching who I am and who I appear to be. In AA, you didn't trouble too much about "having a spiritual awakening." You troubled yourself instead with the qualifier—"as a result of these steps." You "worked the steps," they said, like the steps were Stairmasters, going around and around. You never get to the end of them, but without arriving, you're becoming physically fit.

Here, too, this twelfth step, constancy, seems less about arriving and more about becoming. Will we know this place when we become it? Probably not. But there's still a summit, a bit of a rest, a place with a view, before we begin again.

For Benedict, the summit of this ladder, so carefully constructed and painfully ascended, is perfect, fearless love. Humility is a slow business, says one commentary on the subject—at least if it's authentic humility. "A realistic estimate of the time needed to get to the summit would be forty or fifty years."[6]

I'm going to run out of years, at least on this end of eternity. Maybe I'll get there on the other side. It will be worth the effort, the daily exercise of humility, to reach the summit of perfect love:

> *Through this love, all that he once performed with dread, he will now begin to observe without effort, as though naturally, from habit, no longer out of fear of hell, but out of love for Christ, good habit and delight in virtue.*[7]

The view seems worth the effort.

# Coda
## *The Summit*

On a day of no particular interest or importance, Felix walks by my little desk at home. Like any self-respecting ten-year-old might be doing, I'm up to my elbows in an art collage I have named "Circus." Cut-up magazines, glue sticks, exacto knives, scissors, ink pads, and watercolor pencils are scattered all over, on, and underneath my desk. My CD player is spilling out Hawaiian falsetto singers in concert, as it's been doing without pause since we returned from vacation months and months ago.

"You know," he says, as I begin stomp-stomping the rubber stamp overlays, "if you're that homesick, I'll put together a little travel package for you. Just you and L'uke for a week on the islands. How would you like that? You can see your teacher and the group again. It will be a little uke retreat for you."

The rubber stamp stomp-stomping stops. "Okay," I say. As I go back to art-for-play's sake, I'm already beginning to make lists in my head: lose five pounds, get teeth whitened if you're going to keep smiling like this all the time, learn to play "White Sandy Beach" on ukulele so you'll be ready when you finally see Auntie again.

I get ink stains all over my hands, and apply glue to the wrong side of an image because my head has suddenly departed from where my hands and feet are. I'm back in Hawaii, strumming with my group, keeping up now instead of holding everybody back the way I did in the beginning.

Oh, Auntie—I look at the little photo Felix took of us then, neither of us very tall, but how you put your arm around this mainland outsider

231

and kindly smiled into the camera, while I looked bashful and proud. "Hey, I can play the ukulele! I have a $130 used tenor uke named L'uke, and I can play C and F and sometimes the G7 chord, if I try hard." I played "Christmas on Christmas Island" until it was practically Easter because it reminded me of you, and "You Are My Sunshine" because I didn't need any music for that one, and it was the first song you taught me. When I took my leave, you all strummed me gone, like any and all the guests you welcomed as Christ, like shells washed in on the shore and washed away again with the next tide, the next cruise ship, the last flight of the day.

And now, back on this island, as I wait for the group to assemble on this overcast, warm December day—I got here two hours early because I couldn't wait any longer to be here—I'm ready. I'm ready to take my place here again, a place I hardly occupied in your mind, but in mine, every night when I practiced in Lake San Marcos, tuned by inner ear to your instrument, as the student must.

Oh, Auntie—the instrument I play now is an antique Martin soprano ukulele I called Nana, which is the name my culture would use instead of your culture's Auntie or Uncle. She is simply one of the best instruments made, with a fine clear voice that this old former choir soprano loves to join in the song.

She's come with me to a master ukulele class, where we learned to unfold our attitudes about music, singing, and practice under the eye of a master teacher. ("There's such a thing as a master class for the *ukulele?*" a co-worker asked in disbelief. "Are you getting *serious* about that toy instrument?" Yes, there is. Yes, I am. No, she is not a *toy!*)

At first, I was a little embarrassed—maybe self-conscious is the better descriptor. I played piano from when I was eight until I was eighteen years old. I sang choir, then majored in music, then sang opera briefly, before I put it all away. And now here I am, lugging a little uke case with me on lobbying trips to Washington D.C. ("I used to *love* playing the violin when I was a child," says the first officer when he sees me with Nana deplaning. Do I have any guts? Do I admit that this is not a violin? I smile and keep walking. No guts, no glory, no sissy violin.)

I drag her off to the monastery and try not to ruin silent retreats by playing softly in the Retreat Lounge. I confess to Abbot Antony how every night when I come home from work, I play Nana for a half hour or more. It must be bad since I love it so much?

"Like David," he murmurs approvingly. "He sang praises on stringed instruments."

Ah, the singing part. "Sing praise to the name of the Lord Most High," as the psalms say. The ukulele is always about singing. You said to transpose the music into a key I could sing in, but transposing was hard, so I just played the notes. The guy who owns Kealani's where we play on Saturdays was setting us up for a gig until he found out we just played, never sang. "What's a uke group without singing?" he asked, like he couldn't believe he'd let us use his space and name. And the old ones around here would tell you that a uke without a voice was like a hot dog without the roll.

Oh, Auntie—I kept at it. I really did. You'd be surprised—and, I'm hoping pleased—at how I kept at it. I mostly played Hawaiian songs at first, because I was homesick for your home. But it wasn't my home, and I couldn't pronounce the Hawaiian, and it wasn't my voice. I tried California surfing songs, and one or two of the ballads moved into my repertoire book. I tried camp songs and then 1960s songs, and I got another couple of songs into my repertoire book, a little bit more voice.

And then, Auntie—then I found church songs with chords, the same glorious old songs I'd sung as a little kid at that Episcopalian camp where the House of Silence was, singing them as a junior choir member, and a few from when I was a soloist. "How Great Thou Art," "Will the Circle Be Unbroken," and "Nearer My God To Thee"—there it was: the match was struck, the hot dog wrapped in a roll, the little old soprano uke with voice, *my* voice, praising God with stringed instruments, "like David."

St. Augustine would approve. In a discourse on the psalms, he says,

See how [God] provides you with a way of singing. Do not search for words, as if you could find a lyric which would give God pleasure. Sing to him "with songs of joy." This is singing well to God, just singing with songs of joy.[1]

Such joy! I sit in my sunroom at night, singing my heart out, all praises to God, like Father Stanislaus talked about, and it is all praise, all prayer, all love, and a hell of a lot of fun. The first word of the psalms is happy. My uke has a voice, and it's a *happy* voice at that.

Oh, Auntie—my uke has its voice, and I have recovered mine. I have thirty-three songs with me in my repertoire book. Three of them are memorized, and I'll have at least three more memorized by the end of this uke retreat my husband gave me for no particular reason except he thought I looked homesick. My repertoire has fifty-six chords now, including the most amazing B-flat minor 6th I have ever heard. I can play five different riffs, and two of those riffs are ones I wrote myself. Are you proud of how far I've come, Auntie? Are you glad to see me again?

She is running a bit late this morning, but her eyes grow wide when she takes in this week's group. "How nice of you all to be here," she says. "Let's introduce ourselves, since we have some new and some returning players."

We go around with our names. I am Carol and returning. The couple from Ohio who spend their winters here and their summers practicing the ukulele in their garage where no one can hear them are also returning. "Welcome back!" Auntie says with her kind, inclusive smile. "What a *wonderful* ook-a-le-le," she adds, pointing to Nana. I beam back. I have made myself ready to enjoy our time together. I have been practicing the steps necessary to be ready.

"Sydney, from Seattle," says a young man two chairs over. "I'm here for a seminar and I saw the ad for free ukulele lessons. I'm only here until tomorrow."

"That's okay," says Auntie. "Here's your ukulele to use today." She pulls one of the cheap plastic ones out of the box and hands it to him. "Everybody, tune to my instrument please."

"I've never played anything before," says Sydney from Seattle, sounding a little panicked. "I don't have to stay and hold you all back."

"Not at all," says Auntie firmly. "First we show you a C chord. Luanne will show you a C. And then the F chord. Everybody, play the F chord. Let's play the C and then the F chord a few more times. Now we're ready for "You Are My Sunshine." Is everybody ready? C, F, C, F, C. Okay. Now, begin: "You are my sunshine, my only sunshine . . . ""

We begin to play, the six regulars, the returning mainlander, and Sydney from Seattle, who plunks a chord or two as we start off. "You are my sunshine. . . ." It isn't quite the reunion I practiced for, but it's the reunion I get. I'm here, we are all here together, all tuned a little differently, despite Auntie's direction, all at wildly different levels. And it all blends until we can only hear ourselves in each other, and it's good. But it's only the beginning after all.

"You'll never know, dear, how much I love you . . . " I forgot that's how the song continues. As we sing it, I look at Auntie, and she looks at me. This is where humility brings you. It's love and it's good. It's all good.

# Notes

## Prelude: The Preparation

1. *The Rule of St. Benedict in English*, chapter 7, verse 8. All references to Benedict's Rule use the RB1980 edition edited by Timothy Fry, OSB (Collegeville, Minn.: Liturgical Press, 1982).

2. Genesis 28:12. All biblical references, except where otherwise noted are from The New American Bible, copyright © 1991, 1986, 1970 Confraternity of Christian Doctrine, Inc., Washington, D.C.

3. Esther de Waal, *A Life-Giving Way: A Commentary on the Rule of St. Benedict* (Collegeville, Minn.: Liturgical Press, 1995), 46–47.

4. Rule 7:7.

5. Luke 14:11.

6. Genesis 28:15.

7. Genesis 28:16.

8. Genesis 28:17.

9. Luke 1:46–47.

10. Luke 1:68.

11. Luke 1:79.

12. Norvene Vest, *Desiring Life: Benedict on Wisdom and the Good Life* (Cambridge, Mass.: Cowley Publications, 2000), 44.

13. Rule, Prologue:1.

## Chapter 1: The Gift

1. Luke 2:14 (King James Version [Nashville: Thomas Nelson Publishers, 1976, originally translated in 1611]).

2. Rule 7:10.

3. Rule 7:11.

4. Rule 7:14–25, summarized.

5. Anonymous (Bill Wilson), *Twelve Steps and Twelve Traditions* (New York: Alcoholics Anonymous World Services, 1987), 72.

6. Ibid, 74.

7. Rule 7:13.

8. Joan Chittister, OSB, *Wisdom Distilled from the Daily: Living the Rule of St. Benedict Today* (San Francisco: HarperCollins, 1990), 58.

9. Ibid.

10. Matthew 22:37.

11. 1 Corinthians 12:4.

12. William Willimon, "From a God We Hardly Knew," in *The Christian Century*, 105, 39 (1988): 1173–75.

13. Rule 68:1.

14. Patrick Henry, ed., *Benedict's Dharma: Buddhists Reflect on the Rule of St. Benedict* (New York: Riverhead Books, 2001), 86.

15. Willimon, 1175.

16. Brennan Manning, "The Shipwrecked at the Stable," in *Lion and Lamb* (Grand Rapids, Mich.: Chosen Books/Baker Book House, 1986), 180–81.

## Chapter 2: The Star

1. Evelyn Underhill, *Light of Christ* (Wilton, Conn.: Morehouse-Barlow Co., 1989), 18–19.

2. Giovanni Papini, *Life of Christ*, Dorothy Canfield Fisher, trans. (New York: Harcourt, Brace, & Co., 1923), 21.

3. The antiphons are found in *The Divine Office: The Liturgy of the Hours, vol. I (Advent/Christmas)* (New York: Catholic Book Co., 1975), 647.

4. Matthew 2:13–17.

5. Christian Community Bible, translated, presented, and commented for the Christian Communities of the Philippines and the Third World; and for those who seek God. (6th ed.; the Philippines: Claretian Publications/St. Paul Publications/Divine Word Publications, 1990), 9.

6. Ibid.

7. Psalm 8:4–6.

8. Andrew Murrary, *Humility* (New Kensington, Pa.: Whitaker House, 1982), 10.

9. Rule 7:31–32.

10. Michael Casey, OSB, *A Guide to Living in the Truth: St. Benedict's Teaching on Humility* (Liguori, Mo.: Liguori/Triumph, 2001), 90.

11. de Waal, *A Life-Giving Way*, 48.

12. 2 Corinthians 3:6.

13. Joan Chittister, OSB, *The Rule of St. Benedict: Insight for the Ages*, Crossroad Spiritual Legacy Series (New York: Crossroad Publishing Co., 1999), 66.

14. Psalm 3:8.

15. Luke 17:17–19.

16. Susan Annette Mutto, *Steps Along the Way: The Path of Spiritual Reading* (Denville, N.J.: Dimension Books, 1975), 41.

## Chapter 3: The Temptation

1. Mark 1:13.

2. Aelred R. Rosser, *Workbook for Lectors and Gospel Readers, Year A* (Chicago: Liturgical Training Publications, 2001), 60.

3. Luke 21:3.

4. Catholic Information Network, "Ask Father Mateo," taken from the website www.cin.org/mateo/mt960304.html (March 1996).

5. Ibid., www.cin.org/mateo/9512291.html (December 1995).

6. Rule 49:1.

7. Rule 49:4.

8. Rule 49:7.

9. Rule 7:34.

10. Benet Tvedten, OSB, *A Share in the Kingdom: A Commentary on the Rule of St. Benedict for Oblates* (Collegeville, Minn.: Liturgical Press, 1989), 35.

11. Chittister, *The Rule of St. Benedict: Insight for the Ages*, 67.

12. Matthew 22:21.

13. Romans 13:1.

14. Casey, 23.

15. Psalm 51:3a.

16. Luke 18:13.

17. Psalm 51:3b.

18. Psalm 51:4a.

19. Psalm 51:6b.

20. Psalm 51:9b.

21. Psalm 51:13a.

22. Psalm 51:14a.

## Interlude: The Passing of our Blessed Father Benedict (Solemnity)

1. *Novena to St. Benedict* (Collegeville, Minn.: The Liturgical Press, 1993), 12.

2. 1 Timothy 4:7.

3. Psalm 51:21a.

## Chapter 4: The Passion

1. Father Richard John Neuhaus, *Death on a Friday Afternoon: Meditations on the Last Words of Jesus from the Cross* (New York: Basic Books, 2000), 160.
2. Lavinia Byrne, *Sharing the Vision: The Spiritual Lessons of the Religious Life* (Cambridge, Mass.: Cowley Publications, 1989), 75.
3. Neuhaus, 111.
4. Byrne, 75.
5. Matthew 10:22, from The Jerusalem Bible, as used in The Rule of St. Benedict (Meisel and del Mastro, trans.). Image, Doubleday, New York, 1975.[IITS26]
6. Psalm 66:11–12.
7. Benedicta Ward, SLG, trans., *The Sayings of the Desert Fathers: The Alphabetical Collection* (Kalamazoo, Mich.: Cistercian Publications, 1984), 139.
8. Luke 22:44.
9. Casey, 118.
10. Ibid., 120–21.
11. Chittister, *Wisdom*, 59.
12. David Krogh, *Smoking: The Artificial Passion* (New York: W. H. Freeman and Company, 1991), 80.
13. Matthew 26:29.
14. Father Victor Hoagland, "Why devote a web site to the Passion of Jesus?" from www.cptryon.org/xpipassio/indexwhy.html.
15. Priest: "We adore you, O Christ, and we praise you." All: "Because by your Holy Cross you have redeemed the world."
16. Vest, *Desiring Life*, 107.
17. Byrne, 36.
18. Tvedton, 18.
19. Divine Office, vol. III, 1544.
20. Neuhaus, 2.
21. Psalm 90:7–8, 12–13.
22. Divine Office, vol. II, 496–98.

## Chapter 5: The Morning

1. Francis X. Gaeta, *The Great Fifty Days: Savoring the Resurrection* (Totowa, N.J.: Resurrection Press, 2000), 9.
2. Ibid., 21.
3. Colossians 3:3–4.
4. Neuhaus, 247.
5. Ibid., 249.
6. Chittister, *Wisdom*, 61.

7. de Waal, 50.

8. Anonymous (Bill Wilson), *Alcoholics Anonymous: The Story of How Many Thousands of Men and Women Have Recovered from Alcoholism* (3d ed.; New York: AA World Services, 1976), 72.

9. See Chittister, *Wisdom*, 60; de Waal, 50.

10. St. Francis de Sales, *Introduction to the Devout Life*, Michael Day, trans. (Westminster, Md.: The Newman Press, 1954), 77.

11. Ephesians 4:26.

12. Casey, 61.

13. Psalm 131:1–2.

14. Psalm 32:1–2.

15. 2 Corinthians 4:17–18.

## Chapter 6: The Comfort

1. Luke 2:11.

2. Acts 1:9.

3. Acts 2:13.

4. Phyllis Tickle, *Ordinary Time: Stories of the Days Between Ascensiontide and Advent* (Nashville: The Upper Room, 1988), 12.

5. Acts 2:36.

6. Acts 2:6.

7. Gaeta, 89–90.

8. Acts 8:14–17.

9. 1 Corinthians 12:7–10.

10. Rule, Prologue: 45.

11. Rule 7:49.

12. Chittister, *Wisdom*, 61.

13. Mark L., *Stairway to Serenity: A Spirituality of Recovery* (San Francisco: Harper & Row, 1988), 2.

14. Laura Swan, *The Forgotten Desert Mothers: Sayings, Lives and Stories of Early Christian Women* (New York: Paulist Press, 2001), 40.

15. de Waal, 51.

16. Chittister, *Insights*, 69.

17. Casey, 56.

18. Vest, 89.

19. Genesis 28:16.

20. Monks of New Skete, 116.

21. Galatians 5:25–26.

22. John 14:9.

## Chapter 7: The Whole

1. Rosser, 178.

2. Tickle, 13.

3. Ibid., 15.

4. Rev. Peter John Cameron, OP, ed., *Magnificat*, 14, 3 (May 2002): 308.

5. See Brother Craig's biography of Blessed Elizabeth of the Trinity on the website www.monksofadoration.org/bleseliz.html.

6. Ibid.

7. Shirley D. Sullivan, "Blessed Elizabeth's Prayer to the Trinity" *Spirituality*, 8 (Mar/Apr, 2002): 87–90.

8. 2 Corinthians 13:13.

9. Rosser, 179.

10. Deuteronomy 7:7.

11. Rule 7:51.

12. Chittister, *Insights*, 70.

13. de Sales, 104.

14. Luke 14:11.

15. Casey, 18.

16. Chittister, *Wisdom*, 62.

17. Patrick Henry, ed., *Benedict's Dharma: Buddhists Reflect on the Rule of St. Benedict* (New York: Riverhead Books, 2001), 116.

18. Matthew 20:16.

19. Thomas à Kempis, *Imitation of Christ*, Ronald Knox and Michael Oakley, trans. (London: Burns and Oates, 1963), 21.

20. Ibid., 109.

21. Bishop Donald W. Wuerl, *The Catholic Way: Faith for Living Today* (New York: Doubleday, 2001), 46.

22. Galatians 5:25.

23. *Magnificat*, 4, 4 (June 2002): 2.

## Interlude: Safe Place

1. Woodeene Koenig-Bricker, *365 Saints: Your Daily Guide to the Wisdom and Wonder of Their Lives* (San Francisco: HarperSanFrancisco, 1995), meditation for May 24.

2. Chittister, *Insights*, 64.

3. Psalm 100:1.

## Chapter 8: The Gathering

1. *Alcoholics Anonymous*, 58.

2. Rule Prologue:45.

3. Rule 53:3.

4. Rule 22:8.

5. Rule 50:3.

6. Rule 19:7.

7. Rule 72:11.

8. Rule 7:55.

9. Rosser, 154.

10. Monks of New Skete, 5.

11. Byrne, 20.

12. Casey, 46.

13. Patrick Henry, 106.

14. Ibid., 76.

15. Rule 7:5.

16. 2 Timothy 3:10.

17. See www.camaldolese.com.

18. Swan, 35.

19. Psalm 2:7b.

20. Divine Office, vol. III, 1530.

21. Ward, 103.

## Chapter 9: The Dream

1. Luke 9:33.

2. Romano Guardini, *The Lord* (Chicago: Henry Regnery Co., 1954), 236.

3. Matthew 18:20.

4. Monks of New Skete, 313.

5. Ibid., 250.

6. Roger Housden, *Retreat: Time Apart for Silence and Solitude* (San Francisco: HarperSanFrancisco, 1995), 7.

7. à Kempis, 31.

8. *Speechwriter Newsletter* (August, 2001): 5.

9. Guardini, 236.

10. Carroll Stuhlmueller, C.P., *Biblical Meditations for Ordinary Times, Weeks 10–22* (New York: Paulist Press, 1984), 212.

11. Exodus 34:29.

12. Guardini, 237.

13. Divine Office, vol. IV, 1285.

## Chapter 10: The Call

1. Mark 2:14.

2. Matthew 6:28–30, King James Translation, which would have been the one the florist used. More prosaic translations such as The New American Bible translate the verse as, *"Learn from the way the wild flowers grow,"* which has the same meaning, but would never inspire a naming opportunity.

3. Jean Prescott, "Sit back, relax, and get ready for a good cry," Knight Ridder News Service, in *San Diego Union-Tribune*, September 24, 2002, E12.

4. Casey, 169.

5. *Alcoholics Anonymous*, 315.

6. Ephesians 4:14–15.

7. Bernard of Clairvaux, *A Lover Teaching the Way of Love: Selected Spiritual Writings*, introduced and edited by M. Basil Pennington (New York: New York City Press, 1997), 53.

8. *Magnificat*, 4, 7 (September 21, 2002): 297.

9. Jacques E. Levy, *Cesar Chavez: Autobiography of La Causa* (New York: W. W. Norton & Co., Inc., 1975), 25.

10. Matthew 25:16, King James translation.

11. Matthew 25:14–29.

## Chapter 11: The Church

1. Rule 53:15.

2. Rule 52:1.

3. Monks of New Skete, 115.

4. William Strunk, Sr., and E. B. White, *Elements of Style* (3rd ed.; New York: MacMillan Publishing, 1979), xiii.

5. Sirach 3:17–18.

6. Luke 14:11.

7. Tvedton, 36.

8. Casey, 177.

9. Monks of New Skete, 55.

10. Psalm 84:2, 3a, 5.

11. Psalm 1:1.

12. Father Daniel Homan, OSB, and Lonni Collins Pratt, *Radical Hospitality: Benedict's Way of Love* (Brewster, Mass.: Paraclete Press, 2002), 63.

13. de Sales, 63.

14. Psalm 84:4.

15. Hebrews 9:24.

16. Psalm 24:1, 3.

## Chapter 12: The Saints

1. Ward, 95.

2. Koenig-Bricker, meditation for September 19.

3. Ibid., July 24.

4. *Alcoholics Anonymous*, 60.

5. de Waal, 54.

6. Casey, 66.

7. Rule 7:68–69.

## Coda: The Summit

1. From a discourse on the psalms by St. Augustine, in Divine Office, vol. IV, 1577.